The Trouble at L.S.E.

The Trouble at L.S.E.
1966-1967

HARRY KIDD

London
OXFORD UNIVERSITY PRESS
NEW YORK   TORONTO
1969

Oxford University Press, Ely House, London W. 1

GLASGOW NEW YORK TORONTO MELBOURNE WELLINGTON
CAPE TOWN SALISBURY IBADAN NAIROBI LUSAKA ADDIS ABABA
BOMBAY CALCUTTA MADRAS KARACHI LAHORE DACCA
KUALA LUMPUR SINGAPORE HONG KONG TOKYO

Printed in Great Britain by
Butler & Tanner Ltd, Frome and London

For
Marie, Susan, and Vicky

Preface

I began this book in the belief that it would be as well, for the sake of the many to whom L.S.E. is an object of warm interest and devotion, to explain a little more clearly what happened there in 1966–7, to correct some of the wilder legends of a conflict of villains and heroes (interchangeable according to taste), and to set in their place an account, necessarily prosaic, of the muddles and misunderstandings, but also the adherence to conflicting principles, of men and women faced with unfamiliar—and often uncomfortable—situations.

Recent events have, however, given me an additional purpose. 'For the first time in the history of the United States', Dr. Clark Kerr has written, 'university students have been a source of interest for all the nation; a source of concern for much of the nation; and even a source of fear for some of the nation.'[1] What Dr. Clark Kerr wrote of the United States is now of closer application. What is going on amongst our students? Social analysis had best be left to the sociologists, but it is essential that the actual course of events in our various upsets should first be set out in some detail, so that the purely local and personal factors can be disentangled from any that may be of more general interest. As one of the necessary case-studies, therefore, I offer the present work. In chapter 1 I first set the scene; it is intended to do no more than that, and is certainly not intended as an analysis of the School's nature and problems. In chapters 2 to 9 I then narrate the relevant events. Reflection on causes and issues follows in chapter 10, and I conclude with some discussion of two general topics which have come to the fore in our troubles: the contribution of students to university government, and the principles and machinery of university discipline. (I should perhaps record that chapter 12 was submitted by way of evidence to the Hart Committee on Relations with Junior Members at Oxford.)

It was at the suggestion of Lord Bridges, then Chairman of the Governors of L.S.E., and with the agreement of its successive Directors, Sir Sydney Caine and Dr. Walter Adams, that I first undertook this task; but it is not an official history, and no one but myself is committed to the views

[1] Dr. A. Clark Kerr, 'The New Involvement in Society', *Dialogue*, I, 1, p. 34.

expressed in it. I cannot pretend to be dispassionate; L.S.E. has meant too much to me for that, too many of my friends were involved, and I was not a detached observer; but I have hoped, within the limits of my knowledge, to avoid being unfair.

It remains for me to thank those who have helped me with information or advice. Too numerous to name individually, they include Governors, members of staff, and students of the School; colleagues past and present. My gratitude for their help is unbounded, as it is for those who have shared the task of deciphering and typing my manuscript, and of seeing it through the press.

For access to information and permission to quote copyright material my thanks are due to the London School of Economics and Political Science, its Students' Union, the National Union of Students, the University of London Union, the Collegiate Press Service, the Controller of H.M. Stationery Office, and to the proprietors and editors of *The Church Times*, *The Daily Mail*, *Encounter*, *The Guardian*, *Isis*, *The Observer*, and *The Times*.

H.K.

Contents

Plates

1 The Background

At the time, in October 1966, when my main narrative begins, the London School of Economics and Political Science, a school of the University of London, comprised not far short of three thousand full-time students, with over eight hundred part-time in addition. The composition of this student body departed in a number of ways from what is normal in the British universities. About a third came from overseas, four hundred—more than from all Asia or Africa—coming from the U.S.A. Nearly forty per cent of the students were doing graduate work. As a whole the student body was distinctly older and distinctly more cosmopolitan than is usual. In range of studies, however, the variety was much less than in most British institutions of comparable size. The natural sciences were unrepresented, but there was heavy concentration on the social sciences—economics, politics, sociology, anthropology, geography, statistics, law, and history.

The students were taught by a body of some 270 teachers, to whom the combination of the comparative narrowness of the School's range with its numerical size opened attractive possibilities of specialization. They were, I believe, above the average of university teachers in talent, and of great liveliness of mind. The demands upon them were heavy. There were the demands of their own teaching. There were the calls of participation in the administration of the School at a time of rapid development. There were the demands of society, growing more aware of the value of expert help in its self-improvement: government committees, for example, to be served on, advised, or researched for. There were commercial undertakings in need of advice. There was the public to be informed, through articles in the Sunday newspapers, through broadcasts, or through comment on television. Though sometimes criticized by devotees of complete academic detachment, this *vulgarisation*, as the French call it, is a valuable teaching activity, and has served to raise perceptibly the level of the average man's understanding of the world in which he lives and works; it was interesting to note that it meant no diminution of service to students, since those who were thus engaged in teaching the general public were nevertheless among the most devoted teachers of the School's own students.

There were also the needs of what the staff were sometimes apt to call 'their own work'—their research. Much of it was done, I am sure from, love or inner compulsion; but it led to promotion. Within the School itself excellence in teaching was in theory taken into account in judging claims to promotion, though by what processes it was divined remained a mystery. Quality of published work provided a clearer criterion, of more compelling power; quantity of published work was even more palpable. It was a man's professional standing outside the School, moreover, that might lead to his being offered a professorship elsewhere, and that standing depended almost entirely upon published work, for what did other universities know of a man's teaching?

A young teacher's chances of promotion were good. The School's own promotion policy was liberal, and the rapid growth of departments elsewhere provided ample opportunities. In 1962, for example, there were in this country seven professors of sociology. If all the universities that were seeking to fill such professorships had been able to do so, there would have been almost four times as many a mere two years later. It might be thought that the plenitude of prizes made the competition for them less fevered; it did not. It is one thing for a man to live with the knowledge that he could not be promoted this year because nobody was retiring, and quite another to live with the knowledge that there were the places, but he had not been found worthy. The band-wagons, too, were passing, and might soon be gone. The expansion and the opportunities that it brought might not last for ever. So the haste to publish was great.

The life of the staff, then, was anxious and full, not easy; it says much for their quality and devotion that so much teaching was so well and carefully done, and it is not altogether surprising that there were defaulters.

The great pride of the staff, their treasure and the chief tool of their craft, was the School's library. Of over a million items and well over half a million bound volumes, it was one of the world's greatest specialist collections, standing to the social sciences much as the Cavendish Laboratory in its hey-day stood to physics. Despite the library's disadvantages, it was a joy to have its riches at hand; but the disadvantages were serious, especially by international standards (and what other standards of comparison would be used at L.S.E.?). The library lacked funds to keep up with the rapidly increasing output of books and periodicals within its range, and it lacked space for the adequate deployment of its contents. The acquisition of an additional building for it was, and still is, one of the most pressing needs not only of the School but also of the social sciences in Great Britain.

Shortage of space and shortage of money have been the constant complaints of the School—one of the respects in which it conforms to normal expectations, as the University Grants Committee would no doubt confirm. The blame—if there is blame—rests in part upon the School itself. For many years it did the lion's share of the teaching of the social sciences in this country. If it rejected an applicant, it would be hard for him to find elsewhere the teaching that he sought. Reluctant, therefore, to turn him away, the School acquired the habit of taking in more students than it could comfortably provide for, of stretching its resources to the limit and perhaps beyond. Some were grateful; others believed that the School did it for the sake of their fees—a belief that displays complete ignorance of the finance of our universities, which make a substantial loss on every student that they take.

Most families contain some member who will always help, always undertake new burdens. The fact that the burdens are voluntarily assumed reduces neither their weight nor the chance that they will be resented and complained of. There is something of this habit of mind about L.S.E. It regularly undertook more than could reasonably have been expected of it; not only, some would say, more students but more research projects, more lines of teaching. And then it complained. There are many less endearing faults.

In recent years, however, there had been some easing of the pressure. Buildings were acquired and converted, and more were on the way. The Court of the University of London, always generously aware of the School's physical needs, provided capital grants on a scale of which even the most hardened complainers could not speak without gratitude. The School's income was not increased perhaps on so generous a scale, but enough to make it possible, as the following tables show, for the number of teachers to grow faster than that of students, though with occasional setbacks.

TABLE I *London School of Economics and Political Science 1955–6 to 1967–8: Growth of numbers*

	Full-time students	Full-time teaching staff	Seats in library
1955–6	1,948	162	625
1956–7	1,960	165	625
1957–8	2,027	172	625
1958–9	2,062	175	666
1959–60	2,103	187	666
1960–1	2,179	202	666
1961–2	2,276	215	790
1962–3	2,323	212	790
1963–4	2,450	220	790
1964–5	2,498	237	920
1965–6	2,493	245	920
1966–7	2,865	270	970
1967–8	2,753	283	970

TABLE II   *Index of growth* (1955–6 = 100)

	Full-time students	Full-time teaching staff	Seats in library
1955–6	100	100	100
1956–7	101	102	100
1957–8	104	106	100
1958–9	106	108	107
1959–60	108	115	107
1960–1	112	125	107
1961–2	117	133	126
1962–3	119	131	126
1963–4	126	136	126
1964–5	128	146	147
1965–6	128	151	155
1966–7	147	167	155
1967–8	141	175	155

TABLE III   *Ratios*

	Student/staff (both full-time)	Full-time students per seat in library
1955–6	12	3·1
1956–7	11·9	3·1
1957–8	11·8	3·2
1958–9	11·8	3·1
1959–60	11·2	3·2
1960–1	10·8	3·3
1961–2	10·6	2·9
1962–3	11	2·9
1963–4	11·1	3·1
1964–5	10·5	2·7
1965–6	10·2	2·7
1966–7	10·6	2·9
1967–8	9·7	2·8

It is probably significant that 1966–7, the year of the troubles with which my narrative deals, was a year of set-backs. Though, as the figures for the following year indicate, they did indeed prove only to be set-backs and not a reversal of the trend, their impact was severely felt. The gradual improvement had passed unnoticed, but it was suddenly felt that matters were worse. What had gone wrong was that a tendency to excessive caution in the numerical control of admissions had been over-corrected at a moment when several independent factors—such as an unusually high success-rate in examinations and a reduction in 'drop-outs'—combined to swell numbers. After seriously under-shooting the targets in the previous year, we over-shot them in October 1966, and in consequence felt more than usually over-crowded. At the best of times the School's buildings were among the most intensively used of any university premises in the country. It was no great consolation, perhaps, to reflect that so they should, since the land on which they were built was the most expensive. The School was hard-pressed and knew it, yet not perhaps in all respects as hard-pressed as it felt. The 2·9 full-time students competing for each seat in the library compare with a national average of 3·6 in 1965–6 (the last year for which national figures are yet available). Were students from other London colleges taking up more and more of those seats?

Over the destinies of the School presided the twin authorities of the Court of Governors and the Academic Board. The School's written constitution was that of a company limited by guarantee, of the pattern of the beginning of the century; since that time it had gone substantially unrevised. Its sketchy outlines had been filled in by conventions and understandings, but they had not always been reduced to writing and were sometimes difficult to ascertain with precision. The supreme body was the Court of Governors, some eighty strong, presided over by Lord Bridges, formerly Secretary to the War Cabinet and Head of the Civil Service. The Governors —civil servants, businessmen, members of the professions, academics from other universities—were a self-perpetuating body for the most part, but they included representatives of the University of London and of London local government, and five elected representatives of the academic staff, known, despite the fact that they did not have to be professors, as 'the professorial Governors'.

Although in the eyes of the law the Governors were the School, and all its powers and rights were vested in them, they had delegated those powers to their Standing Committee, a body of about a dozen, including three of the professorial Governors, and to the Director, at this time Sir Sydney Caine, a man of sixty-four, himself a graduate of the School. After a distinguished career in the civil service he had served for four years as Vice-Chancellor of the University of Malaya, and was a Governor himself, though absent overseas, in 1956 when the Court appointed him Director of the School from the following January in succession to Sir Alexander Carr-Saunders.

Caine's primary function—but a largely unrecognized function—as Director was to hold the School together. Without its administration a university would fall apart into a collection of semi-autonomous and un-co-ordinated departments. As Director, Caine was chairman of most of the School's committees. He had to make them think, and think with sufficient precision, both about problems immediately facing the School and about those that could be foreseen. He sought to extract the consensus by which academic bodies prefer to be governed, hating as they do to vote and be

B

divided. He had to ascertain the general will of the School, to help the academic committees to shape it and express it, and then he had to seek to give effect to it. He was in a sense a monarch, his formal position as near as any to be found in Britain to that of an American university president; but he was by his own choice an ever more constitutional monarch. The delegation to him and to the Standing Committee of the formal powers of the Governors was subject to a convention, whose range he was constantly but deliberately widening, of consultation with academic persons and bodies. To them the real power of decision was gradually being transferred; the process had been begun by his predecessor, Carr-Saunders, but he himself was carrying it further. The last area of major importance awaiting transfer was that of allocation of resources between the competing claims of academic departments, the library and other services. In this area he was seeking to improve the mechanism by which decisions were arrived at and to extend its scope—to reduce the extent to which things just happened to the School and to increase the extent to which they happened because they were desired and had been planned.

The power to make decisions of policy was gradually being transferred, then, from the Governors and their Standing Committee to the academic staff. This transfer, which had been going on for thirty years at an accelerating rate, was undoubtedly right. A university must approach to being a self-governing community of scholars, though that self-government is inevitably (and, I believe, desirably) subject to some moderation by lay people and external forces. The way in which the transfer was carried out, however, quietly and gradually, perhaps almost unconsciously, and without explicit recognition, had serious disadvantages. Legal authority still rested with the Governors, and might need to be exercised by them in an emergency, but they came more and more to lack the intimate knowledge of the School necessary to enable them to decide wisely, and they lacked legitimacy in the sense in which the term is used by political scientists: authority recognized by those over whom it is exercised. The more the decisions were taken by academic bodies, the less knowledge of the background to them the Governors had, and so the less ability to make future decisions; and at the same time, and by the same process, the more it came to be expected that all decisions would be taken by academic bodies, and to be felt that they should. It was with a slight shock that it was occasionally perceived that decisions on a particular matter rested still, *de facto* as well as *de jure*, within the powers of the Governors or the Director. The Governors—and this was true even of the Standing Committee, though still more of the Court—were left with less and less to do, uncertain of their role and uncomfortable; cold-shouldered collectively by the academics, and pushed out of touch with the life of the School, yet still, as I have indicated, possessed of the final authority, especially in a crisis.

Nor were the academic decision-making organs yet capable of discharging satisfactorily all their growing responsibilities. The principal academic body, the Academic Board, was essentially a sort of town-meeting, a structureless body of about three hundred members, less than a third of whom would on any occasion be likely to attend a meeting. Well suited for general discussion, it was ill-adapted to executive functions, unless supported by an efficient and trusted committee-structure. This was lacking. In such structure as there was, the principal place was held by the Board's General Purposes Committee, which played its leading role with a singular lack of success. In a surge of egalitarian feeling a few years earlier it had been reconstructed to reflect in its membership the various grades into which the staff (as at most British universities) were divided—five professors, four readers or senior lecturers, four lecturers or assistant lecturers.

The structure of the General Purposes Committee, though well-intended, proved totally irrelevant to the various lines of controversy on which the School was from time to time divided—the economists and their allies against the sociologists or the historians, the devotees of pure learning against the devotees of practical application, of graduate study against undergraduate, the expansionists against the firm believers that enough was enough, but never once the senior staff against the junior. The balanced representation of grades was a useless irrelevance when what was needed was a balanced representation of academic disciplines and habits of mind. This was the place in the structure where one might most reasonably have expected to find what any such institution greatly needs, a caucus, a body so constituted that its opinion can be depended upon generally to reflect that of the institution as a whole. This we most notably lacked. There was no body, among either the Governors or the academic staff, to which Caine could turn for ready advice or a swift decision on which he could act in confidence that it would be generally accepted.

The same need was felt by academic persons. In order to bring about, for example, the teaching of a subject new to the School's curriculum, a professor would have to see to it that the University of London approved regulations for a degree-course in it, that the School agreed to teach it, that staff were budgeted for and appointed, accommodation provided, a quota of undergraduates and a quota of graduate-students allocated, and relevant books bought for the library. Every one of these steps was vital, and each was the responsibility of a different body. Helping the academic to steer his way through this maze, making sure that step followed step and that initiatives did not get lost in the mechanism, was in itself an important part of the work of the Director and the administrative staff, which provided such co-ordination as there was. That staff, of which I was the head as Secretary of the School, responsible for its work to the Director and the Governors, acted as a kind of central nervous system for the School, giving the Director and the committees such information and advice as they needed, drawing their attention to problems in need of solution, and also attending to the paying of the bills, the keeping of the records, and the hundred and one unobserved functions without which the institution's life could not continue.

Caine and many of his colleagues already knew that the machinery of government needed attention. A little while before the narrative begins, a paper on the subject, representing the fruits of a couple of years' thought and informal discussion, had been presented to the Standing Committee. They had had difficulty in finding time for its discussion. There were always more immediate, even if less important, matters to discuss. The problem was adjourned, but during the summer of 1966 a memorandum about it was circulated to all members of the Court of Governors for them to consider at leisure.

It may be useful to describe how some kinds of decision were arrived at. Appointments to professorships and readerships, the senior posts on the academic staff, were made by the Senate of the University of London. The Senate acted on the advice of a Board of Advisors, on which the School was represented by the Director, two professors (chosen *ad hoc* by the School Appointments Committee, of which all professors were members) and one Governor. Appointments to other teaching posts were made by selection sub-committees of the Appointments Committee, each consisting of the Director, two or more teachers from the department concerned, and one or two from related departments. All appointments required the concurrence of the Governors, but this was given on their behalf by their Chairman, to whom the report of the selection sub-committee was immediately submitted. He usually gave his approval by return of post, and was never known to refuse it, so that the real decision was always made by academic persons.

Similarly, the promotion of members of the academic staff required the approval of the Standing Committee of the Governors, but they invariably approved the recommendation of the Appointments Committee; that body reached its own decision after considering reports of sub-committees which scrutinized the claims of individuals. At no time did the Governors seek to intervene in the determination of academic questions.

In the allocation of resources, the Standing Committee, acting on the advice of the Director, would determine how available funds should be divided between the library, the establishment of academic posts, the cost of promotions, and other needs. Within the total allocation for each purpose, the detailed distribution was determined by academic bodies.

There were two administrative problems that normally required little attention but were to become the subject of controversy in 1966-7—communication with the press and discipline. From its foundation the School had been particularly sensitive to allegations that it was a centre for political propaganda rather than for academic study. A lively institution devoted to the study of the world of politics and economics is inevitably concerned with the critical study of contemporary society. Its academic reputation for integrity depends on a certain detachment; but the liveliness of its thought depends on a certain warmth. The two are not easily combined and balanced. Sometimes roughly handled by the press in the past, the School had gathered to itself unfounded legends that it lacked the self-confidence to laugh off. It might have done better to accept cheerfully the attribution of intellectual liveliness and to shrug off with a wry smile the suggestions of political bias, knowing that they were unfounded, and indeed that to believe L.S.E. a hot-bed of revolution was a clear symptom of the crudest political and economic naïvety. The School remained, however, absurdly sensitive on this subject, its Governors perhaps most sensitive of all.

In the early 1930s matters had come to a head: Professor Harold Laski's political activities, for example, attracted a good deal of attention; the Professorial Council (precursor of the Academic Board) and the Court of Governors resolved that 'while members of the staff . . . should . . . be free from regulation or censure by the Governors of the School in respect of their writings or public speeches, they should regard it as a personal duty to preserve in such writings or speeches a proper regard for the reputation of the School as an academic centre of scientific research'. Uneasiness continued; in 1934 an increasing number of letters bearing the School's address had been appearing in the press, and had tended—or so it was feared—to give the impression that the School was a centre of political activity and discussion rather than of teaching and research. The Court of Governors therefore made a regulation which precluded members of the School, staff and students alike, from using its name and address without the Director's permission when sending out resolutions or letters to the press. The regulation was revised ten years later, when the Governors also recorded the opinion that it would be wrong for the Director to permit the sending out of resolutions on political matters by the Students' Union, to which all students had to belong; but voluntary societies were exempted, and might publish their resolutions, provided that the numbers voting were shown. What underlay the distinction was, I think, principally a feeling that the Students' Union was part of the formal constitutional machinery of the School and must keep within its terms of reference; all students belonged to it, and could not resign even if they disagreed with what a Union meeting resolved in their name. Voluntary organizations were not in the same way part of the School, and could say what they liked. If the numbers voting were shown, the significance of their resolutions could not be exaggerated; and members who disagreed could resign. In 1955 it was decided by the Standing Committee that there should be separate regulations for the staff and the students. The staff continued to be subject to the restriction on communication with the press, but three years later the Director was authorized to give them general permission to use the name of the School when writing to the newspapers, on the understanding that they would use proper discretion and would not, for example, use the permission in such a way as to lead to the attribution to the School as a whole of any particular political view. For students the regulations were in 1955 revised—in consultation with a joint staff–student committee, be it noted—and took the form set out in Appendix I.[1] Between that time and 1966 they had caused no trouble. Permission was very occasionally refused, but no one seemed to mind, and the amendment of the regulations was not called for. There were more urgent problems.

Discipline also caused little trouble. Occasional offences called for a mild rebuke from the Director, who had never had to use his power to suspend or fine. A Board of Discipline, armed with more extensive powers, was appointed every year by the Governors (the Academic Board nominating two of its five members) but membership was known to be a sinecure. The Board had not met since 1951, when a student had tried to sell to a second-hand bookshop books from the library; and it was not expected ever to have to meet again, though its members were once or twice informally consulted by the Director. One of my own responsibilities was to assist the Director in matters of discipline, but that part of my work took up no more than a few minutes in the average year.

In the government of the School the students had little voice. They shared in membership of committees that advised on the management of the refectory and the health service; and, more generally, they had their half share of the places on the Academic Board's Staff–Student Committee, which had existed for many years without exercising any notable influence on the course of events. Only recently had its proceedings become sufficiently formal to have agenda and minutes: and its place in the committee-structure was negligible, chiefly because it never, or hardly ever, reported or made a recommendation to any of the School's governing bodies; and perhaps, in lesser degree, because the wrong criterion governed the selection of its staff members. The Academic Board too often chose people, usually without other committee-membership, who were, as the phrase is, 'good with students' or 'interested in students', rather than deliberately selecting people (not necessarily less 'good' or 'interested') who played a role in the general committee-structure and could bring student views to bear on it. Not merely was the committee ineffective, therefore, but its existence constituted an unintended deception, raising for its student members false hopes of participation in the School's affairs. It is not altogether surprising if they felt baffled and cheated.

The responsibility for representing students in their dealings with the School rested with the Students' Union, and especially its Council. Membership of the Union was automatic (a result of student-status, and inseparable from it). A separate Athletic Union dealt with sporting matters, and a Graduate Students' Association provided a few social occasions for the graduate students, who, though they were members of the Students' Union, played little part in its activities. This was hardly surprising. Apart from occasional excursions into the world of politics, and the despatch of

[1] See p. 162.

telegrams of protest to errant governments, the Union's preoccupations had too often been narrowly confined. Either it was concerned about the refectory, alleging that the prices were outrageously high or the quality of the food too low; or it was concerned with 'student apathy'. The apathetic student was the student who took little or no part in organized student activities. What was apt to be overlooked was that in a more important sense he might not be apathetic at all: he might be someone who found other things in life more interesting than the affairs of a Union which spent an undue part of its time in intricate procedural wrangles, involving frequent points of order and motions that the Chairman do leave the chair, of surpassing interest no doubt to students of the Union's own constitution, but to others sterile. As the Union's own newspaper, *Beaver*, had said in November 1963, 'Of course the main body of students is apathetic: there is very little incentive for them to be otherwise. At weekly Union meetings we watch small boys playing games in a political manner: behind this democratic facade there lurks, so the old dog of rumour tells us, a process of self-generating nepotism.' Students, it ended, 'don't give a damn about the Union and, let's face it, there is no earthly reason why they should'.

In newer universities the Students' Union building is apt to be a palatial edifice controlled by the students themselves. L.S.E. had nothing of the kind—a gap more and more noticeable as it was filled in more and more of our sister institutions in the provinces. The need was part of the general need for more space. A completely separate building was probably out of the question in an area where land values are very high, and where it was at the time governmental policy to give preference to provision for postgraduate rather than undergraduate needs. The best hope was that, if new premises could be obtained for the library, a number of the large rooms and ancillary offices that it vacated could be made over to the Union as a separate block of accommodation that could be shut off,[1] when it was so desired, from the rest, and could be controlled by the students themselves. This solution, however, lay, as it still lies, in the future, and perhaps the distant future. Meanwhile the Union had in the basement of the St. Clements Building its bar, named 'the Three Tuns Bar' in commemoration of a demolished public house, and a small number of other rooms used as offices or for recreation.

A notable part in the history that follows was played by *Beaver*, the Students' Union newspaper. Published about a dozen times a year, it was widely read by students. Its editor was appointed by Union Council, but importance was attached to editorial independence and *Beaver* was not the official voice of the Union. Its staff were students and inexpert in journalism. Standards of competence and of journalistic ethics varied as editor rapidly succeeded editor, but were rarely of a high order.

The management of the Union's affairs was entrusted to a Union Council of elected officers, of whom the senior was the President. Tiny as was the

[1] By gates, no doubt. [1 May 1969]

minority of students generally interested in Union affairs, a somewhat larger number—though still a small fraction of the whole number—participated in the election of the President, who tended to be above average in academic ability as well as in other ways. In the early spring of 1966 there was elected (with the support of 585 votes) Mr. David Adelstein, nearly twenty years of age, and a South African by birth. When he was fifteen he had come with his parents to this country and had been a pupil of Manchester Grammar School, specializing in science. He had entered L.S.E in 1964, and had been elected External Affairs Vice-President of the Union during his first year. He is one of a small number of sons of émigrés from South Africa who played a considerable part in the School's affairs in 1966–7. Of great personal charm and of considerable ability, he was a member of no political party, but the experience of a racialist authoritarian government had left him with a certain suspicion of paternalist authority— perhaps of any authority—wherever he found it. As President of the Union, he made clear, he stood for closer consultation between the School and its students, and for student representation on academic and administrative committees. In the Union itself he wished to reduce the power of the Union Council and to leave decisions to full Union meetings. We shall have cause later to note this populist strain in his practice.

His election had come at a time when the School's relationships with its students were already engaging close attention. Two years earlier Mr. Trevor Fisk, President of the Union (now President of the National Union of Students), had asked that the Union should be represented at meetings of School committees when matters specifically relating to students were being discussed. The Standing Committee of the Governors and the Academic Board had agreed that they would be very ready to receive student representatives for discussion of specific issues. In further exchanges, however, practical difficulties had emerged. The students could hardly say when they wished to be received unless they knew what was to be discussed, and the Academic Board rejected a proposal by the Director that he should regularly show their agenda-papers to the President. The Board had, indeed, been inclined to doubt whether its previous decision had been correct. The presence of students, who would not be able to take part in discussion as equals, would hinder constructive debate, and there was no evidence of student discontent on any serious issue that would justify their admission.

Changes in the Union presidency interrupted the discussion. It was resumed early in 1966 by Adelstein's predecessor, Mr. Alan Evans, at the end of his term of office. In reply to enquiries which he made the Director said that, though he foresaw great difficulty in the way, he would, of course, be willing to submit a reasoned memorandum on the subject to the Academic Board.

A number of other subjects of dispute had emerged during Evans's year of office. He had submitted a request for a doubling of the Union's grant of £4,000 a year. Comparison of the Union's finances with those of similar bodies elsewhere was difficult, owing to differences of responsibility. Athletics fell outside the scope of the L.S.E. union, and it had, unlike students' unions elsewhere, neither athletic grounds nor its own premises to staff and maintain: but, however difficult the precise comparison, it was clear that the Union was in serious need of better resources. The Standing Committee of the Governors, therefore, agreed to an increase of £2,000 a year, £500 of which was to represent a contribution towards the salary of a full-time graduate administrator to be appointed, at the Committee's suggestion, to relieve the Union officers of some of their administrative work. The Standing Committee had indicated their sympathy for a proposal that the financial autonomy of the Union be increased by replacing the grant from the School by a compulsory Union subscription to be charged as part of a student's fees. The School was not free, however, to make this change immediately, since the Committee of Vice-Chancellors were discussing more generally the method by which students' unions should be financed, and the School had been asked not to act on its own; had it been free to do so, I have little doubt that the students' proposal would have been accepted.

More difficulty was presented by a proposal that the Union should be freed of a restriction contained in its own constitution, which precluded it from making grants to political and religious societies. The Standing Committee of the Governors did not think it right that funds derived from the School should be used in support of the advocacy of particular forms of political or religious belief and rejected this proposal, perhaps a little woodenly. The discussion of political and religious faiths is a natural and important part of the activities of students—especially students of the social sciences—and hardly less deserving of support than the promotion of particular forms of sport. Where, however, discussion ends and advocacy begins is less clear. The issue was to remain a serious bone of contention.

Another proposal advanced by Evans in the last year of his presidency was that a 'sabbatical year' be allowed to the President of the Union, that is to say that in compensation for the time spent on his presidential duties he should be allowed an extra year of study in preparation for his degree examinations, the cost being met directly or indirectly out of public funds. By the time that this proposal came before the Academic Board, Evans had already been succeeded by Adelstein, and they were allowed to appear together before the Board to plead their case. They argued it well. The Board was sympathetic, but felt that wider issues were raised by implication, since it had been argued that uneasiness among students was one of the factors that were increasing the burden that had to be carried by the Union and its President. There was, many members of the staff agreed, a serious malaise amongst students. The proposed sabbatical year represented no more than palliative treatment of a symptom. It might even have nothing at all to do with the real problems, especially if, as some suspected, many students regarded the Union itself as irrelevant to their troubles. It would be better that the real causes of the malaise be sought, and a committee was constituted to enquire into them.

This body, officially known as the Committee on the Relationships between the School and its Students, came to be known as 'the Ad Hoc Committee', to distinguish it from the long-standing and ineffectual staff–student committee to which I have already referred. Its appointment was briefly noticed in the press. The *Daily Mail* (13 May 1966) reported:

... things have got so bad ... now that the authorities have set up a committee to see how staff–student relations can be improved. David Adelstein, the 19-year-old President of the Students' Union, says: 'Students have talked of striking. The dons have had to do something or the L.S.E. would have had its name dragged through the mud, which wouldn't have been good for its image or for attracting applicants.'

Adelstein assured me that he had said nothing of the kind, but this was hardly an auspicious start. The committee began its work by canvassing the views of colleagues and preparing for a survey of student opinion, to which great importance was attached. Some members of the committee were anxious that it should be completed before they met the Union officers, since they expected the survey to throw considerable light on the extent to which students generally regarded the Union as truly representing their interests. The delay, however, in consulting the Union officers was resented and was damaging to relationships between the authorities and the Union. Union officers may not have been representative in one sense, that is to say they may not have been a typical set of students and they may well have been out of touch with their members, by only a small minority of whom they had been elected. In another sense, however, they certainly were representative; they and they alone had been elected to speak for the students, and they should have been heard.

The survey of student opinion was duly carried out by a sub-committee under the chairmanship of Professor B. C. Roberts, and a forthright report on it was presented to the committee in October. A small random sample of undergraduates had been interviewed and asked to talk about their life as students at the School, and any ideas they might have that might make it more satisfactory. The report, though not perhaps so alarming as one or two later references to it in the press have suggested, was critical of the performance of some of the School's teachers. That there was genuine ground for such criticism, I have little doubt, but even less doubt that the criticisms would have been re-echoed in other universities if similar enquiries had been made. There were and are many university teachers whose lectures are clear, well-delivered, and felt by the students to be relevant. There are others, however, of whom this is not true. Universities have only recently even begun to teach their teachers how to teach. The relationship between teacher and pupil has been regarded too often as sacrosanct, taboo, something on which organization must beware of casting a profane shadow. Co-ordination of lecture-courses with the teaching of small classes, supposedly on the same syllabus, has often been rudimentary or completely neglected. Nor is it unknown for the neurotic teacher to work off his frustrations by making or seizing an opportunity to turn his class towards discussion of departmental politics. Young teachers, little older than their students (occasionally at L.S.E. a little younger) can be scared of them or arrogantly conscious of their own hard-won academic honours and determined that the course shall be no easier for their pupils. Others are ready enough to shock, by telling pupils, perhaps no more than half seriously, that teaching is a distraction from research. Their wide-eyed hearers repeat this and a legend grows. Such legends need to be received with caution, and one needs to remember that the pupil cannot necessarily recognize good teaching when he receives it, though he may come to value it more highly when he looks back in later years.

It was clear enough, nevertheless, that there was room for considerable improvement in the School's teaching performance, and I have no doubt that its imperfections, and especially the neglect of duty by a small minority of teachers, were contributory causes of unrest. There is no reason, how-ever, to suppose that it was more than a small minority that was in default, nor yet that matters were significantly worse at the School than at other institutions, as the experiences of young friends of my own who have studied elsewhere bear out. The quickness of the School's academic departments to respond to criticism and the readiness with which they improved their organization indicated a powerful desire to do better, and I have no doubt that there is now much less ground for complaint.

In the course of the year 1965–6 another problem of great importance had come before the School. Caine, the Director, had made clear his intention of retiring in 1967 at the age of sixty-five, two years before the compulsory retiring-age, and a successor had to be found. Previous selections of Directors of the School had been made by a small group of Governors, and consultation with the academic staff had been belated and minimal. In preparation for this occasion, however, a selection committee had been constituted, containing not only eight Governors but also six members of the Academic Board, to find a new Director, ascertain his willingness to accept appointment, and submit his name to the Court of Governors. The members of the committee were authorized to 'ascertain discreetly' the views of other Governors and members of the academic staff. Partial disclosure in a newspaper of names that had been discussed by members of the committee with their colleagues (though not necessarily by the committee itself) caused embarrassment, and the process of 'discreet ascertainment' had to be abandoned; the kind of speculation that had been reported must, if it continued, have made the committee's work more difficult. They proceeded with it in secrecy, and at the meeting of the Court of Governors in the summer term of 1966 the appointment was proposed and approved of Dr. Walter Adams.

Adams had begun his career as a history teacher at University College London, but had given up his appointment in 1933 to become Secretary of the Academic Assistance Council, which helped to resettle more than two thousand academic refugees from totalitarian countries. In 1938 he had become Secretary of L.S.E., but had left it two years later for war service in political intelligence. After the war he had served for ten years as Secretary to the Inter-University Council for Higher Education in the Colonies, helping in the establishment of new universities in the developing countries of the colonial empire. In 1955, after acting as secretary to a commission that recommended the establishment of a new multi-racial university college at Salisbury, Rhodesia, he had been appointed first Principal of that college. His task there, never easy, had become extremely difficult after the Rhodesian unilateral declaration of independence, when some wished his college to be used as an instrument of political protest, striking the gesture of institutional suicide to mark disapproval of the actions of the Rhodesian 'government'. Adams, however, believed it to be his duty to continue the educational work for which the college had been founded, patiently seeking by tactful negotiation to improve the conditions under which it worked. In the midst of this task he received and accepted an invitation to become the School's next Director.

The selection of the new Director was something in which students had for the most part taken no great interest. There was, however, one exception. A Socialist Society, formed in October 1965 as a result of disillusion with the Labour Party, had soon begun publication of a magazine *The Agitator*. In its early numbers *The Agitator* proclaimed its commitment to fight not only for the overthrow of capitalism but also for militancy in the Students' Union, which it described as corrupt, effete, and bureaucratic. In its seventh number, in March 1966, it proclaimed its intervention in the choice of a new Director. For years, it said, this post had been filled without any consultation with students or rank-and-file staff: now they were invited to take part in an election of a new Director, to be held on 3 May. There was little response to the invitation, and no more was heard about the election. *The Agitator* had not, however, as we shall see, lost interest in the subject.

2 The Pamphlet

Early in the Michaelmas Term, on Friday 14 October 1966, I was told by a journalist that a pamphlet attacking Adams's appointment as Director had been prepared by a group of students and was to be published in a few days' time. It had been circulated in advance to the newspapers, which reported that its publication was to be the opening of a sustained campaign to secure the cancellation of the appointment. If it won widespread support an attempt would be made to organize a boycott of lectures on 11 November, the anniversary of the unilateral declaration of independence by the Smith regime in Rhodesia. In preparation for its publication thirty students had requested Adelstein to call a special meeting of the Union to consider a motion condemning Adams's appointment.

The pamphlet, entitled *L.S.E.'s New Director—A Report on Walter Adams*, appeared on Monday 17 October as 'an *Agitator* publication', produced by an anonymous group of about twenty students. It claimed to be based in part on interviews with four of nine lecturers at the University College of Rhodesia who had been arrested in the previous July, and with students and ex-students of the College; and in part on an examination of the following documents:

1. The Birley Report, written by Dr. Robert Birley, formerly headmaster of Eton and at the time Visiting Professor of Education at the University of the Witwatersrand. This was a confidential report to the Council of the University College of Rhodesia on recent disturbances amongst students there and the action of some of the staff in supporting them. It was never intended to be a report on the College as a whole. Any reference to the virtues of those in charge at the College would have been irrelevant. On the other hand, references to mistakes they had made were clearly relevant. The hasty decision to publish the report, though taken with the agreement both of Birley and of Adams, has proved unfair to the latter, as it has been read by some as a general assessment of the College.

2. A counter-blast issued by fifty-five members of the staff of the University College, including lecturers who had expressed their disapproval of Adams's actions at the time. They felt that Birley had been unfair to themselves.

3. A confidential report prepared for Amnesty International by Mr. Louis Blom-Cooper, a member of the English bar, in July and August 1966, based simply on conversations with members of the staff of the University College

who had happened to be available for consultation during the few days of his visit to Rhodesia; he had never met Adams. The extracts from this report were published without Blom-Cooper's permission.

From their examination of the evidence the authors of the pamphlet deduced four main criticisms of Adams:

1. that he had been unwilling to make a stand for academic freedom;
2. that he had on important occasions avoided making decisions;
3. that he had been extremely isolated both from staff and from students;
4. that he had been inefficient as an administrator.

The pamphlet argued these conclusions with lucidity and skill; it was a very professional piece of work. Its faults began to appear, however, when one could compare its text with the evidence on which it purported to be based. Birley himself said in a letter to Lord Bridges: 'It is an atrocious document. It takes single sentences from my report and uses them to support views quite contrary to those I had expressed.' This is best illustrated (as Mr. William Hanley, a student of the School, first noted) by setting side-by-side a passage from Birley's text (page 20) and the relevant part of the pamphlet (page 8):

Birley	*The pamphlet*
The Principal left for London next morning, Saturday, 19 March. It is clearly not my duty to judge whether the decision that he should go was justified, but I think I may say that I have learnt enough during the last ten days to realize the extreme importance of the meetings which he was due to attend. The future of the College might be said to depend on them. I might add that one senior member of the staff told me that he had strongly disapproved of the decision but that, after he heard on his return of what the Principal had accomplished in London, he came to the conclusion that he had been entirely wrong in his first judgment. It is clear, however, that the absence of the Principal during the next few days was most unfortunate.	As is mentioned above, the Principal was due to leave the College for London on Saturday, March 19th. This he did. The fact that on the day before he left, the police order described above had come into effect, that there were at least 30 police with dogs, six police landrovers, several police cars and plain-clothed detectives on the campus, that all the African students of the College (about 200) and a number of European and Indian sympathizers were boycotting lectures, that already 23 members of the Staff considered themselves on strike, did not stop him. No! Leaving matters in the hands of a Committee of six, Adams went to London to attend financial negotiations on the future of the College; a decision which to quote Dr. Birley again 'was an unfortunate one'. Indeed, this whole business provoked Dr. Birley into even harsher criticism. 'It is clear', he reports, 'that the absence of the Principal during the next few days was *most* unfortunate' (p. 20 our emphasis).

As Birley said in a letter published by *The Times* on 4 November,

> In the context it was obvious that I meant that the situation was made much more difficult by the absence of the Principal, which was, perhaps, a glimpse of the obvious. There was no criticism of the decision, let alone a harsh criticism. I feel that any reader of the pamphlet who is influenced by isolated quotations from my Report and does not refer to the Report itself, may be led far astray.

I have quoted a glaring instance of the way in which the pamphlet used its authorities. There are others, not capable of as brief a demonstration; and it is not my present purpose either to write a review of the pamphlet or to write an appreciation of Adams's work in Rhodesia, a task for another hand on another occasion—though I cannot forbear to quote Birley's description of that work as 'one of the few constructive pieces of work on behalf of multi-racialism during recent years on the continent of Africa'. For the present context it is enough to say that those of us who knew Adams and had read the documents on which the pamphlet purported to be based regarded it as a deliberate piece of propaganda rather than an airing of honest doubts about his appointment. The effect, however, on those who had not read the primary documents, especially Birley's report, and who did not know Adams, was powerful. The pamphlet was, as a student has put it to me, 'free from all the usual Socialist Society ranting', lucid and well-presented. L.S.E. students were already angry about the Rhodesian declaration of independence, especially angry that they could do nothing about it. Here was something connected with Rhodesia that they could do something about.

On the day of the pamphlet's publication Adelstein wrote to the Chairman of the Governors, enclosing a copy of it, and asking how much of the information contained in it was true, and had been known at the time of Adams's appointment; what had been the reasons for overlooking the criticisms, and whether there was now a case for reconsidering the decision. He went on to say that his own role in the affair was difficult and to ask for all the information possible. The Union was going to discuss a private motion condemning Adams's appointment. Perhaps someone who was connected with the appointment could therefore explain the position of the selection committee to the meeting, so that the Union would not be attacking it without knowing what the counter-arguments were.

Two days later Lord Bridges replied as follows:

> Thank you for your letter of 17th October 1966. I am sure that, on reflection, you will appreciate that it is not possible for me, or any other representative of the School, to engage in public debate on the merits of an appointment which the School has made. Since, moreover, the proceedings of the Selection Committee are confidential, and it is on that basis that its discussions took place and advice or information was sought or received, I

am not at liberty to answer your questions (b), (c), and (d). I am therefore left only with your question (a), to which my reply must be that the pamphlet cannot be accepted either as a complete account, or as an accurate account, of the matters with which it deals.

As ill-luck would have it, this letter was delayed by a trivial misunderstanding and did not reach Adelstein until the following week, after the Union meeting. Meanwhile, however, on the day of the pamphlet's publication, and without waiting for a reply from Bridges, the Union Council had decided to support the motion, to be moved at the forthcoming Union meeting, condemning Adams's appointment.

The Union meeting on the Friday was one of the best-attended for a long time, and attracted many students who were not normally interested in Union affairs. The motion for the condemnation of Adams's appointment was moved by Mr. David Lazar, Treasurer[1] of the Socialist Society and a friend of Adelstein. Like him, he had come from Johannesburg in the early 1960s. He had then been at School in Highgate with the seconder of the motion, Mr. Stephen Jefferys, the able and energetic Vice-Chairman[1] of the Socialist Society. The Union was not prepared to take a quick decision; the motion was amended by replacing the word 'condemn' by the words 'seriously question'; Adams was given a limited time in which to reply. In its final form the resolution, passed by 425 votes to ten, read:

> Union, in the light of the information from the Birley Report, the report on the University College of Rhodesia, and the report by Louis Blom-Cooper on behalf of Amnesty International
> (a) seriously questions the appointment of Dr. Adams as successor to Sir Sydney Caine,
> (b) urges the Academic Board and the L.S.E. Branch of the A.U.T.[2] to consider a similar motion.

> Union instructs the President to obtain from Dr. Adams, within eighteen days, a reply to the serious criticisms contained in these reports and if Union considers the reply to the allegations unsatisfactory will oppose his appointment.

Next morning the Chairman of the Governors conferred on the telephone with Caine and myself. It seemed wrong that Adams should be expected to defend himself to the Union. He was still in Rhodesia, and his communications subject to censorship. He was still Principal of the University College, and hardly free to discuss its internal affairs. More important, the quarrel was, strictly speaking, between the students and the Governors, who had appointed him. If the students were minded to make an issue of the matter, it was with the School that the issue must be joined. I was therefore asked to send Adams a cable requesting him not to

---

[1] So designated in a return to the School authorities, but the Socialist Society sometimes denies the possession of officers.
[2] Association of University Teachers.

enter into communication with the Union for the time being; this was confirmed a few days later by the Standing Committee, and Adelstein was
so informed.

We had meanwhile been considering the question whether any reply
should be made to the pamphlet. Public defence of Adams's appointment
—either to the students or to any other group—was out of the question.
Gossip about academic appointments is common enough, but formal
defence of them by the appointing institution is unheard of, and for two
very good reasons: first, any such discussion must involve public comparison of the merits of the person appointed with those of others, and
discussion of the possibility, or otherwise, of persuading others to accept
the post. Full and frank discussion on these lines would not be tolerated,
and would constitute an invasion of privacy and a breach of confidence.
Second, the appointing body has done its work, for which it is not answer-
able to anyone; and the appointment, having been made, cannot be un-
made; to discuss what cannot be done (or undone) is a waste of time. In
our particular circumstances, moreover, the notion could not be coun-
tenanced for a moment that the appointment of the Director-designate
could be upset, or even put in question, by an anonymous pamphlet no
better than this one.

On the other hand, there was considerable public interest in the controversy, and on the advice of a small group of members of the academic
staff, Lord Bridges agreed to write to *The Times* to explain why no formal
comment on the pamphlet was being made by the School. His letter appeared on Tuesday, 25 October:

As chairman of the Governors of the London School of Economics and
Political Science, and chairman of the selection committee which recommended to the Governors the appointment of Dr. Walter Adams as Director
of the school, I write to express the indignation which many of us feel at the
recent deliberate campaign against the character of a man whose help before
the war to refugees from racial tyranny in Europe, and whose services over
the last two decades to education in many lands, constitute a record of most
honourable achievement, notable particularly for the courage which he has
shown in founding and fighting to maintain in most difficult circumstances
a multi-racial college in Rhodesia.

The campaign against him is one to which I would think it neither
necessary nor indeed proper that any reply should be made by L.S.E., nor
would it be right for us to comment on the internal affairs of another university college, but I should not wish to run any risk that silence might be
misinterpreted. It is on this account that I write this letter.

Meanwhile attempts were being made to involve the staff. On the day
of the pamphlet's publication a student told a newspaper reporter that he
knew of several members of the staff who were against Adams's appointment and that he hoped that they would have the courage to sacrifice
political expediency for moral principles. In the Union debate the seconder

c

of the resolution condemning the appointment had said that the Union had a responsibility to maintain as much pressure on the staff as possible. The debate itself was seen by some students as an attempt to force sympathizers among the staff to make a move. A newly arrived American graduate student, Mr. Marshall Bloom, sent to the Collegiate Press Service, an American student press organization for which he acted as correspondent, a despatch saying that the Union did not expect a direct response from Adams. 'In the meantime, however,' he reported, 'some students are working to bring faculty opposition into the open, hoping to force Adams' resignation.' Several faculty members, especially in the law and sociology departments, had indicated their private disapproval of the appointment. 'Students', the despatch concluded, in as frank an avowal of purpose as one might ask, 'are unsure about their chances of forcing Adams to resign. "But if we can keep student support united, and if the bloke *is* stopped, it will be a fantastic victory", commented Union President David Adelstein of Johannesburg, South Africa.'

The Observer (23 October) that week-end reported Caine's denial of strong opposition to Adams among the staff; but, they said, there was evidence of disagreement with his view, though some members of the staff were reluctant to voice their opposition to Adams for fear of losing their jobs or their chances of promotion. If this is so, the members of the staff of whom *The Observer* spoke must have been as lacking in knowledge of the principles governing academic appointments as they were lacking in the courage of their own convictions. Clearly, however, in view of these remarks and of other hints that were appearing, it was time for the staff of the School to see and declare where they stood. An informal meeting of the professoriate was held on the following Wednesday in preparation for a meeting of the Academic Board, to follow a week later on 2 November. The Board then resolved by a substantial majority that it dissociated itself from, and deplored, attacks on the character and integrity of Dr. Walter Adams. It would continue to give full support to the School under the duly-appointed Director.

That was the end of the matter, so far as the staff were concerned, but not for the students, who regarded Lord Bridges' letter to *The Times* as an attack on their Union. The Union Council agreed to bring before the next Union meeting a motion deploring it, and Adelstein was urged to write to *The Times* himself in reply. He prepared a draft letter and took it to show to Caine, who reminded him that he needed permission to send it,[1] and reserved his decision until the following day. He then told Adelstein that he would not give permission. He confirmed his decision by letter:

26 October 1966

You have asked for my permission, under regulation 10 of the Regulations for Students, to address a letter as President of the Students' Union to the Editor of *The Times* commenting on the letter from Lord Bridges, Chairman

[1] Under Regulation 10; see p. 162, and also chapter 1, pp. 9, 10.

of the Court of Governors of the School, which appeared in *The Times* of 25 October 1966 relating to Dr. Walter Adams. I have refused to give that permission and am writing now to set out grounds for my refusal.

Your proposed letter related to the appointment of Dr. Adams to be the next Director of the School and the procedure which the Students' Union desired to follow in enquiring as to the suitability of Dr. Adams for that appointment. I cannot agree that these matters fall within the competence of the Students' Union; I accordingly concluded that it would be improper for me to authorize you to make public any views on these matters on behalf of the Students' Union.

Under the existing constitutional procedures of the School the decision in the appointment of a Director is a matter for the Court of Governors. To assist them in that decision the Court some time ago decided to set up a Selection Committee composed partly of members nominated by the Court itself and partly of members nominated by the Academic Board, together with certain *ex officio* members. No provision is made for any participation in the process of selection by the Students' Union or its representatives.

It is important that the status of the Students' Union should be clearly understood. It is a body set up under the authority of the School, to which all students of the School are compelled to belong; it has a defined constitution and purposes and a definite (and important) role to play in the School's affairs. It is, however, my duty to see that that role is kept within the limits implied by the School's constitutional arrangements as well as the Students' Union constitution itself and I must therefore bear those limits in mind, rather than the criteria which might apply to action by an individual student, in deciding whether to give permission for a communication of the nature you proposed.

In addition to the grounds stated in his letter Caine had, as he told me at the time, another reason for his decision; if he had given permission he would have been condoning an attack both on his chairman and on his own designated successor. He did, however, point out to Adelstein that, if he made one or two minor amendments to his letter so that he was sending it as a private individual from his private address, he would then need no permission.

This decision to refuse permission was one of the critical points of the year. Was it right, and was it wise? There was no interference with the freedom of expression. Adelstein, or any other student who wished, was free to publish the letter as a statement of his personal opinion, so long as he did not write from the School or claim to be writing on behalf of a constituent part of the School. At the level of expediency, too, there was a good deal to be said for the decision. At the time when it was made we were still living in an era when decisions were normally accepted, and Caine had every reason to expect that this one would be—as it very nearly was.

Adelstein made clear to Caine that he was disappointed, but he accepted the decision. His letter was amended, signed by himself and other Union officers as individuals, and sent to *The Times*. Pressure was brought to bear upon him at two informal meetings to change his mind, disregard the regulation, and write as President; but still he would not. At the Union meeting that Friday, 28 October, the majority were clearly in favour of instructing him to do so, but were able to avoid open defiance of the regulations by adopting the view expressed by two junior members of the teaching staff of the Law Department, both comparatively new to the School, that the Director's interpretation of the regulations was wrong; the Union was a society whose membership was voluntary, and under Regulation 9[1] the resolution could be communicated to the press without permission. It may be found surprising that before telling the Union that the Director was wrong they did not mention the matter to him.

Their view, as I have said, was adopted by the Union, which resolved by 306 votes to 23 as follows:

Union deplores the view of the Director that it is forbidden to communicate its views and resolutions to the Press without the consent of the Director; the Union considers this view to be inconsistent with the governing rules and regulations. Hence in accordance with these rules it authorizes and instructs the President to communicate the resolutions and deliberations of this body. Union instructs the President to reply to the letter by Lord Bridges in *The Times* and instructs Union Council to prepare a petition to be submitted to *The Times* as a letter.

Adelstein spoke to Caine on the telephone shortly after the meeting ended, telling him of the terms of the resolution and asking him whether he would change his decision; he also asked what the situation would be if Caine did not agree and he nevertheless signed the letter to *The Times* as President. Caine replied that he did not feel able to change his mind; and if Adelstein nevertheless sent the letter as President it must be regarded as a serious breach of discipline. He suggested that Adelstein should refuse to accept the instructions of the Union meeting and should therefore resign, but should forthwith stand for re-election, thus appealing over the head of the meeting to the student electorate at large. A little later Adelstein spoke to him again. After further thought, he said, he had decided to send the letter officially as President, in accordance with the Union's view that to do so would not involve any breach of the regulations; and in doing it he did not intend to break the regulations.

The staff of *The Times* were asked to amend the letter accordingly. It was intended that they should also omit the signatures of all the other members of Council, but there was some misunderstanding, and their signatures remained on the letter, which appeared in *The Times* next morning, 29 October. Its effect[2] was to indicate that it was regretted by the students as much as Lord Bridges that what had been intended as reasoned criticism of Adams's appointment should have been taken as

[1] p. 162.
[2] I should have wished to quote it in full, but have been unable to obtain permission of Mr. David Adelstein to do so. I should wish to make clear, however, that its terms were in themselves in no way objectionable.

personal denigration. The criticism had cast doubt on the appropriateness of that appointment. The Union had rejected a motion condemning it in favour of one giving Adams an opportunity to reply. Lord Bridges, the letter continued, had suggested that it would be wrong to comment on the internal affairs of the University College of Rhodesia; but how, Adelstein asked, could one avoid discussing Adams's record as an administrator there when he was being considered for the Directorship of the School? (A question which overlooked the difference between private discussion while the appointment was under discussion and public debate some months after the appointment had been made.)

Caine had kept me fully informed of the course of his discussions with Adelstein and of the warnings that he had given him, and reminded me that, while the matter must clearly be brought before the Board of Discipline, it would not be right for him to bring it before them himself, since he was a member of the Board and could not properly act both as prosecutor and as judge. The responsibility, therefore, was mine as Caine's assistant in disciplinary matters.

On the following Monday morning I accordingly wrote to the signatories of the letter, informing them that they appeared to have committed an offence against the regulations of the School, and seeking their comments. I received from all except Adelstein an explanation that their signatures had appeared as a result of a misunderstanding. After making enquiries, I informed them that their explanation was accepted and that disciplinary proceedings against them would be dropped; but against Adelstein the proceedings had to continue.

Adelstein wrote again to Lord Bridges on 3 November 1966, to tell him of the following resolution of the Union, also passed on 28 October:

Union strongly deplores the letter by Lord Bridges in 'The Times' of 25th October 1966 in that
(a) he did not consider it appropriate to address the Students' Union on this issue,
(b) it was written knowing that, in the light of the decision by the Standing Committee of the Court of Governors, a reply on behalf of the Union might not be permitted.

Adelstein explained the Union's concern that Lord Bridges had refused to address the Union because he did not want to make a public statement. The Union, however, was a private forum, not a public one, and Lord Bridges had made a public statement, in the shape of his letter to *The Times*. In that letter, moreover, he had not made clear to whom he was referring, but had said that he felt no reply on behalf of the Selection Committee was called for. Adelstein, as the only person who, so far as he knew, had asked for a reply, had had, he said, to assume that the reference was to him, so that Lord Bridges had appeared to attack the Union in public when he knew that a reply on behalf of the Union might not be permitted.

Lord Bridges replied in the following terms on 14 November:

I have your letter of 3 November 1966 conveying to me the terms of a motion passed on 28 October 1966. I have some doubts whether I should enter into correspondence with you on a subject which relates so closely to one on which a complaint against you is under consideration by the Board of Discipline. But I would like to dispose of certain misapprehensions on which your letter is based. In my letter to *The Times* I expressed indignation at what I described as a recent deliberate campaign against Dr. Walter Adams's character. I said that the campaign was one to which I thought it neither necessary nor proper that any reply should be made by the School, but I did not wish to run any risk that silence might be misinterpreted. For reasons which I do not understand, you appear to think that I was replying to you. So far as I know, you had then made no public utterance of which readers of *The Times* would be aware. Our press cuttings show over thirty references to the affair in the press before my letter was published. In only five of those references are you mentioned—in two as having been summoned by the Director to see him, in two as the person whom the Students' Union had directed to write to Dr. Adams, and in one as commenting on the original pamphlet. There is nothing whatever in these references to lead anyone to think that my letter was about you.

When I wrote of a deliberate campaign I should have thought it was quite obvious that I was referring to the scurrilous pamphlet (which Dr. Birley, in a letter to me, has described as 'atrocious'), and to the steps which were evidently taken to secure that the maximum notice was taken of it by the newspapers. You may therefore rest assured that I was in my letter not referring to you or the Students' Union, which has, I believe, disclaimed any responsibility for the pamphlet. I would add that I should not regard it as appropriate that the Chairman of the Governors should use the columns of *The Times* for controversy with the President of the Students' Union.

Your other point is that I refused to address the Union because I said that I did not want to make a public statement. In fact if you will look again at my letter of 19 October 1966, you will see that what I actually said was that I could not engage in public debate on the merits of an appointment which the School had made. That remains my view, and in this context a debate held by a body as large as the Students' Union must be regarded as a public debate.

The two teachers who had addressed the Union, Mr. Lee Albert and Mr. Alexander Irvine, meanwhile felt it necessary to state their views on the matter more publicly, and a correspondence ensued in the columns of *The Guardian* which proved to have an important and unexpected bearing on the subsequent course of events. It began with a letter signed by Albert and Irvine that was published on Monday 31 October:

It must now be beyond doubt that Dr. Adams's record has been put to grave question by the Birley and Amnesty Reports, a summary of which has been sent to him by the L.S.E. Students' Union along with a temperate request for a reply. But the Standing Committee of the L.S.E. Court of Governors has requested and advised Dr. Adams to make no reply.

Dr. Adams is not alone. Even those at the L.S.E. with access to information favourable to Adams have been forbidden to speak. None the less, five days after stating this position, Lord Bridges, Chairman of the Governors, made public his own views, but did not deign to treat the Union charges as worthy of an argued response. The Union was moved to reply, but was forbidden by the Director of the L.S.E. By the Union President's courageous decision to publish a reply, he now runs the risk of fine, suspension, or expulsion.

We hope our academic colleagues at the L.S.E. recognize that the vital issue now at stake is preservation of the freedom of teacher and student alike to think and speak without fear of reprisal.

Feeling ran high in the Law Department that morning, and seven of its members—including one who had a few days earlier written to *The Times* expressing doubts about Adams—sent a letter themselves, published by *The Guardian* next day, in which they denied that anyone at the School had been forbidden to say anything on the question of the appointment of Dr. Adams or any other matter. Adelstein had been refused permission to send his letter in the name of the Students' Union, but it had been made clear that any student was free to write to the press as an individual. In these circumstances they could not accept that there had been any infringement of or threat to the freedom of teacher or student to think, speak or act in any way; and they were not aware of any pressures on themselves to refrain from public discussion of this question.

Caine too had decided that the letter from Albert and Irvine should not pass without reply, and *The Guardian* of 1 November also published the following rejoinder from him:

Mr. Albert and Mr. Irvine, in their letter published by you yesterday, state that the Students' Union was forbidden by me to reply to the letter sent by Lord Bridges to *The Times*. They also say that the issue now at stake is the preservation of the freedom of teacher and student alike to think and speak without fear of reprisal. This is not the case.

The regulations, with which all students undertake to conform when they are admitted to the School, contain no general prohibition of students communicating with the Press; what they do provide is that the School's name or address shall not be used in any such communication without the permission of the Director. One object of this is to avoid identification of the student body as a whole or the School itself with any particular point of view; another is to avoid the expression by individual organizations of views on matters outside their competence.

Under the constitutional procedures of the London School of Economics the Students' Union has no part in the appointment of the Director of the School. I accordingly informed Mr. Adelstein last week that, while I should take no exception to letters being addressed to the Press by him and other students as individuals, I could not give him the permission which the School's regulations require to use the name of the Students' Union in doing so, since the subject of his letter did not fall within the competence of the Students' Union. I should add that Lord Bridges in his letter had made no reference to the Students' Union so that, in my view, no question of a 'reply' arose.

As to members of the teaching staff, I am at a loss to understand the suggestion that they have been forbidden to speak on this or any other subject or are not free to speak 'without fear of reprisal'.

The issues now at stake have therefore in my view nothing to do with the freedom of teachers or students to think and speak without fear of reprisal; they have to do with the respective functions of the Court of Governors and the Students' Union in the conduct of the School's affairs, and the compliance of students with a disciplinary code which is not illiberal.

Albert and Irvine returned to the charge on 4 November:

We must reply to the charges made against us by the Director and our colleagues at the L.S.E. (Letters, November 1). In particular, we repudiate the innuendo that teachers at the school are under any restraints.

What we asserted, and reassert, is that there has been a studied policy on the part of the L.S.E. Governors and Director to prevent the Students' Union from considering the Adams appointment and from making known their collective views. Your correspondents have now amply justified our charge that the issue at stake is the freedom to think and speak.

The union is expressly authorized 'to promote the welfare and corporate life of the students'. Surely this object includes consideration of the person responsible for the administration and tone of their University. Yet it is the Director's view that because the Union does not participate in the process of appointment it has no competence to criticize the appointment. If so, it is right that citizens in a totalitarian State should have less claim to criticize their leaders than citizens in a democracy. It is for this reason alone that the Director withheld his consent to a Union reply to Lord Bridges, who publicly expressed indignation in the name of the L.S.E. 'at the recent deliberate campaign against' Adams.

The Director invokes a student regulation dealing with the right of students individually to use the school name in communicating with the press. We speak of the more significant right of the student representative association, the Union, to communicate in its own name. (Disciplinary proceedings for 'serious offences' are now pending because the Union president obeyed its instruction to publish.) This right is dealt with in another regulation, which permits a *voluntary* society to publish without consent.

Presumably the Director denies the Union this freedom by deeming it a *compulsory* association—and this though participation in the Union is nowhere required and dissociation nowhere inhibited! The notion of compelled association is thus used to fetter representative expression. If the L.S.E. students are so inhibited, they are unique among students at British universities, according to a recent survey by the National Union of Students. It would be ironic for a controversy which began with denials of academic freedom at the University in Rhodesia to end with violations of those freedoms at the L.S.E.

3 The First Trial

The Board of Discipline, before whom my complaint against Adelstein was to be brought, had, it will be recollected, last met fifteen years earlier. There had on that occasion been no dispute about the facts, and no doubt they constituted an offence. The procedure then followed provided no useful precedent in the present circumstances. In the absence of any such precedent or prescribed procedure, therefore, the Board now had to have a preliminary meeting to decide what rules to lay down for the conduct of its business. Before even that could be done, however, the membership of the Board presented problems. Appointed by the Court of Governors as part of the routine business at their annual general meeting in the summer, it consisted of the Chairman of the Governors, or in his absence the Vice-Chairman; another Governor, Dr. Leslie Farrer-Brown; and the two nominees of the Academic Board, Professors D. V. Donnison and G. S. A. Wheatcroft, with the Director *ex officio*. The Chairman felt that he should not serve on the Board on this occasion, since it was to a letter from him that Adelstein claimed to have been replying; the Vice-Chairman was overseas and not available; and Farrer-Brown felt that he, too, as a friend of Adams, should stand down. The vacancies had to be filled before the Board could meet. Fortunately an extra meeting of the Standing Committee had been arranged for the following Thursday, 3 November, and could act for the Governors in filling the two places.

Before the meeting of the Standing Committee, Caine discussed the general situation informally over lunch with a group of governors and academic colleagues. There was general agreement that it was important to establish that an offence had been committed, and so to validate the Director's interpretation of the regulations, as well as to vindicate his authority in a difficult situation; on the other hand it was agreed that it would be right in the circumstances of this particular case not to seek the imposition of any penalty. Adelstein was an outstanding President, who was doing good work in turning the Union away from its customary sterilities towards taking an interest in what the students really came to the School for—its academic work and its teaching programme. He had been put into a very difficult position. The Union had not merely pressed him but positively instructed him to publish the letter as from itself. Two teachers of law had expressed the opinion to the Union and to himself that he would be committing no offence if he did as the Union told him. If they were wrong the blame for the offence attached rather to them than to him, and it would not be right that he should be punished for the offence. It would perhaps have been as well to let both Adelstein and the Board know that the proceedings were to be of the nature of a test-case for the interpretation of the regulations, and that no penalty was to be sought. Much trouble and anxiety would then have been averted. It was decided, however, that this would be going too far. It was for the Board to determine in the light of the evidence whether or not to inflict any penalty, and it would be wrong to prejudice their position and to limit the freedom of their action; but it was agreed that everything possible should be done to get the matter disposed of quickly.

After this informal discussion a meeting of the Standing Committee was held to consider the vacancies on the Board of Discipline. Of the persons selected one proved to be on the point of going overseas and another was unwilling for personal reasons to serve; but we did at last get the composition of the Board settled, and it met on Tuesday, 8 November, consisting of the Hon. C. M. Woodhouse (who was elected Chairman), Miss M. G. Green (now Dame Mary Green), Donnison, Wheatcroft, and Caine. I designated a member of my staff to act as secretary to the Board.

On 7 November Adelstein had written to me with the following requests, which he said he believed to be essential conditions to a fair and adequate hearing:

1. *That he be allowed legal representation and the presence of his tutor.* He indicated that he wished Mr. Albert to be his 'counsel of record'—an American law term. The use of the phrase 'legal representation' bedevilled the matter. There was no objection to Adelstein's being assisted by any member of the staff that he might choose; but legal representation is normally understood in such a context to mean representation by a member of the legal profession acting professionally. This right had not normally been conceded in university disciplinary hearings in this country and it was very doubtful whether the School should concede it—especially as Adelstein did not want it, since it would, oddly enough, have ruled out Albert, who was a member not of the English but of the American profession.

2. *That he be allowed to hear and question adverse witnesses, that everything on which the final decision might be based be introduced in evidence, and that the burden of proof be upon the prosecution.* All this was clearly unexceptionable.

3. *That 'accurate minutes' be kept and made available to him.* This was puzzling; whenever we took minutes of a meeting we hoped that they were accurate, but this was not a committee-meeting and notification of the conclusions reached was all the record that was likely to be kept. It became clear later that what Adelstein really wanted was the keeping of a verbatim

record of the proceedings which could serve as the basis for a possible appeal or even for taking the matter to the courts. As I did not expect that any penalty would be imposed, nothing was further from my mind than the possibility of an appeal, and a verbatim report would be an unnecessary expense.

4. That a '*decision in response to the arguments to the Board be rendered and made available*' to him. Of course the decision would be made and communicated to him; there would not be much point in the proceedings unless it were. Time, however, showed that that was not what he meant; he was asking for a reasoned statement of the decision.

5. The most difficult request—*that the Director should not serve on the Board*, for two reasons: first, that he was an interested party; second, because he had expressed himself publicly about the matter in his letter to *The Guardian*. The latter ground perhaps did not receive initially as much attention as it deserved; nobody who knew Caine could think him prejudiced, and he was against the imposition of a penalty. More attention was directed to the general question of principle. The Director would be likely to be concerned in one way or another with a high proportion of the cases that might go before the Board, if its life were to enter a more active phase. It would all too often be his permission that had not been obtained or his orders that had been disobeyed. If Adelstein's argument were accepted, therefore, it would mean that Caine could hardly ever serve; but the Governors, by making him a member *ex officio*, had indicated a desire, if not a command, that he should normally do so. His position on the Board, moreover, was different from that of other members; they were responsible for discipline only while they were actually sitting as a Board; his responsibility continued all the time, and it was undesirable, therefore, that he should be excluded from the Board's deliberations, since he would have to deal with their consequences. So we saw it. His position was in some ways comparable to that of the Proctors at the older universities, and no one had in those days seriously suggested that they were prejudiced. Caine, it should also be remembered, was in his last year of office, and concerned not to weaken the position of his successors.

I passed Adelstein's letter on to the secretary of the Board with an indication that I would wish to contest some of his requests. It crossed with an invitation from him to Adelstein to appear before the Board next day, when it was to settle its procedure. Unfortunately he decided that he should not appear without his 'legal representative'; this meant that he could not appear before the Board until it had conceded his request for representation. What this meant in practice was that an opportunity for discussion and the removal of obscurities was missed, and that full scope was given for correspondence to create further misunderstandings and for Adelstein and his friends to detect them. I do not for a moment suggest that this was their intention—indeed, I am sure that it was not—but it was the result of their decision.

The Board decided to state its procedural conclusions in a letter, which was to be sent in identical terms to Adelstein and to me; its terms took several days for the members of the Board to settle. The passages that were to be the subject of controversy read as follows:

3. The Director informed the Board that he had considered Mr. Adelstein's request that he should not sit on the Board, but that he could see no reason for avoiding his responsibilities as an *ex officio* member of the Board. . . .

8. The Board do not regard it as appropriate for either party to be represented by solicitors or counsel but have no objection to Mr. Adelstein being accompanied at the hearing by one member of the staff of his choice who will have an equal right to address the Board and question witnesses. Hence there is no objection to Mr. Albert attending the hearing if Mr. Adelstein so desires. The Board may wish, in addition, to hear Mr. Adelstein's tutor.

9. The general procedure envisaged by the Board is as follows, but the Board reserves the right to alter or modify this procedure if in the course of the hearing it appears to them to be desirable to do so.

(a) The Secretary will first outline the nature of his complaint against Mr. Adelstein and will submit evidence in support of it.

(b) Mr. Adelstein will then outline the nature of his answer and submit evidence in support of that answer if he desires to do so.

(c) The Board may, if it thinks fit, call for such further evidence (if any) as they require for the purpose of this enquiry.

(d) During the hearing the Secretary and Mr. Adelstein will be permitted to put any proper and relevant questions to any witnesses giving evidence to the Board.

(e) The Secretary and Mr. Adelstein will be asked to address the Board on the question whether an offence has been committed.

(f) The Board will then retire to consider whether the complaint is or is not justified.

(g) If they consider that the complaint is justified they will then hear the Secretary and Mr. Adelstein on the question of what penalty should be imposed.

(h) The Board do not propose to take a verbatim record of what takes place before them, but members of the Board, its Secretary, and the Secretary of the School and Mr. Adelstein may make such notes as they think proper of the evidence and arguments.

This was sent to Adelstein and to me. The ambiguity of the words 'legal representation' had led the Board to try to avoid them by spelling their intentions out in detail in paragraph 8. The words 'an equal right to address the Board' puzzled Adelstein; it is difficult to see how they could be interpreted in any sense hostile to him, and they were intended to mean that Albert would have equal rights with Adelstein. Their right to call witnesses was stated in paragraph 9(b) in terms identical with mine, but they appear to have thought it to mean only that Adelstein himself could give evidence. That so much misunderstanding could be engendered would be almost comic if its results had not been so very destructive.

Albert replied to this letter on 17 November, asking the Board to make clear that Adelstein could be represented by him at the hearing and could present witnesses. He also repeated the request that the Director should not sit, and the request for a verbatim record, explaining why it was desired. He expressed his readiness to attend a separate hearing on procedural matters if the Board so wished. The Secretary of the Board consulted its members by telephone and replied next morning, the Friday before the day fixed for the hearing, that the Board could not add anything to their earlier letter on procedure, but were willing to hear Albert and Adelstein on these points at the beginning of the proceedings on Monday, 21 November. Provisional arrangements would be made for a verbatim note to be taken.

Meanwhile, without waiting for Albert's letter to be received by the Board, let alone answered, *Beaver* had, on the day that it was sent, 17 November, asserted that the Board had rejected or ignored all the points that Adelstein had put forward as conditions necessary for a fair hearing. This, it proclaimed, substantially changed the situation in which the Union had—as was indeed the case—decided on the preceding Friday against a boycott of teaching. Adelstein's entire future was at stake, and the procedure to be followed, it was alleged, denied him many of the rights to which he was entitled as a matter of natural justice.

Not surprisingly, in the light of what they were thus told, the Union resolved by 516 votes to 118 at a special meeting held that afternoon that

Union deplores the threat of disciplinary action against its President for carrying out Union's instructions in writing to the Press in its name. Normal channels of communication between Union and School (a) being inadequate and (b) now having ceased to function at all, Union asks its members to boycott all lectures, classes and seminars on Monday November 21 for the whole of the day, and to hold a peaceful demonstration outside L.S.E. to coincide with the meeting of the Board of Discipline. Union takes this action in order to draw the attention of the School Governors and administration to the desire of L.S.E. students to be able freely to express their opinions on matters of concern to them. Union (a) asks all members of the academic and research staff at L.S.E. to support this boycott; (b) instructs Union Council to organize pickets, the production and distribution of leaflets explaining the purpose of the boycott, and a report-back meeting on Monday afternoon to discuss further action.

Next morning, Friday 18 November, Irvine spoke to me on the telephone and asked whether there was any way out of the deadlock in which we seemed to find ourselves. As matters stood, Adelstein was likely to refuse to appear at the hearing on Monday, and the Courts were to be asked to intervene and bring our proceedings to a halt. I explained to Irvine the misunderstandings that had arisen, and we agreed that the only real point outstanding was the Director's membership of the Board. On that we arrived at what seemed to be a possible compromise. Caine could, if he chose, withdraw from the board on the ground that in his letter to *The Guardian* he had stated a view on matters related to the disciplinary hearing. His withdrawal on that ground would not prejudice his position or that of his successors as members of the Board on future occasions, but would enable the present proceeding to be got out of the way. Caine, whom I at once consulted, agreed. Irvine and I agreed that the understandings reached should be confirmed at a meeting with Albert and Adelstein that afternoon, but Caine made it a condition that they should not be revealed until the Board met. His reason was that he had told his colleagues on the Board that he was going to sit, and he felt that he should tell them himself before he announced his change of mind. Adelstein pointed out that this meant that he could not call off the boycott. Caine was prepared to put up with that, since the truth of the situation would come to light after Monday's hearing. This faith in the ultimate triumph of truth was in my judgment a serious weakness on our part. Truth will out if it has a public relations officer, but not otherwise.

On Monday, 21 November 1966, the Board of Discipline duly met. Their first act was to admit Mr. W. Savage, the President of the National Union of Students, to act as an observer. The Director then spoke. The regulations, he said, contained nothing to suggest that he should not serve as a member on a case arising from an infringement of his own authority; on the contrary, his own interpretation of the regulations was that they were designed *inter alia* to give him the necessary powers to enforce that authority. Accordingly he could not agree that there would be anything improper or undesirable in his serving in a case of the present kind. It had, however, also been suggested that a public statement that he had made about the circumstances of the case implied a bias. He did not himself regard it as prejudicial, but was anxious to avoid any shadow of suspicion that the proceedings were affected by any bias, and had decided not to sit. He would, however, be available if his evidence as a witness were desired; and if—but only if—the Board had in mind to impose a penalty, he would, in view of his continuing responsibility for the conduct and welfare of the School, ask for the opportunity to make a submission to the Board.

Caine then withdrew, the Board confirmed their agreement to Albert's representation of Adelstein, and the proceedings began. About the facts, which I have already recounted, there was little dispute, save in respect of an alleged agreement between the National Union of Students and representatives of the Committee of Vice-Chancellors and Principals. The President of N.U.S. had written to Caine that an assurance had recently been given that it would be unthinkable to the Vice-Chancellors that an elected student representative should be disciplined for carrying out the stated wishes of those who had elected him. The secretariat of the Committee of Vice-Chancellors had said that this letter was based on a misunderstanding. The discussion in question had been about student participation in university government. One of the representatives of the N.U.S.

had said that a student officer should not be held personally responsible for views expressed in a representative capacity. This had been accepted, but was very different from the proposition, which had not, they said, been put forward at the meeting, that a student acquired immunity from the rules of his university if he was acting in execution of the stated wishes of his Union; that is to say, that if his Union instructed him to break the rules he would commit no offence by doing so. There appeared at first to be some inclination to proffer this as a possible line of defence for Adelstein, but it was explicitly abandoned by Albert during the cross-examination of a representative of the N.U.S.

The defence actually presented on Adelstein's behalf was that he was acting under Regulation 9,[1] his letter amounting to the communication to the press of a resolution of a voluntary society recognized by the Students' Union. The reply to this was that

1. the Union was not a voluntary society; membership of it was automatic, students could not resign from it, and the reference to voluntary societies was there to distinguish them from the Union;
2. the Union was not a society recognized by the Union;
3. Adelstein's letter was not the communication of a resolution;
4. even if it had been the communication of a resolution, voting figures were not stated, as the regulation required.

After the evidence had been taken and the argument completed the Board invited the Director to attend and give evidence, in the course of which he spoke of the courtesy which Adelstein had shown, and the fact that he had clearly been moved by his feeling of loyalty to the Union and still more by the legal advice he had received. These were factors that should be taken into account if the Board found that an offence had been committed.

After closing speeches by myself and Albert the Board withdrew to consider their conclusions. When the hearing was resumed, the Board delivered their conclusions as follows:

We find that there was a breach of Regulation 10 by Mr. Adelstein. Regulation 9 (which was invoked on Mr. Adelstein's behalf) has, in our view, no application to communications to the press on behalf of the Students' Union.

Under Regulation 10, as now framed, the Director is responsible for controlling communications to the press by students writing in the name of the School or of any body including the name of the School in its title. This responsibility the Director could not avoid. He exercised it in this case only after the most careful consideration and gave a full statement of the reasons for his decision.

We find also that Mr. Adelstein acted in good faith and in the belief that he was not infringing a regulation of the School. In accepting this belief under strong pressure and following incorrect advice, he committed an error of judgment.

[1] See p. 162.

We have decided to impose no penalty.

We wish, however, to make it clear that so long as the Regulations remain in their present form, we should be bound to take a serious view of any further infringement.

This was exactly the result that I had, as instructed, aimed at achieving. The procedure announced in advance by the Board had provided,[1] however, that, if they found the complaint justified, they would hear myself and Adelstein, in that order, on the question of what penalty should be imposed. This would have been the proper stage for me to indicate the desire of the School authorities that no penalty should be imposed, and it was then that I intended to do so. By omitting that stage (after, to be sure, an unduly wearisome and protracted hearing) the Board gave me no opportunity of doing so, and of showing that it was clarification, not blood, that we were after. The result was to give the militant students, as we shall see, a chance to proclaim a victory as their achievement.

The Board's proceedings had taken place in an oasis of civilized calm during a troubled day. During the morning, from 9.30 until 11.30, there had been an official demonstration; all students were asked by the Union to congregate outside the School, but to try to avoid obstructing traffic. A meeting was held in Houghton Street at 11 o'clock. A boycott of lectures, classes, and seminars continued all day, but personal tutorials were unaffected, and the library and refectory were fully used. A courteous apology was extended to the members of the academic staff for any inconvenience that might be caused them, and they were asked to support the boycott. It was recognized that the great majority of them would be unwilling to support a total boycott, but they were asked, if taking lectures or classes, to cancel them if a substantial proportion of students did not attend. The staff were told that the Union had decided on the boycott because it felt that Adelstein should not have been called before the Board for carrying out the Union's instructions, and that the Board's procedure implied a denial of natural justice, so that there was no assurance of a fair hearing. The belief that Adelstein was being denied the procedural safeguards for which he had asked was evidently the principal reason for the boycott, against which the Union had decided a week earlier. How much ground there was for that belief the reader will be able to judge.

The boycott itself was orderly, and there is no doubt that a high proportion of students did take part in it; but as lectures are not compulsory at the School and attendance is not recorded it is impossible to be precise—there are no normal attendance figures available as a base for comparison. A large crowd gathered outside the School bearing banners—'Free L.S.E.' and the like, and one which read 'Berkeley 1964: L.S.E. 1966: We'll bring *this* School to a halt too.' The official demonstration was not enough, however, for some, notably members of the Socialist Society, who went up to

[1] See p. 32, para. 9 (g).

the seventh floor of Connaught House, near the room where the Board of Discipline were sitting, and sat on the floor. They sang songs from the civil rights repertoire, some suitably amended—'We shall overcome,' 'We shall not be moved,' and 'We're gonna bury Walter Adams down by the riverside.' Surprisingly, the noise did not penetrate to the room where the Board were sitting; the walls and doors were solid, and we knew nothing of it until the Director sent a message up apologizing for the disturbance and saying that he could not remove the sitters save by calling in the police, which he was reluctant to do.

One attempt was made to reason with them, by Professor B. C. Roberts, whose room was nearby. They told him that their complaint was not against the teachers but against the administration. He told them that he was a Governor of the School and a member of sundry committees; this made him part of the administration, and they could talk to him. They asked him why communications were so poor, and he replied that one of the reasons was that administrative decisions were taken by committees, which often took a great deal of time to reach their conclusions. Then how, they asked did the committee which fixed up the disciplinary board hearing manage to operate so quickly? His reply is not recorded, but the question was an odd one, since students had been complaining as long as a fortnight before about the delay in disposing of the charge against Adelstein. Roberts went on to discuss with them some of the pros and cons of student representation, and also some of the shortcomings of the School.

The conclusion of the day's proceedings was described to the press by Adelstein as ' a substantial victory'. It showed that boycotts did not harden matters, he said, but in this instance had softened them. He was also reported by Mr. Nicholas Lloyd of *The Daily Mail* to have said 'Before the boycott I was refused the right to have a hearing under the rules of natural justice, but because of the boycott I was allowed a fair hearing with no interested parties on the Board, a legal representative and recorded minutes.' It is hard to see how Adelstein can possibly have believed that this was all due to the boycott; but, as experience has taught me, what a newspaper says that a man said is not necessarily what he did say. Yet Mr. Nicholas Lloyd is a careful and honest reporter.

There was, indeed, some dispute amongst students about the responsibility for the victory that they claimed. The more militant said that it was due to the boycott, but the National Union of Students said that it was due to the intervention of their solicitors. 'Adelstein pardoned by Board—NUS legal advice wins LSE day,' ran the headline in their *Student News* of 5 December. The actual verdict and the decision not to impose a penalty had in fact not been influenced either by the boycott or by the solicitors. Of the procedural issues, the only one that had in reality still been outstanding on the previous Friday had been the question whether the Director should sit as a member of the Board, and that had been settled before the letter from the N.U.S.'s solicitors had been received; but the lawyers can claim some responsibility for its settlement. It was not so much that we feared (as perhaps we should have feared) that the Courts would take the view that the Director should not sit; it was much more that we wanted to see the end of the matter; legal proceedings would, whatever their result, seriously delay the achievement of this object. What counted most, however, was the possibility that Adelstein would not present himself at the hearing if the Director sat.

This all goes to illustrate a lesson that will become apparent again in the course of my narrative. Besides the overt struggle with the School authorities there was another conflict, in some ways more important, going on amongst the students themselves, on the question whether the traditional reasoned negotiation with the universities and other public authorities should be replaced by more militant tactics. Each party to this conflict, which was now at a critical point, needed to show that its tactics worked. Militant students needed to claim the outcome of the disciplinary proceedings as a victory, and as a victory for militancy (as anything that happens at the time of militant action will, if it comes in handy, be claimed as a victory for militancy); the leaders of the N.U.S. and those who supported them had to respond by claiming the victory for their own tactics; neither could admit the possibility that it was not a victory, though the result achieved was what the School authorities had sought. The School authorities would not claim a victory; nor would any responsible university authorities in any circumstances claim a victory over their students. Victory is not what they want; to grind students into subjection would be a disaster. Even the talk of victory is—and was—harmful. It continues and exacerbates the conflict.

Not only had the concepts of victory and defeat, foreign to any satisfactory relationship, been introduced; a substantial body of students had been roused to a more militant attitude to the School authorities. The Union spoke for a more substantial following than ever before, and spoke for them in strident and belligerent terms. Deep suspicion of the good faith of the Director and the Governors had been created and energetically fomented; it was reciprocated; and there had appeared some signs of serious division amongst the staff.

The anti-Adams agitation was still continuing amongst the students. Adelstein made clear that he regarded the Union as now committed to opposition to Adams, and more protest as likely unless they were convinced that it was wrong for them to have any views on the subject. The Union Council themselves had brought out on 11 November a second but briefer pamphlet about Adams. The Socialist Society were reported to be planning a daily sit-in to block the administrative offices when Adams arrived at the School. Moves for 'student power' were rumoured—at the extreme a demand for equal participation with the staff in the running of the School and the election of the Director and Governors.

To such demands as this, even if they were meant to be taken seriously, no concessions were possible. On the other hand, remedies were being sought for what were believed to be the basic causes of student unrest. Academic departments were being pressed to improve the organization of teaching, and to introduce better arrangements for consultation with students in their care. If ordinary moderate students could be persuaded that their grievances were being attended to as rapidly as possible, the extremists could be isolated. One of the difficulties in the way was that of communication with the ordinary student. The whole of the School's student population could not be assembled in one place and addressed; we had no room nearly big enough. The normal channel of communication, the Union, could not be relied on; its officers were hostile and suspicious. A direct message must be sent to all students. It was drafted and printed during the Christmas vacation, and sent to all students before the beginning of the new term. It is reproduced in Appendix II.[1]

There was, of course, no possibility of reconciling the irreconcilables—*les enragés*—who were opposed not only to the School authorities but to the nature of contemporary society. We must do all we could by swift remedy of grievances to deprive them of support, but they were themselves evidently bent on causing more trouble. If so, no attempt, Caine felt, should be made to avoid it, which would merely have the result that they would hold their fire until Adams came. For him to have to deal with it in his first few days at the School would be unfairly difficult. It would be far better to have it out before he came.

There remained, in between the irreconcilables and the ordinary student, the Union and its hierarchy. The first meeting of the Ad Hoc Committee with the Union Council had been intended for a date earlier in the term but had had to be postponed because of the involvement of some of us in the disciplinary proceedings. Two or three meetings now took place. The discussions were intended to be exploratory, and were difficult at first, though on each occasion they eased noticeably after we had all had a buffet supper together at half-time. When they were concluded, it was with the understanding that they would be followed by other meetings in the new year, to discuss first the committee's draft report on the academic relationship with students—which the committee regarded as the more important and urgent part of their work—and then the subject of student representation and participation in the government of the School; the committee were inclined to propose the establishment of a Students' Representative Council. Its structure would be carefully devised to make it as truly representative as possible, and it would be separate from the Union, which would continue to carry out its welfare functions, and to act as a debating forum. The precise relationship between the two organizations was to be left open for further discussion. Our progress was not perhaps over-swift; but, as *Beaver* itself said in an editorial note, more important than achieving a rapid solution was achieving the right solution.

[1] See p. 165.

One moment of awkwardness arose. Adelstein applied for a sabbatical year—an extra year of preparation for his final examination, which he would otherwise have to take in the summer of 1967. Caine initially refused, but granted the application after Adelstein had appeared before the Ad Hoc Committee to present his case more fully.

On 2 December Caine addressed a meeting of the Union at their invitation. He was able to report that the Academic Board had agreed to set up a committee with equal membership of staff and students to review the disciplinary regulations, and that academic departments had all been asked to review arrangements for consultation with students, and were being encouraged to set up joint staff-student committees. Whether student representation on the principal committees of the School, however, would be effective or useful was not a matter for him to decide. It would be carefully considered by the bodies concerned, but he expressed his personal reservations about it. Of demands for autonomy for the Students' Union he said that the School was sympathetic to the idea of voluntary membership, but so long as membership remained automatic for all students the School had an inescapable obligation to watch the interests of minorities; the Union, moreover, was financed out of public funds and it was not right that public funds should be used for the support of particular political or religious opinions.

So the term ended, with problems unresolved, though with some hope of making a better start on solving them in the new year; but also with student militancy, hitherto unknown, a positive and powerful factor in our affairs. The small sit-in on 21 November had given us a useful warning of the way in which a small number of determined recalcitrants could, if they chose the right time and place, caused disruption out of all proportion to their numbers. I therefore gave some thought to precautions that we might take against future occasions of trouble. When the Court of Governors met on 8 December I thought it possible that there might be some kind of demonstration, and a small task force stood by under the command of a senior member of my staff: his instructions were to do everything possible to prevent obstruction or insult to Governors, but to give first priority to attempting to obtain evidence (including if necessary photographic evidence) that would enable disciplinary proceedings to be brought with success against malefactors. In fact, the occasion passed off quietly enough.

4 The Thirty-First of January

In January 1967 militancy was very much in the air. For some time there had been discontent with the National Union of Students and its methods. More radical students did not believe that it was opposing the educational policies of the Government sufficiently vigorously or effectively. They believed that what they called 'Tio Pepe diplomacy'—patient, reasoned negotiation with the authorities by a few well-briefed representatives, supplemented by informal contacts—should give place to mass lobbying of parliament and nation-wide demonstrations in which weight of numbers would be the principal means of argument.

Nor was it only on methods that they differed. The N.U.S. was debarred by its own constitution from discussing political issues not directly related to education. The radicals argued that it was useless to urge that more money should be spent on education unless they were at the same time prepared to show where the money could be found. If they proposed that it should be by savings on defence they were inevitably—and, as they believed, rightly—drawn into discussion of political issues about defence and foreign policy.

Those who took this view were engaged in the formation of the 'Radical Student Alliance', not as a rival body but as a 'ginger group' within the N.U.S. (which they perhaps hoped to capture). At the Council meeting of the N.U.S. in 1966, communist students, Young Liberals, and members of the National Association of Labour Student Organizations (N.A.L.S.O.) reached agreement on two major issues of policy, Vietnam and Rhodesia. From this agreement developed conversations between activist members of N.U.S. and officials of N.A.L.S.O., the Union of Liberal Students, and the National Student Committee of the Communist Party. During the summer, contact was developed with syndicalist student bodies in Europe, and in October 1966 the Radical Student Alliance published its initial manifesto; the twelve signatures to it were headed (presumably for alphabetical reasons) by that of Adelstein.

The manifesto called *inter alia* for

1. The right of students to complete control over their own unions;
2. their right to effective participation in all decisions that affect them;

3. full maintenance grants with no means test for all full-time students in further education;

4. a classless and comprehensive educational system;

5. resistance to undemocratic pressures in college government;

6. collective action by students on matters of social concern, such as racialism;

7. active co-operation with students in other countries;

8. the pursuit of a more active and militant policy in furtherance of the objectives of student organizations.

Before long the government gave the radicals the opportunity that they needed. On 21 December 1966 they announced very large increases in tuition fees for students from overseas at British technical colleges and universities, whose grants would be reduced correspondingly. For some time an influential body of opinion, including some vice-chancellors, had felt that university tuition fees should be substantially increased so as to make possible a reduction of direct government grants, on which the universities were becoming too dependent. The Robbins Report had expressed support for this change.[1] One of the major difficulties in its way was that it would cause a massive shift in the financial burden of higher education from central government to local authorities, by which the fees of the great majority of British students are paid. This difficulty did not, however, stand in the way of an increase in the fees of overseas students. It seemed absurd, moreover, that it should be cheaper for an American student to cross the Atlantic and come to a British university than to go to a graduate school in his own country, and that this benefit should be provided by the British taxpayer. The government's decision, therefore, has more to be said for it than some critics have admitted, but it was closely related to emotionally charged issues—academic freedom, the autonomy of the universities, even racial discrimination—and needed more careful preparation and presentation than it was given. The universities were not consulted in advance, and their sense of outrage was great.

The radical students seized upon the issue as one that they could exploit and handle more effectively than the N.U.S. (though they can claim no success: the government's decision still stands unaltered in 1969). On 20 January the Radical Student Alliance and the L.S.E. Students' Union Council jointly called for immediate and strong protest against the government's decision, and announced the inaugural convention of the Alliance, to be held on 28 and 29 January.

For much of the week that preceded this convention Adelstein was away from the School. At Hull he attended an informal meeting of representatives of students' unions at which a suggestion won favour that students at all universities should boycott their lectures on 22 February as a mark

---

[1] *Higher Education: Report of the Committee appointed by the Prime Minister under the Chairmanship of Lord Robbins: Cmnd. 2154*, paras. 652 seqq., especially 655.

of protest. In a debate there he was one of the proposers of a motion, carried by a large majority, expressing lack of confidence in the philosophy of the N.U.S.

At the week-end, on 28 and 29 January, the inaugural convention of the R.S.A. was held at L.S.E. Adelstein was elected to its Council at the top of the poll. The convention was welcomed by 'Paddy' O'Connor, the Mayor of the London Borough of Camden, himself a man with some experience of social protest, who told the students 'militancy is worth a good deal more than negotiation'.

Meanwhile militants were at work at L.S.E. *Beaver* appeared for the first time in the new year on 19 January, under a new editor. Its main banner headline on the front page read: 'ADAMS' COLLEGE EMPTIES'. The article that appeared below these words gave a gloomy and misleading account, based on inaccurate information or half-truths, of the present state of the University College of Rhodesia. A leading article, under the heading 'STOP ADAMS', read:

Adams should not come. It is not a question of whether or not he is a good man, whether or not he is a racialist. You don't choose the Director for these qualities or the lack of them. The case against Adams is quite simple: that he is not the man for the job. *Beaver* has gone into the whole business deeply, and we are satisfied firstly that he did co-operate with the Smith regime, and thus permit a gross infringement of academic freedom; secondly, and in our view far more important, he is not an efficient administrator nor in good enough contact with his students for a candidate for the position of Director of LSE. LSE needs a Director with good administrative abilities, an active concern for the welfare of the students, and above all a certain dynamism which is needed to get the place out of the present rut. It does not need a stopgap, nobody's first choice or even second choice.

Something must be done and quickly. Union should choose a group of people to devote themselves solely to stopping Adams. The campaign must be organized at national level to put as much pressure as possible on the Administration to change their minds. This can be done, if it is done quickly.

On an inner page an article was headed 'WHO REALLY WANTS ADAMS? a despicable or a noble man—two views and more facts.' It gave an account of Adams's past career, and of views favourable to him; and then went on to sum up the case against him, concluding:

STOP HIM. A mistake has been made in the method of selection. It can be reversed for two reasons: firstly, because the appointment is only for a relatively short period, secondly, Sir Sydney Caine would retain his post for another two years to make time for a more suitable successor to be found.

The renewed campaign to 'stop Adams' for which *Beaver* called was soon under way. An *ad hoc* organization, not chosen by the Union, and fluid in character, was already in being with the object of finding ways and means, if possible, of stopping the appointment.

At a meeting held on Wednesday 18 January 1967, Union Council discussed a proposal that they should summon a special Union meeting to consider calling a sit-in to express opposition to Adams's appointment. As only five of the eight Council members present voted in favour they judged the support insufficient and dropped the proposal. At their next meeting, a week later, they agreed that Marshall Bloom should arrange a 'teach-in on sit-ins', on Tuesday, 31 January, to which outside speakers would be invited. On the following Friday, 27 January, it was announced at the regular Union meeting that there would be a meeting on Tuesday at 4 p.m. about Dr. Adams.

On Monday, 30 January, after the R.S.A. convention, Adelstein was back in the chair at a meeting of Union Council. It devoted most of its time to discussion of oversea students' fees, but found time to agree also that the meeting organized by Marshall Bloom on ways of opposing Dr. Adams should be held on Tuesday afternoon.

Apart from a rumour, which we had not taken seriously, that 'a teach-in on sit-ins' was to be arranged for 31 January, nothing of this came to the notice of the School authorities until Monday, 30 January, when leaflets, of which the following is a specimen, were distributed in the students' refectory:

STOP ADAMS
STOP ADAMS
HOW
Come to a meeting to decide further
action

TUESDAY.   31st January.   OLD THEATRE.   4 p.m.

One of them was brought to me after lunch by one of the secretarial staff. I took it to the Director, and on making enquiries we found that the Old Theatre was booked for the time specified in the name of the Graduate Students' Association, an organization hitherto more somnolent than militant. We discussed what should be done. Caine had always been very reluctant to interfere with the free expression of student opinion, but the proposed meeting seemed to be going beyond reasonable limits. Should it not be stopped, he asked. After reflection we thought not. It would be as well to know how much support the meeting attracted. If it were poorly attended, that would be useful and encouraging to know. Even if it were well-attended it would be better that we should know, and have a chance of finding out what was planned for the future, than drive the agitation underground and remain in ignorance. Caine decided to let the meeting continue, therefore, but, since it was advertised as an open meeting, he agreed also that I might arrange for one of our staff to attend it and see what happened.

That evening, after the Director had entertained the Union officers to dinner, he and I went to have a look at the advertisements for the meeting. They consisted generally of a reproduction of the front page of *The New Statesman* of 26 May 1956, containing an article criticizing Adams for permitting separate halls of residence to be maintained for European and African students at the University College of Rhodesia. Across the page a strip had been added, reading: ' "Compromises" on essentials did not begin at University College, Rhodesia, when UDI was declared. Rather, the college was founded on racialist distinctions negotiated and defended by LSE's new director, Walter Adams.' At the foot were manuscript additions, various in content. A typical specimen read: 'WANTED: new Director. 3½ year sinecure for aloof, irresponsible, unprincipled man. Any offers?' We agreed that some of these posters were intolerably libellous and we took them down.

On the following day, 31 January, the day on which the meeting was due to be held, further leaflets in the following form were in circulation:

STOP ADAMS   STOP ADAMS   STOP ADAMS   STOP ADAMS

Soon a man who is an inefficient administrator, a man who considers it no part of his duty to protect his staff and students against intimidation, censorship, imprisonment and deportation by an illegal regime, a man who has had a vote of no confidence passed against him by his own teaching staff, will become *your* Director.

The basic facts are not controversial: all the reports on University College, Rhodesia, whether written by a headmaster of Eton, Amnesty International, the International Students Conference, or fifty-five lecturers at the college, have strongly criticized Adams.

The selection of this man as L.S.E.'s new director is symbolic of a host of problems including the place of the students in their college, and there is no better place to begin work for a different L.S.E. than by opposing the appointment of Adams. Although the selection committee itself is unlikely to reverse its decision given his own health, Adams might resign if it were clear that enough students did not want him.

We must make it clear that we still don't want Adams and are prepared to take direct action to prevent his becoming our Director. Come to a meeting on Tuesday, at 4.0 p.m., in the Old Theatre, to discuss what can be done to stop him.

An alternative version was identical save for the omission in the third paragraph of the words 'given his own health'. Both versions were on yellow paper and came to be known as 'the yellow leaflets'.

I picked up one of these leaflets at midday and showed it to Caine. His first thoughts of the previous day had been to doubt whether the meeting should be allowed to be held in the Old Theatre, and now he was sure that he could not properly allow it. We arranged for the booking of the Old

Theatre to be formally cancelled and for notices to that effect to be put on the theatre doors. Caine sent for Bloom, as the president of the organization that had booked the theatre, to tell him of his decision. He began by asking—in order to be sure that he was speaking to the right person—who was responsible for the meeting to be held at four o'clock in the Old Theatre. Bloom has said that he answered 'the Graduate Students Association Committee and the Union Council'. Caine then told him that the booking of the Old Theatre had been cancelled. He showed him the yellow leaflet and drew attention to its last paragraph. He explained the distinction that he drew between a meeting arranged for discussion and one arranged for planning 'direct action', which he did not feel that the School should accommodate. Bloom took the decision with apparent calm, saying 'I understand your position'. In fact, however, he was in some confusion and was to admit later that he had not understood exactly what had been banned or why. He asked whether the meeting could be held if direct action were not discussed. Caine said not; the reference to direct action, once made, altered the situation. Bloom also asked whether Caine would have taken a similar view if a motion on the lines of the yellow paper had been put at a Students' Union meeting, and Caine replied that he could not say what his view would have been in those hypothetical circumstances. After asking him to confirm his decision by letter, Bloom left.

Caine's decision has been criticized on a number of grounds, which may be classified as follows:

1. that he had inadequate information about the purpose of the meeting;
2. that he made a political misjudgment;
3. that he did not make his decision clear;
4. that he did not give the students an opportunity of discussing the matter with him;
5. that his decision was an interference with the freedom of speech and assembly.

I take these in turn:

1. *the purpose of the meeting.* It is said that the meeting was merely to discuss Adams's appointment; it might or might not, critics say, have gone on to decide on further protest. When a meeting has not taken place and now never will, conclusive evidence of its nature is clearly not to be had; but the best evidence available is then the advertisements of it, taken against the background of the time. The background is provided by *Beaver*'s call for Adams's appointment to be 'reversed', for Adams to be 'stopped'. An L.S.E. student questioning Senator Robert Kennedy at a meeting at Oxford on the previous Sunday, 29 January, had spoken of the students of L.S.E. as 'trying to remove their new Director'. And the advertisements? Monday's leaflets spoke of deciding 'further action' to stop Adams. The yellow leaflet went further; after indicating the possibility that Adams might be prevailed upon to resign, it said 'we must make it

clear that . . . we are prepared to take direct action to prevent his becoming our Director. Come to a meeting . . . to discuss what can be done to stop him.' The issue has become a little confused because of the emphasis put on Caine's equation of 'direct action' with violence or a serious possibility of violence.[1] This has distracted attention from the word 'prevent', which is a very forcible expression to use. There is a world of difference between protesting at an appointment and preventing a man from taking it up. Prevention is more than persuasion, and more than words.

2. *the political judgment.* It is said that the meeting was not going to attract much attention; it was going to come to nothing, and the opposition to Adams would have fizzled out. Caine made it important by banning it. I should certainly agree that the opposition to Adams was most unlikely to be strong enough to force Adams to resign; but, though numerically a small minority, Adams's opponents were determined and organized, and could have been a very serious nuisance to him, especially in his first few days at the School. Be that as it may, however, Caine's decision was not made on grounds of expediency.

3. *clarity of decision.* It is said that Caine did not make clear whether the ban applied to the Old Theatre only or to all parts of the School, and that this uncertainty made it difficult for the students to decide what to do. Bloom cannot have supposed that the ban on the use of the Old Theatre was due to any special circumstances affecting the theatre alone; it was the nature of the meeting, as Caine saw it, which made it unfit for the School to accommodate. Caine's decision therefore carried the implication that he would not allow the meeting in any part of the School under his control. The question whether it could be held in the Three Tuns Bar was not raised by Bloom, and it is expecting a little too much of Caine to say that he should have suggested to Bloom where he could take his meeting. If Bloom was in doubt, he had ample opportunity to ask Caine more questions; but he did not take it.

4. *opportunity of discussion.* Caine has been criticized for not sending for Adelstein to discuss the matter, and also for taking his decision at the very last moment. Adelstein, however, knew comparatively little about the meeting, as was to appear later; he had not seen the yellow leaflet, for example, and he had not been at the School very much during the week while the meeting was being planned. It was essentially Bloom's meeting and Bloom was the man for whom the Director sent. As to shortness of notice, Caine took a little while to make up his mind; banning a meeting is a serious matter; and when he had taken his decision, it took a while to find Bloom, which is not altogether surprising. It is perfectly true that the time left was short; but there was a good half-hour or more left during which Bloom could have discussed the matter further with Caine, or could have brought Adelstein to see him. If Bloom had been a young and inexperienced lad,

[1] An equation more reasonable than some critics allow; violence followed within a few hours of Caine's decision.

timid and hesitant, it might have been different; but he was a graduate, articulate, and Caine was entitled to assume that if Bloom said he understood, then he really did.

5. *interference with freedom of expression and of assembly.* It is said that the students had the right to discuss Adams's appointment and to meet for the purpose as they chose, and that Caine was not justified in interfering with their exercise of these freedoms. Clearly, however, these freedoms are not unlimited. As discussion of illicit action progresses to advocacy of it, and advocacy to incitement, it is a matter of some nicety to determine precisely the point at which preventive action is justified; and it is easier to criticize the decision than to make it. Caine's view was that the yellow leaflets indicated clearly as the purpose of the meeting something beyond what he could properly allow in premises under his control, and he saw it as his duty to exclude the meeting from those premises; it could still have been held elsewhere. Bloom did not attempt to suggest that he was wrong. I find it very hard to understand the contention that it was Caine's duty to allow the School's principal lecture-room to be used for the preparation of action to prevent his successor from taking up his appointment. One man's freedom ends where that of another begins. The students' freedom of speech and assembly ended at the point where their exercise would constitute or contribute to improper pressure upon Adams.

Soon after leaving Caine, Bloom went over to the Students' Union offices. Someone was sent to fetch Adelstein from the library, where he was working, and with four other members he held a Council meeting, which Bloom attended. It was a confused meeting. Bloom said that he did not understand the extent of the ban or the reasons for it. Some of the members of Council present had not read the yellow leaflet, and its relevance does not seem to have been appreciated. Adelstein went out of the meeting to try to speak to the Director on the telephone, to see what he could find out about the ban; but the Director's line was engaged, and he returned no wiser. The meeting broke up; what, if anything, it had decided was to be a question for investigation later, but it is certain that it did not decide either to call the meeting off or to transfer it somewhere else inside or outside the School.

While the meeting was going on, or very soon after, the Union duplicator was being used for running off leaflets, to be described in a moment, proclaiming that the meeting was to be held despite the ban; but it appears that the Council members had no hand in the preparation of these leaflets and indeed knew nothing of them. The leaflets, one supposes, would have been issued whatever the Council decided; but any claims they had to legitimacy would have been greatly diminished if the Council had decided to call the meeting off.

About half an hour after Bloom had left the Director we were told that some of the notices that had been fixed to the theatre doors had been removed, and others defaced; posters were beginning to appear saying that the meeting would be held in the theatre despite the ban. Fresh copies of the Director's notice were put up, and he decided that porters should be stationed at the doors with instructions to refuse entry to students; as the doors could not be locked the theatre light-fuses were removed. This was an odd thing to do, perhaps: but the purpose was a simple one—to keep people out of the theatre during the time that it took to collect the porters.

Leaflets were now being circulated freely. The following is a specimen:

CAINE BANS ADAMS MEETING.

AT 2 p.m. THIS AFTERNOON SIR SYDNEY CAINE SAW MARSHALL BLOOM, CHAIRMAN OF THE GRADUATE STUDENTS' ASSOCIATION TO HIS OFFICE AND TOLD HIM THAT THE 'STOP ADAMS' MEETING SCHEDULED FOR THIS AFTERNOON AT 4 P.M. WAS BANNED.

THIS MEETING WAS SPONSORED BY THE STUDENTS' UNION COUNCIL AND THE GRADUATE STUDENTS' ASSOCIATION.

THIS IS AN ATTACK ON FREE SPEECH—IT MUST BE OPPOSED.

THIS MEETING SHALL TAKE PLACE

4 p.m.   In the OLD THEATRE!

Caine asked me to go to the entrance hall at four o'clock and, if a substantial number of students assembled there and sought admission to the theatre, to tell them that he was willing to come down to explain the reasons for his decision. As that time approached the entrance hall filled up rapidly. Three or four hundred students were gathered there, on the stairs and in the corridor nearby: some of them, no doubt, had come in response to the original notice, not knowing that the meeting had been cancelled; some in response to the leaflets announcing that it would take place despite the ban; and some because they were passing that way at the time.

A little before four o'clock Bloom walked in and took up his place in front of the theatre, facing the crowd. He was followed by a troop of students, several of whom sat down on the floor in front of him. Two of them produced a large banner with the words 'STUDENTS RIGHTS' on it and held it up in front of him. He stepped forward to address the assembly and got involved in the banner, so that to me, turning towards him at that moment, he looked rather like a statue waiting to be unveiled.

The atmosphere seemed light-hearted, and there was badinage between students and porters. Bloom was later to say in evidence to the Board of Discipline that he opened the proceedings by explaining the Director's decision and by saying that microphones had been set up in the Students' Union Three Tuns Bar so that the meeting could be held there. I was meanwhile engaged for a minute or two with a reporter. When I arrived back on the scene someone not known to me was saying 'May I put the suggestion that we send a small delegation to see Sir Sydney Caine in order to ask him to reconsider his decision about whether we can use the Old Theatre?' There was dissent, and someone shouted 'Why can't he come to speak to us?' At this point I went up to Bloom and told him that the Director had left word with me that, if it was desired, he would be willing to come and explain why he had forbidden the use of the Old Theatre. There seemed to be general assent to his being asked to come.

I went to meet him. By the time, five minutes later, that we arrived back in the hall the atmosphere had changed very much for the worse. The crowd was noisier and much less good-humoured, and inflammatory remarks were being shouted. When Caine tried to speak he had some difficulty. Some shouted that he should be heard only if they all went into the theatre; but someone, again not known to me, proposed that he be allowed to speak for two minutes. A student addressed him: 'May I put it to you, Sir Sydney, that it is a great insult to us, as a student body, that we should have to meet you outside here, in these conditions? Would you please reconsider your decision not to allow us to use the Old Theatre?' He replied in the negative, and someone shouted 'What about our rights to the Old Theatre?' Caine replied 'Students have no *rights* to the Old Theatre.' After the word 'rights' there was a roar from many of the crowd, so that all that could be heard by most of them was simply 'Students have no rights.' Not surprisingly this angered many hearers. A small number of people were shouting inflammatory remarks, then forcing their way through the crowd to another position, and shouting again from there. The crowd was turning, or being turned, into a mob.

Nevertheless, Caine got something of a hearing for a very short time. He explained that he had not made any objection to criticism of the appointment of Adams. There had been no interference with *Beaver* and he had not prohibited the meeting so long as he had thought it was simply for discussion of the appointment. At midday, however, he had learned that it was called for the purpose of planning 'direct action' to prevent Adams from taking up his appointment. That implied more than the use of rational processes of discussion; it meant violence. 'It is not', he said, 'to prevent free speech that I have forbidden this meeting, but to prevent direct action against this School.' After he had spoken, he was again asked whether he would reconsider his decision and allow the theatre to be used. Again he refused, saying 'I'm not going to have a meeting on this subject in this atmosphere.' Someone shouted from the back 'You're having it!'

There was a confused and disorderly discussion, in the course of which I saw Adelstein for the first time that day, on the stairs leading down to the entrance hall. He shouted out 'Let's all go to the bar, let's all go to the bar!' Someone else explained again that the Three Tuns Bar had been prepared for a meeting, but there were shouts of 'No!' and booing, and there appeared to be few in favour. Someone stood up on a chair and said:

We have heard Sir Sydney speak, and since he will not let us into the Old Theatre I propose that he now leaves us. Given that we are here, blocking the library entrance, the stairs, the main entrance, and part of Houghton Street, Sir Sydney has two alternatives open to him: he may leave us and allow us to have this meeting, or he may try and move us. Should we decide to go into the Old Theatre it would solve his predicament.

Shortly after this Adelstein came forward and spoke again. Precisely what he said was later to be carefully considered by the Board of Discipline.[1] I have the clearest recollection of hearing him say that the Director's authority had been used arbitrarily; Caine had tried for wrong reasons to say that the students could not discuss something, and the issue was one of free speech. It was a matter of academic freedom that, as students, they should be able to express their opinions in the institution in which they studied. It was a matter of principle that they should, as a responsible body, discuss the subject somewhere. If this was the issue it did not really matter where they discussed it, but he thought, nevertheless, that they ought to discuss it where they had said they were going to, and where they always had discussed things, in the Old Theatre. Reviewing the evidence many months later, I believe that there was a most unfortunate ambiguity in Adelstein's words. When he said that the students ought to meet in the Old Theatre, I am now inclined to think that he intended to convey that they ought to be allowed to meet there, but that the words that he used conveyed to some of his hearers the meaning that if they were to be true to their principles they had a duty to meet in the Old Theatre. Be that as it may, at the end of the speech someone—either Bloom or Adelstein—took a vote on whether they should go to the bar or to the Old Theatre. The vote was heavily in favour of the theatre. Caine was again asked whether he would change his decision, and again refused. There was a movement towards one of the doors of the theatre. Caine and I moved to stand in front of the porters in the doorway, and a number of students, including Bloom and Adelstein, are said to have formed a line to hold the crowd back.

A few minutes later Adelstein spoke once more. He seems to have supposed earlier that there was really nothing except the Director's decision

[1] See p. 69.

to stop the students from entering the theatre, but he now knew that there were porters in front of the doors, and saw that there would be resistance. 'I am sorry,' he said, 'I made a mistake; I did not realize that the doors into the Old Theatre were barred. You can't hold the meeting there.' He asked for further consideration. Would the Director reverse his decision? Caine again refused. Would the porters stand aside? Someone suggested that this was unfair to the porters—they might lose their jobs. Adelstein then took a vote again, this time, it appears, using the words 'storm the Old Theatre' to describe one of the alternatives. Almost as he was saying this, however, the porters at one of the doors were forced back, and at about the same time others entered the theatre by a side door. Confusion increased. There were cries that some students were already in the theatre, and that all must go in, or else the few who were there would be victimized. Adelstein again took a vote, and asked the Director to reconsider his decision. Assaults were being made on the theatre doors. Somebody hit a porter, and the porter hit him back. Caine and I asked one or two students who were taking part in the assault to give their names, but they refused. During the scuffles, Adelstein asked the Director whether he would agree to the meeting being held in the bar (which was Union territory, and outside the Director's immediate control); Caine replied that he would agree, on condition that it was a meeting with a more rational discussion. Would he also agree that, if they moved to the bar, there would be no victimization of those who were already in the theatre? He said that he would agree.

Meanwhile in one of the scuffles several porters had been forced back into the theatre, and one of them slipped and fell to the floor. One of his colleagues ran across the hall to the Porters' Room and said 'they've got Wally!' Those of the porters who were in the room came to the aid of their colleagues. Among them was Mr. Edward Poole, a man of sixty-four with a very weak heart and very near to retiring age. He had nearly sixteen years' service with the School and was very popular with staff and students. He was sitting having his tea, but he hated to be out of things, and came to the help of his colleagues. He took his stand between two of them at the nearest doors, which, as ill-luck would have it, were those at which there was the heaviest pressure. He can only have been there a minute or two when I turned and saw him, grey in the face, slipping down to the floor. Students cried 'Man hurt!' and made way for him to be carried over to the Porters' Room. Adelstein told the crowd 'This is more serious. Don't go in. Someone is hurt. Sir Sydney has given us an assurance that there will be no victimization of those already in the Old Theatre. Will everyone please go to the bar?'

I myself went to the Porters' Room, where the School Nurse was trying to resuscitate Poole. We summoned an ambulance, but it was clear enough that he was dead, from heart-failure, as it was later established; no one had molested him in any way. Caine meanwhile had gone into the theatre to attempt to persuade those who were there to go to the bar. His efforts were unsuccessful, and he was on the point of saying that the time-limit was up and his promise of no victimization withdrawn, when the news was brought to him that Poole was dead. He announced this, and told them to go. Some professed incredulity, but they left the theatre.

In the entrance hall, still very crowded, students were standing, some in tears, as Poole was carried out to the ambulance. For a while all the arguments and differences seemed very trivial. We sent a porter who knew the Poole family to break the news to them, and Caine decided to close the School for the rest of the day. A little later he asked me to come with him to the Three Tuns Bar, where he wanted to speak to the meeting if it was still going on. We found only a few students arguing there in a corner, with someone addressing them passionately about Caine's alleged interference with free speech. Caine told them of the death of Poole, who, he said, had had a very weak heart and might have died at any time; no student should feel himself in any way responsible; but he went on to point the lesson that violence could so easily arise in this sort of situation. After all that had happened it was evidently his first and deepest concern that the students should not blame themselves for Poole's death, and it was repeated on subsequent occasions that they were not responsible. It was true, I suppose; but it remains my opinion that if it had been a normal day Poole would have had his tea and gone home.

After Caine had spoken in the bar, we returned to our offices. Soon after, I was called into Caine's room, where he had the Students' Union Council with him. I was told that they had agreed to issue a joint press-statement, which I was asked to prepare. It read as follows:

The School and its Students' Union deeply regret that, in the course of an attempt by students to gain admission to the School's main lecture theatre for the purpose of holding a meeting for which the Director had refused permission, one of the School porters had a heart attack and died. The porter's state of health was known to the School authorities and he had not been detailed to take any part but came to join his colleagues at the doors of the theatre.

The School and the Students' Union share the deepest regret that the chain of events should have had this tragic end.

As I was leaving later that evening I met Dr. P. Cohen, Adelstein's tutor, who had heard what had happened and was very worried. I tried to be consoling, saying that, as it seemed to me, Adelstein and Bloom had not been responsible for any of the violence, but had been trying to control the crowd. What I said to him then Cohen very properly quoted as evidence for their defence in the later disciplinary proceedings, by which time I had completely forgotten it. Did what I said to him reflect a considered judgment? I think not entirely. That evening we were all suffering from a profound sense of shock, and the desire to blot out awkward memories, close gulfs, reduce tensions, and conciliate was overwhelming. Perhaps we should have been angry instead, but that came with reflection.

E

5 The Decision to Prosecute

The narrative unfolded in the previous chapter has been pieced together in part from what I myself saw and heard at the time; but still more from an examination of evidence that has since become available. On the following day there was a natural desire among my colleagues to learn more of the confused events of 31 January and to discuss them. There appeared to be a strong majority in favour of the institution of disciplinary proceedings against those who were primarily responsible for the disorder that had occurred: but who were they? The Board of Discipline seemed to some the body to which responsibility fell for investigating the question. Such a course, however, might lead the Board into acting first as investigator, then inevitably as prosecutor, and finally as judge. This would be contrary to the rules of natural justice. At a special meeting of the Academic Board called that day, therefore, the Director agreed to appoint a small committee of enquiry 'to make an urgent investigation into the events of Tuesday, 31 January 1967, and to make recommendations as to action to be taken'. Their report was to be presented to me, and was to indicate in particular whether charges against any individuals should be laid before the Board of Discipline. There was a minority of members of the staff anxious that time should be allowed for passions to cool. By them the appointment of the committee was, I believe, welcomed as an occasion of delay; but their opinion was not much voiced at the time.

The Director forthwith constituted the committee, appointing three professors to it. They had their first meeting the same afternoon, and for the next week sat almost continuously every day except Sunday, going on until midnight each night. They issued a general invitation to witnesses to come to give evidence, and about eighty did so, mostly students but also some members of the staff of the School.

As it happened, a special meeting of the Court of Governors had been called for the following day, for the purpose of discussing possible reforms in the machinery of government of the School, and Tuesday's events were of course considered. The Court were satisfied that the committee of enquiry had been appointed, but were anxious that the disciplinary proceedings that would, as they assumed, follow should not be protracted.

They formally expressed their deep concern at recent events and recorded their support for the Director.

In the next few days opposing positions were being taken up by various groups of staff and students. A hundred and twenty-five members of the teaching staff signed a statement condemning 'the attacks made upon the Director designate by some students of the School, and the violence to which they have led, as entirely contrary to the spirit in which the affairs of the School should be conducted and a potential threat to academic freedom'. A smaller number issued a rival statement blaming all parties—staff, students, and administrators—for the situation.

Student voices were at first very critical of their fellows. A group of sixteen wrote to *The Times* dissociating themselves from the activities of their colleagues and urging that they cease from hysteria. Mr. Peter Watherston, Chairman of the L.S.E. Conservative Society, soon to be elected President of the Union, said that there were a number of people at L.S.E. who hoped that the officers of the Students' Union would resign. Fly-sheets were distributed demanding the resignation of 'extremists' and measures to reduce the power of Union officers; Bloom was criticized for interpreting what happened at the School in the light of irrelevant experience in the civil rights movement. Others, however, proclaimed that free speech had been denied and that to censure their leaders would be to reinforce those who were anxious to prevent change, and to lay the way open for future arbitrary action. It was time for students to stand together and press forward with practical proposals. The Socialist Society, in particular, proclaimed opposition to 'a student witch-hunt' directed against Adelstein and Bloom, but also to the committee of inquiry, which would, they said, report to an administration and academic staff that saw the situation 'as an opportunity to destroy the movement for students' rights and to victimize those who have been involved in it'.

On Friday 3 February, the Union Council issued their own account of what had happened. To the narrative as I have related it, it had only one piece of information to add, but that piece appeared to be of considerable significance: 'At 3 p.m. on Tuesday 31st January,' the statement recorded, 'a meeting of five members of Union Council was held and it was felt that the 4 p.m. meeting should continue.' It appeared, that is to say, that the decision to hold the banned meeting had been taken, after Caine's interview with Bloom, by a meeting of the Union Council.

On the day that this statement was issued the Union met; some seven to eight hundred members were present. A motion expressing regret at Poole's death and sympathy for Mrs. Poole was carried by an overwhelming majority and a collection was taken for Poole's family. Adelstein then moved: 'Union never has condoned and never shall condone physical violence.' Watherston moved an amendment, which was accepted by Adelstein, to add 'in the furtherance of student aims', and the motion was carried by a very large majority.

Adelstein then left the Chair to move:

Union

    a. accepts Council's deepest regret that a meeting organized by Council should have resulted in the tragic events of Tuesday 31st January 1967

    b. in view of the situation that has developed asks Council to continue in office.

In moving this he spoke, *Beaver* (No. 68) records, 'with uncustomary lack of confidence and was subjected to the same vicious heckling that his critics claimed had been thrown at them.' Referring to the banning of the meeting, Adelstein stated that it had not been known whether the ban applied specifically to the Old Theatre or to the whole college; this was, he said, 'another breakdown in communication between staff and school'.

Watherston spoke against the motion and called on Council to resign. They were, he said, collectively responsible for what had happened. By calling on them to resign he did not mean to suggest that they were to blame for it all, but he did blame them for deliberately defying, as he saw it, the Director's ban on the meeting and for seeking a direct confrontation with the School without authority from the Union. He also criticized them for allowing provocative posters to be put up on notice-boards.

The first part of the motion, accepting Council's regret, was carried unopposed. During the debate on the second part there was considerable disorder and the debate had to be adjourned for five minutes. Soon after it was resumed the General Secretary announced his resignation, saying that he was not prepared to represent students who changed their allegiances. He proposed that the motion should lie on the table until such time as it could be discussed in a more rational atmosphere, and his proposal was approved by well over a two-thirds majority.

The Union Council had survived the first wave of criticism and could now reasonably expect to remain in office. It was Bloom's turn to face his critics four days later at a meeting of the Graduate Students' Association on Tuesday, 7 February. He said that he had had nothing to do with the publication of the inflammatory posters and leaflets distributed prior to the meeting of 31 January. He had spent the major part of the time trying to calm the meeting down. The tragedy of the whole affair had been the lack of time given to the students to organize properly some alternative to the banned meeting in the Old Theatre, coupled with a certain misunderstanding in that when the Director announced that the meeting had been banned he gave them no opportunity to explain the true meaning of 'direct action', but was under the erroneous impression that it meant violence. A motion accepting Bloom's report was passed by a large majority; and it was agreed by 115 votes to 93 that the Graduate Students' Association should take no further part in Students' Union politics, and that it should take no part in student politics without the authorization of a simple majority of votes at a meeting of the association called for the purpose. A motion of no confidence in Bloom was then debated, but was rejected after a number of speakers had urged that the previous motion provided sufficient safeguards for the future.

The joint Staff–Student Committee met on 8 February and discussed recent events, beginning with a far-reaching suggestion that any action planned by staff or students should in future be referred to the committee so that any misunderstanding could be alleviated or removed. In discussion it was pointed out that the difficulty lay in forecasting which actions were likely to cause trouble, but generally accepted that better arrangements for consultation of student opinion were needed. There followed some discussion of the agitation against Adams. One of the conventions on which academic institutions worked was, it was argued, that, since senior appointments were always likely to be controversial, one nevertheless agreed to work with whoever was appointed. What did the student members think that the School should do, when once an appointment had been made according to the established procedure, if a group continued to agitate against it? The students had not asked for representation on the selection committee during the twelve months when it was sitting; questions had been raised only after the appointment had been announced. Once a man had been appointed, ought the School to stand by and take no action against anyone who mounted a campaign against him? It was natural and reasonable that people should express their reactions to the appointment; that was fair comment; but once there was a contract of appointment, the School felt that it had a duty to protect members of its staff from intimidation. One reason why students were sometimes called irresponsible was that they did not look more than one move ahead. If Adams were to resign because of student agitation, the only type of man who would agree to come in his place would be one who would be prepared to disregard students entirely.

On the other hand it was argued by the students that a large number of them felt that new information had come to light since the appointment had been announced, and had cast doubts on its legitimacy. Adams had not been allowed to reply, and Lord Bridges had not explained to the Union whether the facts concerned had been taken into consideration. It was not for the School to clamp down on any form of agitation. Students should be allowed not only to discuss the appointment of Adams but also to demonstrate when he arrived.

The committee agreed in the end on the following statement:

Student representatives were of the opinion that the Adams issue would die of inanition provided that disciplinary actions arising out of last Tuesday's events did not exacerbate feeling. The staff members of the committee agreed that there was a real danger that strong disciplinary action would worsen the situation. It was therefore agreed that these views should be submitted to those responsible for initiating and taking disciplinary action, if any, and that they should be recommended to take these views into consideration.

I was unable to be present at the meeting at which this conclusion was reached, and my recollection is that the advice contained in it did not reach me until the die was cast, for the report of the committee of inquiry reached me that evening. The members of the committee, while agreed on other matters, had failed to reach agreement on the major issue. It rested, therefore, with me to decide whether disciplinary proceedings should be instituted. In the light of the information contained in the report I reviewed the possibilities. Students had forced their way into the Old Theatre; but their identity was not known, and the Director had granted them immunity if the meeting moved to the Three Tuns Bar. It was true that he had been on the point of withdrawing that immunity, but he had not done so. Students had also prepared and circulated leaflets proclaiming that the banned meeting would nevertheless be held; but again their identity was not known. A considerable number of students were believed to know who they were, but would not reveal it; it was a closely guarded secret, and there was no way of finding out.

The conduct of Adelstein, Bloom, and the four members of the Union Council who had met with them at three o'clock on 31 January—Miss P. G. Jones, Mr. S. Malik, Mr. S. Moss, and Mr. A. P. Ross—seemed from the information available to me to give serious ground for complaint. They had, as it then seemed, decided that the four o'clock meeting should be held despite the ban; and what made it worse was that they seemed to have made no serious effort first to persuade the Director to change his mind. Then they had come to the theatre entrance at four o'clock. For what purpose had they come? To hold the meeting? Did it not look, then, as though they had together conspired to disobey the Director's decision?

I next considered Bloom's other actions. He had come to the theatre entrance at four, and had for a time apparently presided over the assembly in the entrance hall. Was that assembly the forbidden meeting? It had not discussed the subject which that meeting had been called to discuss, it was true, but if Caine had reconsidered his decision when he was asked to do so, the students would all have trooped into the theatre, I had no doubt, and would have gone on with their advertised business. It was, then, the forbidden meeting, though engaged on a preliminary point of business— settling where to meet. It was not made any more permissible by being held in the entrance hall, for two reasons: first, the entrance hall was not a place where meetings were allowed to be held; second, Caine's grounds for banning it clearly extended by implication beyond the theatre to any part of the School over which he had direct control. The meeting, I judged, was the forbidden meeting, and by convening and presiding over it Bloom appeared to have committed a clear offence. Adelstein and Bloom had put to a vote in the entrance hall the question whether the assembly should stay there, go to the Three Tuns Bar, or enter the theatre. The last alternative was forbidden, but they had not drawn attention to that fact, and had let the assembly vote again and again as if the three alterna-tives were on an equal footing. They had been under no obligation to put anything to the vote; the assembly was never a Union meeting, and if it was at the beginning a meeting of the Graduate Students' Association it had by the time the votes were taken degenerated into a disorderly assembly and then a mob. By taking the votes they were, as it seemed to me, conferring a spurious legitimacy on the desire to invade the theatre, and indeed assisting that illicit purpose to be shaped and made known.

Last of all, I examined more closely the evidence of the content of Adelstein's speeches. It appeared to suggest that he had told the crowd that if they thought it a matter of principle that they should hold their meeting in the Old Theatre, then if they held to their principles they must meet there. He seemed not to have suggested that any weight was to be attached to the Director's decision, but, by calling that decision arbitrary, rather the reverse. What he had said seemed to me to amount to encouragement to the mob to demand entry to the theatre.

There appeared, then, to be good *prima facie* grounds for bringing the conduct of the students that I have named before the Board of Discipline. There were arguments which had been presented to me against doing so. Student leaders, when they decided (as it seemed they had decided) to go on with the forbidden meeting, had been subject to strong emotional pressures. Disciplinary action against them might be honestly regarded by a significant proportion of the student body both as an injustice and as an attack on 'student rights'. This was not to say that they ought to be immune from disciplinary action merely because they were, or thought they were, morally justified in refusing to obey the Director's order. If a person made a deliberate choice to break a rule, he must also be prepared to incur the legal consequences. If there were doubts in some minds about the wisdom of instituting disciplinary proceedings against those who appeared to have offended, it was not necessarily because it was thought unfair for them to be subject to the risk of penalty; nor could it be accepted that persons who enjoyed a wide measure of support for defiance of authority, and who were likely to attract a still wider measure of support if any attempt was made to discipline them, must inevitably be exempt from disciplinary action. If that concession were made, the result could well be anarchy. Nevertheless, the view had to be considered that in the particular circumstances of this case disciplinary proceedings against the leaders who had apparently decided to go ahead with the meeting might on balance be contrary to the best interests of the School. The consequence might be to polarize attitudes within the School at a time when there might be grounds for hoping for a steady improvement in the relations between the student body and the School authorities. Whether one took this view must rest mainly on a judgment of the situation in the School and of the extent to which the widespread sorrow caused by Poole's death might provide a period of reflection and calm in which a determined attempt to promote harmony might be successful.

The force of the argument against disciplinary proceedings was somewhat weakened by the fact that the shock caused by the events of 31 January seemed already to have passed without much sign of permanent good result. The students appeared more inclined to blame the Director for making his decision than their fellows for disregarding it. The student officers had not resigned, and were clearly not going to be removed from office. None of them had said a word of regret to Caine for what they had done. Instructions which he had given on what he felt to be compelling moral grounds had been blatantly disregarded. If his decision were not now supported by disciplinary proceedings, it would mean that the School was disowning that decision and his position would be impossible. Neither he nor his successor would be able to give any unpopular instruction with any confidence that it would be carried out.

I did not think it right to be deterred from disciplinary proceedings by the fact that disorder might be the consequence. Appeasement would be no less likely to lead to trouble, sooner or later. There was more trouble to come, and the more of it we had out before Adams came, the greater his chance of peaceful entry into office. If we were seen to be influenced by threats, his task would be harder.

Finally, and perhaps most important, it was not for me as an official to decide the major issues. Both the majority of my academic colleagues and the Court of Governors had been of the opinion that the course of events on 31 January should be reviewed by the Board of Discipline. It was for the Board to decide whether offences had been committed and, if so, whether they should be punished. My responsibility as an official was to lay the issues before them for decision, not to withhold them.

Before giving effect to my decision, however, there was one last thing to be done. We expected that night—though he decided otherwise soon after—that Caine would be serving on the Board of Discipline, and I should not compromise his impartiality by showing him the case against individuals. What I could do, and did, was to discuss with him the arguments against prosecution, and ask him whether he thought them persuasive in our present situation. He found them no more persuasive than I had done.

On Thursday, 9 February, I formulated my complaints for submission to the Board, and sent them to the Registrar, who was on this occasion to act as Secretary to the Board. The press had been enquiring repeatedly for news of the conclusions of the inquiry, since the death of Poole had attracted the closest interest; so I felt it right at this point to tell the press that I was bringing complaints before the Board. I did not, however, reveal the names of the students against whom the complaints were to be brought. Unfortunately some reporters were good at guessing and came to the School to interview those whom they took to be the accused. In one or two cases they guessed right and reached the people concerned before the formal notice reached them from the Registrar. This was a pity, and led to understandable complaints; but the alternative would have been to risk the publication of a garbled version of what was happening.

6 The Second Trial

Having decided to lay complaints before the Board of Discipline, I had to formulate them with sufficient precision and to prepare the evidence for submission to the Board. The committee of inquiry had left with me notes of the evidence given them by the witnesses, mostly students, who had appeared before them. I picked out those who seemed to have the most important evidence to give, and asked them whether they were willing to give it. Most were willing. It does not follow that they agreed with what I was doing; some of them may have hoped that the balance of their evidence would tend to favour the defence; others believed as a matter of principle that the truth about what had happened should be established.

I had also to consider with my staff where the Board should meet. Bearing in mind the small-scale sit-in that had taken place when the Board had met in November, I felt that we had to take seriously the possibility of an attempt to obstruct the Board's proceedings. Such an attempt could be made with success by a comparatively small number of students if they could gain control of the approaches to the room where the Board were to meet. We should be very reluctant—and very unwise—to attempt to remove sitters-in by force, even if we had the resources to enable us to do so. The assistance of the police could only be called for if there were a serious threat of a breach of the peace, or if the obstruction were caused by trespassers—though not with certainty in the latter contingency; for the removal of trespassers is not the duty of the police; it is for the occupier of premises to control access to those premises, to control what goes on in them, and to eject trespassers.

It is, however, the duty of the police to prevent obstruction of the highway; and with this in mind we chose as the venue for the Board's proceedings a lecture-room at the top of a small detached building of the School, the former St. Clement Danes Parish Hall. Very few people needed to use this building in the ordinary way, except those who were attending lectures in the room of our choice. Those lectures were all transferred elsewhere, and we were able to restrict access to the building. It opened directly from the street, so that any attempt to block the entrance would be an obstruction of the highway, which the police would no doubt clear. As a citadel, the building of our choice had its advantages; but as a venue for judicial proceedings it was less than perfect. The acoustics proved poor; and the room, which had for years been used as a meeting-place in the evenings by some Sea Cadets, had a very nautical air. One end contained a ship's bridge, with radar screen and other navigating equipment; there were kayaks slung from the ceiling; on the walls were portraits of Nelson and other distinguished seamen. It would have done very well for a naval court-martial.

In these surroundings the Board met on Thursday, 16 February. There appeared before them myself as complainant, the six students as respondents, and three members of the staff of the Law Department—Professor J. A. G. Griffith on behalf of Adelstein and Bloom, Mr. M. Zander on behalf of Malik, and Mr. B. W. M. Downey on behalf of the other three students. The formal charges that were before the Board are set out in the Board's judgment in Appendix III,[1] and I shall not reproduce them here; shortly, there was the charge of 'conspiracy'—the decision of the three o'clock meeting; charges against Adelstein and Bloom of taking the vote on the forbidden course of action, against Bloom of presiding over the forbidden meeting, against Adelstein of encouraging the crowd to demand admission to the theatre; and finally two minor charges against Malik that I withdrew in the course of the hearing when he gave a satisfactory explanation for what had appeared suspicious actions. I alleged that each of the acts charged constituted disobedience to the Director's instruction.

Pleas of not guilty were entered on behalf of all the respondents. Their representatives then referred to two sentences of the statement issued by the Court of Governors on 2 February:

The Court of Governors, while anxious to say nothing that might prejudice the operation of the School's disciplinary procedures, wish to express their deep concern at recent events culminating in the disturbances of Tuesday 31 January 1967. They wish to record their support for the Director in his conduct of the situation and the measures which he is taking to prevent any recurrence.

The defence argued that the statement was prejudicial and that any Governors who had been present at that meeting of the Governors and were therefore associated with the statement should not be members of the Board of Discipline.

After a short retirement, the Board announced that three of them had been present at that meeting of the Governors. They had considered very carefully what had been said, but felt that it was really impracticable for a domestic tribunal of the present kind to be constituted of people who had not at one time or another expressed views on matters which might arise. They proposed to hear and determine the present proceedings on the basis of the evidence produced to them and to put out of their minds anything that might have been said to them before.

The Board then settled the procedure to be followed, and appointed 24 February for the hearing. On that day, at the beginning of the proceed-

[1] See p. 171.

ings, they agreed that a small number of students might be allowed to be present as observers, and they granted my own request that Dr. Michael Mann, a part-time teacher in the Law Department, be allowed to represent me.

I need not here repeat in full the evidence that was tendered. I have taken it into account in constructing the narrative of the events of 31 January that is contained in chapter 4 above. A principal accusation against all respondents (the only one against three of them) was that they had joined in deciding to hold the forbidden meeting. This accusation referred to the decision said to have been made at the Council meeting which they had attended at 3 o'clock that afternoon. The weight of the evidence showed now, however, that at that meeting they had not decided anything at all. They had all felt that the 4 o'clock meeting ought to be held. They had wanted Adelstein to speak to the Director, who might be persuaded to change his mind; and who were they, they thought, to decide what the students should do? Adelstein had tried to telephone to the Director, whose line had been engaged: he had tried again after a time but Caine had then left his office, probably, I think, already on the way to the entrance hall.

No suggestion, however, had been made at the Council meeting that the 4 o'clock meeting be postponed or transferred to any other place, and somewhat discordant evidence was given by one student, at that time an officer of the Union. He had arrived just after the Council meeting and had met Adelstein, who had, he said, told him that there had just been a Council meeting. They had decided to go ahead with the meeting. Asked whether they were publicizing the fact that the meeting was continuing, Adelstein had said, according to the recollection of the witness, 'Yes. Get as many people there as you can before four.'

After the Council meeting, evidence showed, the possibility of transferring the meeting elsewhere had been considered and it had been decided to make preparations for holding it in the Students' Union Three Tuns Bar (which, it will be remembered, was technically not within Caine's direct jurisdiction). It was argued for the defence, therefore, that there had been no decision at the Council meeting to disobey the Director: even if there had been, a decision to disobey was not in itself disobedience. What was forbidden was the four o'clock meeting in the Old Theatre. That had not taken place. There had therefore been no disobedience. To this last point, which was raised in connection with other charges also, the reply made by Dr. Mann on my behalf was that conduct which was in itself inconsistent with obedience amounted to disobedience.

I have repeated in Chapter Four the account given in evidence of the conduct of Adelstein and Bloom in the entrance hall. Particular points of interest that emerged including the following:

1. Adelstein did not think the Union Council had issued any of the notices advertising the meeting of 31 January. He had not seen the yellow leaflets

that day, and did not regard them as giving a correct indication of the purpose of the meeting. He agreed that they implied that the decision to take direct action had already been taken, but in fact the meeting, had it been held, might, he said, have decided to do nothing.

2. When using the phrase 'storm the Old Theatre', Adelstein had intended simply to bring home the gravity of what was involved in any attempt to enter the theatre.

The case for the prosecution was that in putting to the vote options including that of going into the Old Theatre Adelstein and Bloom were engaging in conduct inconsistent with obedience to the Director's instructions. For the defence it was argued that the putting of the alternative to the vote was not in disobedience to those instructions but provided an opportunity, which would probably not otherwise have arisen, for obedience to them. Adelstein's function was to seek to elicit the opinion of the gathering so that he could communicate it to the Director. This he had done. To have continued to urge students to go to the bar would have been wholly unrealistic. Putting the alternatives kept open the possibility that the students would, as they eventually did, choose the legitimate course.

The charge of encouraging the students to demand admission to the Old Theatre was supported first by the argument that Adelstein, when he repeatedly put the alternative options to an excited crowd, was encouraging the notion that they could insist on holding their meeting in the Old Theatre, and secondly by the language he used in saying that Caine's authority had been used arbitrarily, that the issue was whether students could discuss what they wanted to discuss, and that if that was the issue it did not matter where it was discussed but, he thought, it ought to be in the Old Theatre. In using such words to an excited gathering which he knew wanted to go into the theatre he was encouraging them to demand admission to it. The defence was again that the putting of the alternatives to the vote had provided an opportunity for obedience, and that the effect of Adelstein's conduct, looked at as a whole, was to discourage rather than to encourage the gathering to demand admission to the Old Theatre.

The hearing of the evidence and part of the argument on it occupied two whole days, Friday, 24 February and the following Monday. The Board were unable to meet again until the following Friday, 3 March, when they heard Griffith for the defence. They then announced that they must await the transcript of evidence, consider it, and discuss it before they could meet again. That could not be before Monday, 13 March. The delay dismayed us all, defence and prosecution alike, but the complete transcript did not arrive until 7 March, and after studying it the Board met privately to consider their verdict; they could not have been very much quicker.

When the Board re-assembled on Monday, 13 March, they announced that it had not been proved to their satisfaction beyond reasonable doubt that those who attended the three o'clock Council meeting had in fact decided to hold the four o'clock meeting despite the ban; and they had therefore decided that this charge should be dismissed. This meant that all complaints against Malik, Moss, Ross, and Miss Jones had been either dismissed or withdrawn, and they had already been privately informed of this. The complaint against Bloom of convening and presiding over the banned meeting had also, the Board found, not been proved. There remained the complaints against Adelstein and Bloom of taking the votes and the encouragement charge against Adelstein. These the Board found proved. They had prepared a reasoned judgment and it would be read at the conclusion of proceedings; copies would be available for distribution shortly afterwards.

After a short recess, statements in mitigation were heard from Dr. P. Cohen as Adelstein's tutor and from Professor E. Gellner as Bloom's. Dr. Cohen made clear, as in the previous term, that Adelstein was a good student, doing his work regularly and some of it well. He was not a man who would advocate violence; on the contrary, he had a very firm belief that there were deficiencies in the School's machinery for negotiation and discussion and he would do a good deal to further its reform. Professor Gellner described any punishment that the Board could inflict on Bloom as a little trivial; it would not really do any great harm; his life and his career would not suffer in any serious way if he was not allowed to spend the next term at the London School of Economics. What we should really be saying to him would be that he was not the kind of person we held fit to be associated with us. We should not be doing him any objective harm, but just expressing contempt, which he did not deserve. He was a man of very good academic ability. He had conducted research in a small town of Alabama into the attitudes of its Jewish community towards desegregation, a piece of work of a very high order. He was not a man who just condemned segregationist tendencies; he also wanted to understand them. When he came to the School and found that there was a local issue which, rightly or wrongly, was connected by the students with racialism, it was very natural for him to get involved, and it did him credit. What had led him to take the vote on alternatives of which one was forbidden was his conviction that the will of the community of which he was an elected representative should be followed; if the other students wanted to go to the Old Theatre notwithstanding, he would then allow the general mood to express itself. It did not in any way imply his own wishes in this matter, but rather the opposite. This did not seem serious or discreditable.

Professor Gellner concluded by saying that these were not dishonourable young men and should not be punished severely. They were two among many in these riotous circumstances and in view of their initial attempts to make people go into the bar they were not particularly responsible for the events that followed. If they were punished the Board would be singling out two from a large group, not perhaps arbitrarily but certainly not equitably either. In the interests of staff–student relations that ought not to be done.

Bloom himself then made a statement, primarily for the reason, he said, that, although he was sure the Board would disagree with it, it might give a clear explanation of principles to which some students adhered, but which the Board might disagree with. The first principle was simply the maintenance of the L.S.E. as a community of free enquiry and discussion. If students were denied freedom of discussion, that would reflect on the institution as a whole. Inasmuch as the students saw the ban as a direct threat to freedom of speech, it would have been far more discreditable to the School for them to acquiesce, as if they were school-children and not members of a great university.

The second issue was considerably more broad and complex. Students did not view this Board, hearing charges that student representatives participated in discussions, as serving a legitimate purpose within the community of scholars. However fairly the Board wanted to conduct its hearing, it seemed to students that the logic of convening it had been dictated by the need to pacify a broader public, a public whose interests in the L.S.E. were not real, but whose tastes had been offended by incidents occurring there that they did not understand. The problems of the L.S.E. must be dealt with at their root causes, and symbolic acts of discipline, however excessive, would either be irrelevant or would exacerbate the situation. The relationship of mutual trust and respect between students and the School had been breached. Students had, he said, 'been spied on, misled, and received the indignities of banned meetings and pre-school treatment'. The students wanted a school administration that would constantly seek ways to make it more possible—instead of less—to work closely with the staff. They had, in fact, close and devoted allies among the staff who were as concerned as they were with the unpleasant results of the cultivation of an expanding twentieth-century bureaucracy and a nineteenth-century view of authority. The mark of a great community was the ability to change, and whether the Board of Discipline acquiesced or not there would be positive changes in L.S.E.

Adelstein then spoke of his actions on 31 January. He had been confused; looking back at it now, had he been able to predict what was going to happen, he would have acted differently; but under the circumstances, not knowing what would happen, he believed the way in which he had responded was the right way, given the circumstances at the time; and, secondly, although the Board had found Bloom and himself guilty, he still did not consider that anything they had done was disobedience to an instruction of the Director.

He went on to say something about the way students interpreted the issues. He thought that it was accepted by most members of the administration and of the staff that there was a serious problem concerning communications and that somehow some sort of acceptance of the student vote must be developed in the L.S.E. One thing that was not realized was how the concept of student rights fitted into this. In desiring some meaningful say in the institution students would want to feel that, however contentious the issue that they raised, they would be heeded and taken seriously. Hence when it appeared to them that even within their own Union they were not being allowed to phrase what might be to the staff distasteful issues it meant that the freedom of discussion and speech was being closed. He understood that the criticism of Adams had been extremely distasteful to many members of staff; yet however distasteful it might be there should never be any attempt in an academic institution to inhibit or prohibit such discussion, however odious the administration might feel it. Students had felt that the criticism had been reasonable. They had responded when attempts had been made to prevent their expression and discussion. When he had been instructed by the Students' Union to write a letter to *The Times* the fact that he had not been given permission had been viewed as an attempt to stop discussion. This time there had been a meeting where outside speakers had been invited and it had been stopped. This was interpreted by students, whether for Adams or against him, as an attempt to stop free discussion. It was quite obviously wrong for students not to have the right to free expression and free discussion, and so long as the situation existed in which the authorities did not understand this point of view then students would automatically feel that the avenues of discussion were closed and would respond in ways which would bring the School into disrepute and give rise to the sort of situation which had occurred on 31 January.

Professor Griffith then made his final speech, listing ten points:

1. The disobedience in this case was what a lawyer would call constructive disobedience: it was not a clear disobedience of an order; Adelstein and Bloom did not think they were disobeying and did not intend to disobey;
2. their moral character was not in question;
3. they had not created the situation in which the acts had taken place; the situation in which they found themselves at four o'clock on 31 January was not of their creation, but was caused by the Director's decision and the issue of the leaflets shown on page 49;
4. they were representatives; and representatives were never free agents;
5. it was not clear that they could properly and effectively have acted otherwise than they did;
6. they could have done many things that would have made matters much worse;
7. they had had to act in an emergency with very little time for thought;
8. they alone had exercised over the gathering such control as had been exercised over it;

9. the findings of fact on the putting of votes and the encouragement must have been marginal;

10. others were more to blame; who had prepared and distributed the leaflets, who had put up the posters, who had forced entry into the theatre?

Griffith concluded by saying that the events of 31 January were part of a much wider pattern. The School was clearly passing through a period of great change. We had had a revolutionary increase in numbers, but had assumed that the institutions and the nature of the relationships which were good up to the period of 1946-7 were nevertheless going to continue to be satisfactory. The School in 1967, however, was not very similar to the institution it had been twenty years earlier. He thought it was the fault of the academic staff primarily and the administrative staff secondly that they had not seen that they must make certain sorts of adjustments.

We were all responsible for 31 January, he urged, all of us in the room, as were the Director, all the students and the academic staff. We must now clearly start some measures of reconstruction. He had faith in the student body. He had found this present generation of students very honest, very tough, and highly critical. They were a good generation of students; but there were enemies of the School, some of them within it, some of them outside. These enemies were small groups and they did not command the support of the majority; but they were able (whether for the best of motives or the worst, it did not matter) to move when situations were created for them. His great fear was that the Board might feel compelled to create another such situation. He hoped very much that the Board would think that its existence, the authority of the proceedings, and the publicity given to them, had established and made clear that the authority of the School stood behind the instructions given by the Director. No single act by this Board or any of us could do very much to improve the present situation, but some single acts could do much to harm it.

The Board then adjourned. In the afternoon they reassembled to read their unanimous decision. It is reproduced in full in Appendix III,[1] and I shall here refer only to its most important features. The Board dealt first with the 'conspiracy' charge—that the members of Council had together decided to hold the banned meeting. It was not surprising that it had been brought, in view of the Union Council's statement that they had felt the meeting should continue; on the other hand, though the various accounts of the Council meeting differed in some respects, they all agreed in saying that the meeting was confused and that no actual decision was taken as to future action. The blame for the confusion appeared to the Board to rest mainly on Bloom. Those who had been present at the three o'clock meeting had acted irresponsibly, and they had committed a grave error of judgment in not taking immediate action to call off the four o'clock meeting.

[1] See p. 171.

It was not with that that they were charged, however, but with taking a decision together to hold the four o'clock meeting in defiance of the ban; to support such a charge evidence of some overt act, such as the passing of a formal resolution, was necessary. The Board, after full consideration of all the evidence, felt that there was an element of doubt, and the accused were entitled to the benefit of that doubt.

The Board turned to the charges on the putting of votes. In their view the charges were clearly proved; if any student publicly put a proposal to other students which, if accepted, involved a clear breach of an order of the Director, he was guilty of disobedience of that order. When the students concerned were the Presidents of the Union and of the Graduate Students' Association, whose views carried considerable weight with other students, their disobedience was more serious. It was no answer to say that the proposal was only put as an alternative to a lawful proposal, nor to say that the meeting was disorderly and might well have broken into the theatre even if they had not spoken; it was their duty, if they did speak, to tell the students that the order of the Director should be obeyed, and to refuse to put to the vote any proposal involving disobedience of that order.

The Board next turned to the complaint that Bloom had convened and presided over the banned meeting. They did not regard the meeting in the entrance hall as the banned meeting. Bloom was the person who had originally called the four o'clock meeting, and he was the person to whom the Director had conveyed his order that the meeting be not held. It was his clear duty to take all possible steps to call off the meeting and to discourage a crowd from collecting. He had taken no such steps, but the Board did not consider that he had convened and presided over the banned meeting, and this charge therefore failed.

There remained the charge against Adelstein of 'encouragement'. In the Board's view, Adelstein's action in putting to the vote a proposal that the students should 'storm the Old Theatre' was sufficient evidence to justify this complaint, but there was more. At a time when it was doubtful whether anyone could have persuaded the gathering to disperse peaceably Adelstein had the last opportunity to do it: what he had said must have encouraged the crowd in their opposition to the Director's ban. He had admitted saying that he regarded the ban as an arbitrary action which raised the principle of free speech and that in his opinion the meeting should be held in the Old Theatre. Having heard Adelstein's evidence the Board had no doubt that he said words which clearly meant to the crowd that he would not regard it as wrong for them to enter the Old Theatre if they thought fit to do so. The Board accepted that he was not personally in favour of that course of action. He appeared to have regarded himself as a representative of the students rather than their leader, and to have thought it his duty to ascertain the sense of the meeting and to do what the meeting wanted even though it involved disobedience to the Director's order.

F

In discussing the penalties to be imposed, the Board made clear that they did not regard Adelstein and Bloom as the principal instigators of the disorders on 31 January, and that they should not be penalized for the acts of people other than themselves. They were not before the Board as representatives of students generally but as persons who had themselves committed breaches of discipline. Their own offences, however, were serious. The difficulty of their situation had been pleaded in mitigation, but their own failure to call the meeting off had contributed to that difficulty. The Board dismissed the argument that the meeting had been called only for purposes of discussion, and that the ban on it had been a denial of free speech. It was clear from the evidence, they said, that it had been called for the purpose of taking action to stop Adams from coming to the School and formed part of a campaign to prevent a person who had been duly appointed to an academic post from taking it up. Action of this kind was a denial of academic freedom and could not be defended on the basis of a right to speak freely.

The Board had considered whether to make any distinction between the two students in the penalty imposed on them. Adelstein had been found guilty on two complaints and Bloom on one only. Adelstein had been found guilty on an earlier occasion, but with mitigating circumstances; Bloom, however, was a graduate and should therefore exercise greater responsibility than an undergraduate; and in examining the conduct of both of them prior to the disobedience which they had both committed the Board found greater mitigating circumstances for Adelstein than for Bloom. The penalty, then, should be the same for each of them, and the Board's unanimous decision was that both be suspended from the School forthwith until the end of the Summer Term 1967.

At this point, and without waiting to hear more, the student observers withdrew. In their absence the Board concluded by expressing their expectation and their hope that the work and constitution of the School would continue to develop and change, and that these changes would be debated widely, freely, and sometimes passionately. Such debates and the changes they provoked had been a recurring theme in the life of the School since it began. It was not debate or change that disturbed the Board. In fulfilment of the concept of a university the School embraced diverse schools of thought and many shades of opinion. This very diversity demanded that debate and discussion should proceed in an orderly and rational manner with proper heed for the views and needs of everyone involved in the School. What was needed now was a conscious effort by everyone to think in terms of the well-being of the School as a whole, a school where the various purposes of an academic institution—learning, teaching, and research—could all flourish.

The dismissal of the charge against the members of Council came as no great surprise to me, in view of the evidence that had been received, though it seemed to me that what had saved them was that, faced with an awkward situation and a difficult decision, they had avoided taking it. It was allegedly their meeting that had been called for four o'clock. The Director had forbidden it. That they should then have met, expressed their feelings, and reached no decision was a possibility that had not occurred to me, and had not been indicated by the actual course of events at the time.

Student legend, it is interesting to note, has given them the credit—if credit it be—for the act of which they were not found guilty. *Beaver* on 9 March 1967, in a summary of events, says, under the heading '31 January', 'Five members of Council meet with Bloom and feel that this is a direct curb of free speech so decide to go ahead with meeting planned.' Miss Ruth Cohen, at the time a student of the School, follows this version closely in an article in *Student Resurgence* (London, 1968). The Socialist Society in their pamphlet *LSE: What it is: and how we fought it* say 'Union Council met and sanctioned the attempt to go ahead with the meeting (they were later indicted for this decision)'. Ben Brewster and Alexander Cockburn in *New Left Review*, 43, speak of the 'members of the Union Council who were present when the decision to continue the meeting was made'. The evidence, however, that acquitted the Council members of blame—and disqualifies them for revolutionary laurels—rings true. It is in character with what had gone before. In the previous term Adelstein had not quickly decided to send his letter to *The Times*; before he did so he had faced two informal meetings, had been instructed by the Union, and had had the advice of two members of the staff. Even then he did not say— as many would have heard with sympathy—'It is a bad rule, and I am going to disregard it.' Similarly now, he had not said 'This is a gross interference with freedom of speech, and I will have none of it.' He had talked in the entrance hall of principles, of what people should do if they believed this or if they believed that, but had done very little to reveal his own point of view. It is in character that at the Council meeting he should have concluded that the right thing was to wait to see what turned up, and wait for others to tell them what to do. Gellner referred in his speech to the Board to a populist strain in Bloom's thinking. It seems to be there in Adelstein's practice also; he had acted in what 'was precisely the populist tradition of leadership—the anti-elitist tradition that on no account must you attempt to impose a doctrine on the people, that the people must learn to speak with their own voice and that you must merely give expression to it; that the people's will ultimately always will be right.'[1] A friend of Adelstein had said in evidence 'The student body does not have leaders.' Adelstein seems to have seen it as his function simply to ascertain what the people wanted—even if the people were a riotous mob. In the entrance hall as well as at the Council meeting it was on these lines that he acted.

---

[1] I quote from Professor Leonard Schapiro, speaking of the Russian provisional government of 1917, at a conference in May 1967 on the definition of populism.

It has been argued that it is the job of presidents of unions to ascertain the wishes of their members, that that was what the two presidents did in the entrance hall and that they were punished for simply doing their job. Even at a meeting of a union, however, it must be within the powers of the presiding officer to refuse to put to the vote an illegitimate proposition; and what was going on in the entrance hall was not a meeting of the Union. If it is argued that some kind of personal immunity attaches to the persons of presidents in anything that they do that comes anywhere near to their presidential functions, that is very near to the argument put forward and abandoned in the Michaelmas Term's proceedings, and impossible to justify. In the last resort every man is responsible for his own acts; what Adelstein and Bloom were punished for was what they did, not what any-one else told them to do.

It has been said that Adelstein and Bloom were punished for putting a proposition to the vote, and this sounds monstrous; but it is an over-simplification. It was by the putting of the votes that the majority view, if there was one, in favour of the forbidden course of action was shaped and revealed, and was given such shadowy appearance of legitimacy—a populist legitimacy—as it had; it was what the presidents did that enabled the unlawful consensus to be formed and made known. Even so, if they had only said 'But this is forbidden' when putting the proposition to the vote they would, I am sure, have escaped even more lightly; but they did not. The offence, taken in the circumstances and taken with its conse-quences, was more than technical.

Having reached their verdicts, the Board had to agree on sentences. Reformative, deterrent, retributive, all these punishment can be; I doubt whether the Board had much hope of—or really felt much need for—reforming the characters of Adelstein and Bloom. Was their purpose deterrent? Perhaps, but I doubt it. Retributive? Yes, possibly; but if retribution was their purpose—perhaps a rather old-fashioned purpose—it is hard to tell how the weight of the penalty to be imposed was selected. Perhaps, however, the function of the penalty in matters of this particular kind is declaratory; to be a sufficiently impressive act to maintain the moral force of the rule broken. For this purpose a careful and detailed declaration of censure might have served better.

Academic institutions are always in difficulty about penalties. Minor penalties—small fines (it is only small ones that most students can pay)—may suit minor peccadilloes but are unsuitable for what one may call political offences. There remain suspension and expulsion. The effect of suspension for more than a term is likely to be delay of a year in graduation; and it may sometimes lead to a termination of a student's grant, which can be tantamount to expulsion. The effects of a single term's suspension vary from university to university and from student to student. Were the Board right to inflict it in this instance? There is perhaps a good deal to be said for the view that for a political offence the penalty, at least for a first offender, should either be the academic death-penalty of expulsion or else no penalty beyond censure. Expulsion may be justifiable if the offence is very serious and accompanied by aggravating circumstances such as the use of violence or its instigation; if it has characteristics of moral turpitude or if it shows its perpetrator to be misusing his place at a university and unlikely ever to make good use of it. In fact it ought to be used not so much as a punishment as for separation from the university community of the man whose conduct clearly marks his unfitness to continue in it. To have expelled Adelstein and Bloom would in my opinion have been wrong. There was no suggestion of moral turpitude against either. Neither had advocated violence.

On the other hand, neither Adelstein nor Bloom was victimized, in the sense either of being punished for anything that others had done or of being selected as a scapegoat or specimen for exemplary treatment. The fact that others unknown may have been guilty of greater offences (which, if proved, would have carried a higher penalty) did not absolve these two of their responsibility for what they themselves had done. In the world of school-children it may seem unfair that some are punished while others escape. In the adult world it is otherwise. More criminals escape detection than are apprehended; but the fact that the majority escape is not considered to give the detected any immunity, nor to make their punishment 'victimization'.

The Board unanimously decided on a penalty that they may reasonably have thought light. Adelstein had already applied for a year's extension of his course of study and had been granted it. To spend one of his three extra terms away from the School would do him no harm. Bloom's tutor, pleading on his behalf, had told the Board that his life and his career would not suffer in any serious way if he were not allowed to spend the next term at the London School of Economics.

One is left in the end, however, perhaps in the light of much that is now past but was then in the future, with an uneasy feeling that the sentence was an unsatisfactory and ineffective compromise, that either it should have been heavier, as the advocates of retribution might demand, or that a full and carefully worded act of censure would have been more effective, even perhaps more severe, and altogether more appropriate. I incline to the latter view, but would not have taken it at the time. Wisdom after the event? Perhaps; better late than never. The suspension of Adelstein and Bloom merely confirmed them in their vision of themselves as high-minded men of principle, suffering at the hands of remote, uncomprehending, and oppressive authority, and made them seem heroes. The Board might have done better to try to give them a truer picture of themselves as creators of situations that they could not control. This might have been harder for them to bear; it would also have been more authoritative. Political offenders may sometimes in the public interest have to be treated with the greatest severity. A mere cold-blooded boxing of their ears, however, serves no purpose. Instead of convincing them of the error of their ways, it convinces them of their own superiority. Dead martyrs are bad enough, but live martyrs are quite insufferable.

7 The Sit-In Begins

While the disciplinary proceedings were going on, a small number of students had acted on behalf of the Union as a 'conciliation committee'. They visited a large number of members of the teaching staff and sought to persuade them that those proceedings were a mistake. Considerable hopes were, I think, entertained of the success of their efforts, and it was, I suspect, these hopes that made the Union's reaction to the disciplinary proceedings so mild—until, that is, they came to an end. Yet their efforts were, I believe, misconceived. The conciliators were trying to exert an indirect political influence on the Board of Discipline; but the Board was trying to be a judicial body, not subject to political influence from any direction. We had in the preceding term accepted whole-heartedly the notion that the Board should give its verdict on the evidence submitted to it, and should not take account of any other matters; that, indeed, was what Adelstein and Albert had asked. With such an approach to the Board's responsibilities the work of the conciliators was inconsistent.

The activities of the conciliators had a considerable influence on the subsequent course of events. They were regarded by students as an attempt to use the channels of negotiation, and their lack of success was taken as establishing that negotiation had not worked. Another consequence was that a considerable number of members of the staff were given a full account of the student point of view, that of the defence in the disciplinary proceedings. They did not, however, receive any similar account from the prosecution, nor, indeed, did they ask for it. The case against Adelstein and Bloom was put to the Board of Discipline, but was not explained generally; it would have been thought in some way prejudicial and unfair to engage in what would have been regarded as propaganda against them while the disciplinary proceedings were going on. No such scruples, naturally, restrained the output of propaganda in their favour, so that in the political battle they gained a considerable advantage.

The reliance that was placed upon the activities of the conciliators was, I have indicated, one of the factors that restrained the Union. At its meeting on 10 February the adjourned motion of confidence in the Council was passed, as was a resolution deploring the ban on the meeting of 31 January, calling for the abandonment of disciplinary proceedings, and pledging all lawful means of aiding the defence of the accused. On 23 February a motion proposing a peaceful picket of the disciplinary proceedings was rejected, but a silent vigil of volunteers—hardly distinguishable from a picket[1]—was instituted. On 3 March it was agreed to send a deputation to protest to the Board of Discipline at their slowness. The deputation saw Donnison and Wheatcroft, who explained some of the reasons why the hearing of the case was taking so long, emphasizing the Board's determination to be fair, but pointing out that this involved careful consideration of the points raised during the hearing. The delay was, nevertheless, very unfortunate, especially as some students suspected that the Board were trying to play their proceedings out until the end of term, in order to reduce the chance of organized protest.

Whether or not there would be such protest was hard to guess. Clearly enough, if the Board of Discipline were to expel Adelstein and Bloom, protest would be certain, though how widely based I should not have cared to guess. The Board was most unlikely to go so far as that, however. Even suspension for a year would probably cause a considerable upset. On the other hand, suspension for the rest of the term would be accepted with an ill grace, but not much fuss, but suspension for the rest of the term would be an almost derisory penalty. Suspension to the end of the summer term was likely enough, it was easy to guess; it seemed to be touch and go whether it would be accepted without protest or not. Some signs were hopeful, some not.

Among the hopeful signs was the route of the extremists in the presidential elections on 9 and 10 March. Because of the especially difficult task that would face the incoming president, and to make sure that students of good academic quality were not deterred from standing for election, Caine had guaranteed that the successful candidate would be allowed an extra year of study for his degree. The most colourful candidate was Mr. Edward Parker, of the Socialist Society, whose election poster proclaimed 'Smash the Governors!' (hardly an indication in itself that students were subject to any serious limitation of their freedom of speech). Parker proclaimed the need to wrest from the Governors control (which in fact they had not exercised for many a long year) over staffing and decisions about the curriculum, and to support the working class in the struggle against Capital. He won less than two hundred votes. The successful candidate, Mr. Peter Watherston, with five hundred and thirty-three votes on the first ballot, stood, as did the runner-up, for the re-establishment of informal contacts with the administration and for co-operation with Adams. They also advocated student representation on School committees and the curbing of the power of the President and Council. While one can in the circumstances understand this, it carried with it the danger of going

---

[1] 'The difference between picketing and a vigil is that a vigil is longer and held in a meditative spirit.' M. Oppenheimer and G. Lakey, *A Manual for Direct Action*, Chicago, 1964, p. 74.

further still in the populist direction of letting very important decisions be taken by the mob at a Union meeting. The weakness of the Union at L.S.E. has always been the weak constitutional position of the officers. Adelstein had erred not in being too strong a president, too inclined to go his own way, but in being too responsive to the noisier minority. What the average student wants, I am sure, of his Union is that he should be able to elect a sensible executive to represent him, and be able to leave it to them to do so, while he attends to matters that interest him more. What he does not want to have to do—and will not do—is to attend every Union meeting in order to prevent some well-organized minority from forcing through a resolution to compel the Union officers to do something silly. As a tactic to overcome this difficulty Watherston had in mind a plan, which he was never able to carry out, to make extensive use of the referendum.

Watherston himself was almost as different from Adelstein as he could be; after leaving Winchester he had qualified as an accountant, and had then come to the School to qualify himself for a career in finance. His intention had been to concentrate on study, but as an active Conservative, associated with the Bow Group, he had been drawn into student politics. He was (and no doubt still is) a pragmatist, a believer in negotiation rather than militancy, but a reformer none the less.

A less hopeful indicator of student feeling was a teach-in on the role of students in the government of their universities, held on 10 March. Student after student complained of poor communication between students and the administration, suppression of free speech, and a general atmosphere of paternalism. Some members of the teaching staff who spoke had a hard time making themselves heard, though there was, according to *The Guardian*, incredulous silence when someone suggested that people other than left-wing groups had a right to make their views heard. Mr. Peter Archer, a Labour M.P., was astonished at the violence of the feeling displayed and was himself shouted down when he said that free speech included free speech for Young Conservatives and even racialists.

On the same day *The Times* reported that an 'action group' of about a hundred students had said that they would fight any unfavourable decision of the Board of Discipline. All possibilities of negotiation had been exhausted, and direct action was the only way of preventing victimization. They had prepared plans, they said, to disrupt the main centres of administration of the School. Protest, we had already decided, is one thing, but paralysis quite another, and we had made our plans accordingly. After the Court of Governors had passed an enabling regulation on 1 February the Standing Committee had authorized the Director to appoint members of the staff to act as his deputies for disciplinary purposes, with power to suspend students. Caine appointed three members of the academic staff, all men of good common sense, and all three devoted teachers respected by their colleagues and by students, D. J. Sinclair, Senior Lecturer in Geography, F. J. Fisher, Professor of Economic History, and R. W.

Firth, Professor of Anthropology. Each of these three was free to act on his own initiative within an agreed policy. A demonstration of protest (e.g. a sit-in) would be allowed, so long as no obstruction was caused. If a small number of people caused an obstruction and refused to budge they would be suspended and if possible removed as trespassers, the help of the police being sought if necessary.

The administrative offices were the centre of the nervous system of the School, and we had had in mind even before the warning conveyed by *The Times* that they would be a natural target for the militants, as they have been at other universities before and since. We were determined not to let them pass out of our hands. We were very lucky. The administrative departments had all moved a few months earlier into Connaught House, which immediately adjoins the School's Old Building. At two levels holes had been made in the party-wall, but the local authority had required us to put steel fire-proof doors in the connecting corridors. These doors were closed on Friday 10 March, since we thought it very important to forestall any attempt by militants to anticipate an unfavourable decision by the Board. Access to Connaught House was therefore restricted to the front door, students who came in were required to deposit their registration cards, and the number of them who might be in the building at any one time was strictly limited. A porter was stationed in the building at night, and we thought it was secure.

Having made our preparations, we waited to see what would happen. On the following Monday the Board of Discipline, as I have already recorded, announced their conclusions. Some seven hundred students were waiting in the Old Theatre, where a Union meeting was begun at ten past four, and lasted only forty minutes. A call for the immediate reinstatement of Adelstein and Bloom was carried by acclamation. There was a general desire for a demonstration of protest, but doubt as to its form. For a boycott of teaching there was strong support, but the suggestion of a sit-in in the entrance hall was received with hesitation, especially as members feared that the police might be called in; though what was a fear for many was a hope for some, since the calling in of the police would dramatically call attention to their protest. Watherston made a speech saying that if a protest was to be effective it must be organized, and suggested a vote on the question whether there should be a sit-in that day, the following day, or in the near future. While he was speaking Parker announced that he was now going to start a sit-in; several members left with him. Watherston concluded by proposing two motions, both of which were carried by an overwhelming majority: 'That the Union have a boycott until the sentences are rescinded,' 'That this Union supports the principle of holding a sit-in.' He suggested that those who wished to organize the sit-in should go to the Union Council Room after the meeting, but Adelstein said that the obvious thing to do, having decided to sit in, was to do it immediately. The meeting then broke up, but the sit-in had already started; when Parker and his companions left the meeting they had gone to the entrance hall and sat down.

The beginning of the sit-in was a critical moment for both sides. The students had not planned it, and Watherston himself thought of it as a demonstration of protest rather than as a weapon, and thought of it as lasting for no more than a few hours; it was the boycott of teaching that he expected to continue and to be effective, and he believed this because he was still under the impression that it was the boycott of teaching that had prevented any penalty from being imposed on Adelstein in the previous term.

The students did not know what the reaction of the authorities would be. Some of them expected to be removed by the police, or even arrested. As I have said, however, Caine had agreed with his deputies on the policy to be followed. If a sit-in started, it should be allowed to continue, but any obstruction of stairways, corridors, and entrances to the building should if possible be checked, for two reasons; first, the obstruction of means of escape in case of fire or panic is a danger against which the inhabitants of any large building must be protected; secondly, obstruction fundamentally alters the nature of such a demonstration. A sit-in is in itself simply a form of expression of opinion, and therefore deserving of a certain degree of tolerance, however misguided the opinion and however exaggerated the form of its expression; when it turns to obstruction, however, it becomes an attempt by weight of numbers to make the normal life of the institution impossible, and so an attempt by force to compel acceptance of the views of the participants. This underlying difference showed itself at various times and in various ways throughout the week; the moderate students wished to demonstrate the strength of their convictions in order to persuade the authorities to accept their point of view; the militants wished to make it impossible for the authorities to do otherwise.

Sinclair, who was very quickly on the spot, acted in accordance with the agreed policy. When the entrance hall was completely blocked he announced that unless the students moved he would use his disciplinary powers; but the announcement was greeted with derisive cheers, and no one moved. A few minutes later, Jefferys sat down on the bottom step of the stairs, which Sinclair had instructed the porters to keep clear, and was rude to a porter who asked him to move. After he had repeatedly refused to move Sinclair suspended him until the end of term, told him that he was trespassing on School premises, and instructed him to leave the building. A woman student joined Jefferys; she too refused to move and was suspended, but neither left the building. We now had either to let them be or to call the police in, which we were not yet ready to do.

There was not much else that could be done. Various minor devices were tried, on individual initiatives, in the hope of cooling the ardour of the sitters, but—as was really to be expected—they failed to achieve their object and made matters worse. The radiators, for example, were turned off and the doors were locked open, so that the entrance hall was soon fairly cold. Just as the effect of the suspension of Jefferys had been to stiffen resistance (or, as a student subsequently explained to me, to reassure the demonstrators by proving to them that we really were bad people), so these pin-pricking measures merely served to annoy; students brought up tables and turned them on their sides to block the doorways and keep the draughts out.

Shortly before half past ten, the normal time for closing the buildings, Caine came in and spoke to the students. He told them that they could stay all night if they wished, and would not be molested; but action would be taken if next day they interfered with people who wished to continue the normal activities of the School. He knew that there was considerable feeling among them about the suspensions. Adelstein and Bloom could, he said, appeal to the Standing Committee of the Governors, and would receive as fair a hearing as they had received from the Board of Discipline; but any appeal would not be favourably affected by the demonstration. Despite his words, the sit-in was continued throughout the night by nearly three hundred students.

Encouragement came to the sitters-in from a small section of the academic staff. The Union meeting had been told by Dr. Ralph Miliband, Senior Lecturer in Political Science, that he thought the decision of the Board outrageous, that a number of members of the staff would be meeting later that evening to consider it, and that, while it would be wrong for him to give them counsel, 'it is meet and proper for students at this School, which was once great, to express their solidarity with their elected leaders in any way they think will be effective'. During the evening Alex Finer, Deputy President of the Union, had gone to try to find some of his friends among the staff, who, he thought, might be prepared to make a statement to the press. He told them why he thought it was necessary. Partly he felt that a positive sign of support from staff to students was needed, because it was obvious to him that the first twenty-four hours of the sit-in were crucial and that attempts might be made to break it. During this stage it was necessary for students to feel they had support from part of the staff, which would help them to stand by hasty personal decisions which could have ended in their being suspended from L.S.E., or worse. Equally important was the effect on the press. If the newspapers universally condemned what was happening the sit-in would be weakened, but if a statement were made by some members of staff in general support of the students that evening, for inclusion in the next day's papers, it was unlikely that the student action would be universally condemned or dismissed as irresponsible.

During the evening Miliband announced to the crowd in the entrance-hall that he had just come from a meeting of members of staff, and he read out a statement that fifteen of them had signed, saying 'We are shocked by the sentences handed down by the Board of Discipline against two elected student representatives and believe that their severity is deeply injurious to the interests of the School.'

Already energies of both sides to the dispute were beginning to be distracted to the polishing of their images. We paid heavily in the week that followed for the shortage of other news and for our closeness to Fleet Street; we were a cheap story, on their doorstep. Had we been at Leicester or Hull or Liverpool we might have been mentioned briefly in an inch or two, but as it was we had, on both sides, the privilege of feeling ourselves misunderstood in detail and at length. This made matters worse, and hardened the attitude of both sides. When a position has been publicly taken up, and publicly defended, its modification is very difficult, and likely to be taken—and felt—as a sign of weakness.

On Tuesday both sides issued statements to the press. That of the students read as follows:

WHAT WE ARE DOING AND WHY

Yesterday the Board of Discipline suspended David Adelstein and Marshall Bloom, until the end of next term. For Marshall this is tantamount to expulsion, as next term is his final one when he must take his exams. The suspension, which came into operation last night, means that the two students may not make use of the facilities of the School, such as the Library.

One charge on which they were both found guilty was that of taking a vote at the meeting on 31 January which included as one of the alternatives entering the Old Theatre against the Director's instructions. David was also found guilty of 'encouraging students to demand entrance' to the Theatre.

Students have reacted strongly to the sentences. A meeting of about 800 people in the Old Theatre yesterday afternoon welcomed a proposal from Peter Watherston, President-elect, to organize a sit-in outside the Theatre. There was almost unanimous support for his further suggestion of a 'boycott of classes and lectures until the sentences are rescinded'.

About 400 people immediately started the sit-in and nearly 300 students stayed all night in the college. The sit-in will go on all day and all night for as long as there are students willing to make this important protest in support of their colleagues. At the same time it is vital that all students show their disgust at the Board's decision by staying away from all classes and lectures from now onwards.

The reasons why strong protest of this kind is justified are:

1. David and Marshall were selected from among many students who were involved in the events of 31 January. To single out them alone for such heavy punishment is harshly unjust and incomprehensibly illogical.

2. Although the complaints brought against the students were concerned only with the conduct of the 31 January meeting, members of the Board raised the whole Adams issue during the proceedings. They equated student opposition to the new Director with 'interference with academic freedom'.

3. As has already been pointed out by the Students' Union, the Board of Discipline can be considered to be structurally biased against the students on trial.

4. Throughout the proceedings there was an implicit assumption that all steps taken by the Administration, including the Director's decision to ban the meeting, were correct. The defence was not able to question the Administration's role. This naturally biased the case against Adelstein and Bloom.

5. Throughout this affair the Union has deliberately followed a moderate line, using every possible channel of communication to alleviate the situation. But at each stage the response from the School has been negative. Our patience is now exhausted.

To the statement issued by the authorities we will come in a moment. During Tuesday morning the sit-in continued in the entrance-hall, but there are a number of other entrances to the School's buildings (which are connected by bridges above the streets), and despite inconvenience much that was normal continued. Attendance at lectures and classes was diminished, but they were held. What was to be the pattern of life for the next week was shaping itself. In the entrance-hall the students sat and listened to speeches, from time to time moving to the Old Theatre for a formal Union session. Amplifiers were rigged up in the hall to relay the proceedings from the Theatre. In between speeches there was singing; I well remember 'We all live in a red L.S.E.' being sung to the tune of the Beatles' 'We all live in a yellow submarine'. Sweeping parties of students did their best to keep the entrance hall reasonably tidy, despite the large numbers using it for purposes for which it was not designed.

It was a fairly lively morning. Speeches were made by members of the Socialist Society suggesting that something should be done that really would cause inconvenience, such as an invasion of the Senior Common Room. At times it sounded as though violence was impending, and the police were asked to stand by. In fact, however, although the militants were in the ascendant, the pot did not boil over; a great part of the audience was unreceptive to suggestions of this type. Towards midday a deputation of three students was sent to deliver an ultimatum to the Director, which they did with great politeness, so that it sounded more like a friendly warning—'We're terribly sorry, but unhappily things are going to get worse . . .' If the suspensions were not lifted forthwith, the building would be blockaded. Caine had, of course, to reply that he had no power to lift the suspensions. The announcement of this when the deputation returned was met with jeers, and 'Caine is not Able' became something of a catch-phrase for the next few days. Those who had complained so loudly that he had too much arbitrary power were even more displeased when he made clear that his powers were in fact limited. Be that as it may, the threatened blockade was imposed. Hitherto a gangway had been kept clear for those who wished to pass through the entrance-hall. It was kept clear no longer, and students sat across the doorways to bar them.

Caine held a press-conference that afternoon. It began with the circulation of a prepared statement, reading:

The London School of Economics and Political Science is anxious to remove a number of misconceptions about what is going on at the School at the present time.

1. There is not, and has not been, any genuine issue here about freedom of speech for students. The School has been depicted as an authoritarian and oppressive institution, which has denied its students ordinary freedom of speech. In fact, the School has allowed a far greater freedom than other comparable institutions could have been expected to permit. Criticism, some of it scurrilous, of the duly made appointment of a new Director has been allowed to continue unchecked for some months. The Students' Union has discussed Dr. Adams's appointment at a number of meetings without interference, and their resolutions have been widely reported in the press. Pamphlets have circulated freely, and the Students' Union newspaper *Beaver* allowed what many would consider an improper degree of license. Only when it was proposed that a meeting should be held to prepare direct action to prevent the new Director from taking up his appointment did the Director intervene. He took the view that he could not properly allow the School's main lecture room to be used for such a purpose. Students defied this ban, which has by a mischievous piece of distortion been represented as an attack on free speech.

2. Two of the students who played a prominent part in the defying of the Director's ban have been brought before the Board of Discipline. The procedures followed by that Board have—as the defence has admitted— been scrupulously fair, and the students concerned were represented by members of the staff of the Law Department. A carefully reasoned judgment was delivered, explaining the penalty imposed, suspension to the end of next term—i.e., one term plus a little more than a week of this one. Against this penalty the two students have a right of appeal to the Standing Committee of the Governors, and it is understood that they intend to exercise it.

3. The present agitations are, fundamentally, not against these penalties themselves but against any disciplinary procedures at all. They are being organized by a relatively small number of individuals. The School has three and a half thousand students. Few of the meetings concerned with recent issues have been attended by more than two or three hundred students.

4. The School is a long way from perfect and knows it. It has to adjust itself to the post-Robbins expansion of its numbers, to considerable development in its fields and methods of study, and to the competition of more generously equipped new Universities. Many of its problems are due to its cramped accommodation and surroundings. Over the past year it has been carefully reexamining such matters as its organization of teaching and its formal relationships with its student body. Much care and patience have been devoted to discussion of these topics with student representatives. Adaptations have already been made to meet the needs presented by new circumstances, and more are on the way, but progress has been impeded by the persistent agitations and disorders throughout this session.

Questions followed. An American correspondent asked whether it was true that American students were at the bottom of the trouble; Caine replied that he would not like to attribute anything like complete responsibility to any particular section of the student body, but, pressed further, admitted that happenings in some American universities might have provided something of a model. Roberts, who was present as a professorial Governor, added that some of our American students had been prominent in demonstrations at home, and some had taken up the anti-Adams agitation within a few weeks of their arrival in this country. 'Were the demonstrators politically inspired?' 'I do not think,' Roberts replied, 'that this militancy can be attributed to any one political influence, but it is definitely politically inspired in so far as there is a hard core of militants who are against any form of authority. The people behind this are not a political party as such, but a strongly motivated group who hold views about the nature of society which make them rebel continuously against authority of all kinds. They are opposed to the state, to the School as an institution. All they want is a completely free society where there are no constraints or restrictions and no discipline of any kind.' Were they communists? No, more like anarchists and Trotskyites than communists. They were in sympathy with workers' control, and with the Dutch provos. Because they were generally older and more politically aware than the majority of students, they had influenced the Union Council into supporting the present action. Roberts's remarks were freely quoted in the newspapers, but very selectively, the qualifications being omitted and the highly coloured passages given prominence. The impression was given by some reports that he had said that all or most of the protesting students were anarchists, and those who were not naturally resented it. It would be hard, however, to maintain that what he actually said misdescribed the Socialist Society or the part they had played. They had begun the troubles with the anti-Adams pamphlet. Their propaganda had been continuous and militant during the six weeks before the sit-in. They had begun the sit-in. Their voices had been most prominent during that morning. They were the spear-head and the hard core of the militants. What is very hard to determine is the extent of their influence; would the sit-in have started but for them? That many of the sitters-in were poles apart from them does not prove that they had not been influenced by the constant drip of propaganda. Half the art of leading the multitude by the nose consists in not letting them become aware that they are being led by the nose. Nevertheless, I am inclined to think that, because they made so much noise, we did attribute more influence to them than they had; indeed their vociferousness and picturesqueness drew attention away from the element of moral protest in the sit-in. That element was, however, in reality much more significant than the politics of the Socialist Society. A considerable number of sensible students, reasonably impervious to their propaganda—Watherston himself is the obvious example—took the view that the disciplinary proceedings were wrong and had resulted in gross injustice; and one result of the selective reporting of Roberts's remarks may have been to increase the extent to which moderate and right-wing students took part in the sit-in, to show that it was not all inspired by the Socialist Society.

Sir Sydney Caine (*centre*) talking to students 31 January 1967

Marshall Bloom (*left*)
and David Aldelstein

The beginning of the sit-in

At four o'clock that afternoon a Union meeting was held. Telegrams of support were read, including, predictably enough, one from Bertrand Russell. After they had been read it was moved that unless the suspensions were lifted by noon next day the students would do all they could to paralyze the entire School. There would be no violence used, but the Union was adamant that the School would cease to function unless their request for justice was granted. A substantial majority agreed that this motion should be deferred until after the Standing Committee had met, and in fact consideration of it never was resumed, since the attempt to paralyze the School was made, but unsuccessfully.

At five o'clock that evening the Standing Committee of the Governors met for their normal monthly meeting; an addition to the twenty items on their agenda was to consider the procedure that they should adopt on the appeal by Adelstein and Bloom, notice of which had been lodged by Griffith. They agreed to ask him for a statement of the grounds of appeal, to be submitted by five o'clock next day, when they would meet again. To hear the appeal itself they would meet on Friday, 17 March, at 3 p.m. Adelstein and Bloom should be allowed to be represented by Griffith, and I as the complainant should be allowed to be represented by Mann. The sentence of the Board of Discipline should not be suspended pending the appeal, but Adelstein and Bloom should be allowed to enter the School premises to consult their legal advisers and to arrange the handing over of their presidencies to their successors.

Sympathetic members of staff, the press reported, met that evening to consider the problems that the protest was creating, and were reported as fearing that 'the confrontation would escalate'. Nor were the fears without reason. In the entrance hall militant speakers demanding a more lively boycott were cheered, while the more moderate had a less enthusiastic hearing. Discussions began of various ways of disrupting the life of the School—for example, by sabotaging the telephone system—and at about half past eleven the students broke up into small groups to consider the various possibilities.

At about half past four on Wednesday morning there was a knock on the door of Connaught House, the administrative building. Without opening the door the night porter asked 'Who is it?' A voice answered 'Cleaners'. He opened the door and was swept aside as a party of about twenty students rushed in. Once inside they sent for reinforcements, and about sixty-five more came in. They made barricades of furniture at the entrance and at the points where Connaught House was connected to the Old Building. Most of them settled down on the floor of the narrow entrance hall. Meanwhile the night porter had spoken on the telephone to Mr. William Wall, the foreman porter, who reported in turn to Mr. Edward Brown, the Clerk of Works. Brown had his right arm in plaster, but together they set about recapturing Connaught House. Brown knocked on the front door; a student opened it just enough for him to thrust his foot in, and then his plaster-encased arm. Some attempt was made at first to push him out, but a shout went up 'No violence!' He and Wall were able to enter the building, where two or three porters joined them. Together they took possession of the entrance lobby and pushed the barricade back a few feet. A bridgehead had been established. Sinclair was then roused and told what had happened. He consulted the Director, who asked him to call the police, and I was summoned by telephone just before seven o'clock. When I arrived at the School half an hour later, I found Sinclair with the porters and two press photographers in the lobby at the entrance of Connaught House. He explained to me that he had allowed the press photographers to come in and take photographs on condition that they supplied copies to us so that we could identify the students from them.

Sinclair and I had the task of recovering possession of the building from the students. If they would not leave voluntarily they would have to be evicted as trespassers; but they would not become trespassers until, by being suspended from their status as students, they had been deprived for the time being of any right they had to be in the building. After we had asked them to go and they had refused, Sinclair briefly consulted me on the question for how long they must be suspended. The device of a purely nominal suspension for, say, one day did not occur to me. They had by a mixture of trickery and force invaded a building of the School, and they had refused to leave it when repeatedly told to do so. If they were to be suspended it seemed to me that this merited something more than a nominal period of suspension. If it did not, what would they have to do to merit it—burn the School down? Finally, whatever suspension was now imposed could subsequently be reduced, but not increased. We agreed, therefore, to make it three months; and Sinclair told them that they were suspended for that period. I told them that they no longer had any right to be on the premises, but were trespassers, and, as the representative of the owner of the building, I instructed them to leave. A police inspector, who was now with us, tried calmly and pleasantly to persuade them to go, but was no more successful; so, after they had sung 'We shall not be moved!', his constables carried them out. Their suspensions were not in fact enforceable; the photographer did not send the promised photographs.

Public hostility to the students was meanwhile becoming a serious factor in the situation. The students themselves were aware of it, and some of them were beginning to fear that their local authorities might cut off their grants. Consciousness of being a member of a tightly knit little band of people suffering public hostility in defence of principle increases solidarity. The defeat of the Connaught House invasion, the suspensions which were involved, and brief press reports of what Roberts had said—or was alleged to have said—did a great deal that day to exacerbate feelings, though it is interesting to notice that I have never heard a word of complaint against the calling in of the police. The suspensions, however, were greeted as 'provocative', which was natural enough. In a conflict of this kind every action of the authorities goes into one of three categories: either it is irrelevant, or it is a victory for the rebels, or it is provocative. It was clear into which category the present action fell. A Union representative in a statement to the press said that 'all the students wanted, to call off the sit-in, was a gesture'. Instead they had got the instant suspension of a large number of students. This sounds very well, but what gesture did they want? Sundry gestures were made during the week, but I believe that there was only one that would have brought the sit-in to a voluntary end—the suspension of the penalties inflicted by the Board of Discipline, and the implicit repudiation by their colleagues of those who had served on the Board and had heard the evidence and the arguments.

Great efforts were made that day, nevertheless, to find an acceptable solution of the conflict. A group of students issued an invitation in the following terms:

TO THE MEMBERS OF THE ADMINISTRATION AND STAFF OF L.S.E.:

We are each, as students and as staff, talking to ourselves and not to each other. And yet we are each, by our actions, trying to get the other to understand our separate points of view. Reason has broken down. We have degenerated to the point where we are each trying baldly to force our point of view.

What we as students are insisting upon is our right and need to have our point of view, our interests and our rights, listened to and taken account of in your decisions that affect us. We feel that but for a small coterie of faculty members you have seriously failed us, that you have not listened to what we have been asking, most particularly now by the suspensions of David Adelstein and Marshall Bloom and the refusal to lift those suspensions.

We have been trying to understand what you have been trying to say to us—what you think and why you think it. The recent administration action seems to have been saying to us that the administration will either ignore us or not tolerate our insistence to be heard and listened to. Indeed that they will punish us for challenging the arbitrary exercise of their authority. Simply for disobeying an order, whatever the circumstances and merits of just that order.

Perhaps they have been saying just that; in which case we would remind them that the point of their education is to enable and require us to think for ourselves. Not to accept as valid the excuse that we thought, or acted, simply because another, or a mass of others, have told us to. That we have not foregone our obligation to use our intelligence.

But perhaps they (and you) have been saying something else. Perhaps you have been saying that you do not understand what we have been asking. Perhaps you are saying you are fearful lest 'things get out of control'. Perhaps you are obsessed by the chimera that the students cannot be placated, and want to 'take over'. Perhaps you are simply afraid of 'losing face'.

We do not know why you have been acting as you have been acting, and what you have been trying to say to us.

But we do feel it is essential, if we are to act as civilized and educated men, that we each try to find out what we have each been trying to say to each other. We feel sure that the suspension of 85 more students demonstrates how very far we are from this ideal. We would like to resurrect the dialogue that has died. We think we are right. If you think we are wrong we would like to know why. We are prepared to listen. In simplest terms, some of us would like to prevent even more of a blow up than has already occurred.

At yesterday's Union meeting it was decided that a group of students should try to speak with the faculty and administration near the Senior Common Room.

In keeping with this decision, we would like to propose a dialogue in words to complement the dialogue or non-dialogue in actions that we are all currently involved in. We would like to exchange views.

Three or four of us will be in the room adjacent to the Senior Common Room from 11.30 a.m. Wednesday, 15 March. We invite any and all faculty and administration members to come in so that we can hear each other out. We will report your views back to the Union meeting. We hope that you will not fail us again. That at this critical moment you will not refuse to engage in a dialogue. We look forward to speak with you.

This initiative met with a substantial response from members of the staff, and unofficial conversations continued during the day. In addition a meeting, attended by both students and members of the staff, was addressed during the afternoon by two Members of Parliament, who were trying to explore the possibilities of a settlement. It was followed by a meeting between members of the Union Council and two of the professorial Governors, Roberts and Donald MacRae, Professor of Sociology. The discussion was in very general terms; Watherston said afterwards that there had been no negotiations, but an exchange of ideas. At five o'clock that afternoon the Standing Committee met. The first question considered was whether the police should be called in and asked to remove the sitters. There was a disposition to feel that something should be done to restore control of the School's buildings—perhaps, indeed, a desperate urge to do *something*, instead of leaving all the initiatives to be taken by the students. The invasion of Connaught House and an intensified blockade of the School's buildings during the day seemed to show that matters were getting worse, and that the militants were in charge of the situation. The Standing Committee therefore agreed that, while efforts should continue to be made to win over the moderates, the police should be asked, at least provisionally, for assistance in removing the sitters. The Committee then received a paper, signed by four members of the staff, setting out a 'peace plan', providing for the calling off by the students of physical obstruction of the premises, the grant to Adelstein and Bloom of permission to use the library during the Summer Term, and the setting up of a committee of five representatives of the Governors and staff and five students to undertake informal discussions. Two deputations were received, the first of four professors, and the second of three members of staff and three students, sent as a result of the conversations begun in response to the morning's invitation. The importance was urged of giving the moderate students some support, and attention was drawn to the almost paranoid suspicion from which the students were said to be suffering. It was essential that the appeal be heard by a clearly independent body, acceptable to both sides. It might be constituted by co-opting the selected persons on to the Standing Committee and then leaving them to hear the appeal, all the other members staying away; and the hearing should not be legalistic in character.

The Standing Committee did not feel able to accept these suggestions, but drew up a statement, which the Director was asked to read to the Union. He had at the same time to open the way to possible removal of the sitters by withdrawing any permission, express or implied, that they had to be on the premises overnight. He began his speech to the Union by saying 'I am not what some people think I am—the dictator of this School' and went on to say that he took his instructions from various bodies, including the Standing Committee, a message from whom he had come to read. It ran as follows:

1. Appeals against the decision of the Board of Discipline have been made by Mr. Adelstein and Mr. Bloom. They will be considered in due form by the Standing Committee with the minimum of delay. Lord Bridges and Mr. Farrer-Brown, who were members of the Board of Discipline, will not take part in the hearing; nor will the Director (who is a member of the Standing Committee) since he was a witness in the case.

2. The Director and Mr. Sinclair will consider any representation made to them in writing by the students involved concerning the suspensions imposed on 15 March.

3. The School will also consider any representations from a student whose eligibility to sit for a University or School examination is affected by a suspension.

4. When the School has returned to normal functioning, the Standing Committee will be happy to meet student representatives to carry further the discussions which have already been started for improvements in the arrangements for consultation with students on the School's affairs.

Caine went on to say 'The School, as you know, is normally closed at 10.30. On Monday I gave, I think explicitly, permission to all students then sitting-in to remain. I did not give that permission yesterday and it is not made for tonight. I hope, therefore, that students will go home at 10.30.' He was asked whether his statement meant that he was forbidding a sit-in after 10.30 and said that this was a question he might have to consider later on. What he had said was a statement of hope rather than intent. He could give no undertaking that if the students abandoned the sit-in no disciplinary action would be taken against them. Asked whether he was going to call the police in, he refused to answer, and the mood of the meeting became increasingly angry. When he was asked to suspend the suspensions of Adelstein and Bloom pending the hearing of their appeals, and replied that he had no power to do so, he was greeted with jeers. Nevertheless, the meeting, which had been hostile at first, gradually warmed to him, recognizing that he, just as much as anyone else, was a human being caught up in a complex situation and not enjoying it. Finally a former student in the audience, a lecturer at a College of Technology, said 'We have had our differences, but I have never thought of you as a tyrant. I appeal to you as a human being skilled in administration to help us, to use your influence as a human being to bring back some sanity.' Caine replied 'I think that is a good note on which to leave.' Some observers felt that the moment was one at which an opportunity was missed, and that a passionate defence of academic freedom, an explanation of the way in which it was involved in the controversy over Adams, and an indication that the School had no room for those who denied that freedom, might have won the audience over. Others see it as the moment for a concession. In a sense each of these views goes some way to disprove the other. More to the point, Caine never was a rabble-rouser, a man to make a stirring oration. His gifts were those of discussion, negotiation, argument in small groups, but he lacked histrionic ability. He had already announced the small concessions that the Standing Committee had authorized, and could at that time offer no more without betrayal of what mattered to him most in all this conflict, the maintenance of constitutional processes and rational argument as a means of settling differences. He could not respond immediately to the moving appeal addressed to him: very few men could have done so in that situation, but he did give in due time what he was asked for, the use of administrative skill to bring the conflict to an end.

As we left the theatre, we agreed that there could be no question of calling in the police that night, and I cancelled the arrangements that I had been instructed to make with them. I spent the night in my office, talking much of the time with colleagues and with one of the students who had appealed that morning for a resumption of dialogue. In the middle of the night I played host at a buffet supper in the Staff Dining Room kitchen to a small party which included Adelstein, to whom I went on talking in my office—trying to persuade him that he really was guilty—until he was tired and went home. After clearing up some of the arrears of paper-work on my desk I caught an early train home to have breakfast and come back.

It is time to take stock. The position of the students—the minority of the School's students, that is, who were sitting in—is reasonably clear. They objected to the suspension of Adelstein and Bloom. They were incensed, perhaps even more, by the fact that their views were being disregarded. The sit-in and the boycott were designed to persuade 'the Administration' to rescind the suspensions. A minority of the participants was not perhaps primarily concerned with the well-being of Adelstein and

Bloom, but wanted to use the conflict as a weapon against authority, which must be humiliated and broken. Would anything short of the rescission of the suspensions have satisfied the students and ended the sit-in? It is possible that the temporary lifting of the suspensions pending the appeal might have done so, but only, I suspect, because it would have been regarded as an indication that the appeal was to be successful—as a promise, that is to say, by the Standing Committee before examination of the evidence that they would allow the appeals whatever the evidence. This had little to commend it.

The establishment of a special appellate body perhaps had some superficial attractions, but closer examination reveals serious difficulty. The defence lawyers were, properly enough, watchful for any procedural irregularity that might enable the courts to review the case. The setting up of a new appellate body would have involved such irregularity, which could have been overcome only by obtaining the consent of Adelstein and Bloom. This would have given them a veto on its membership, and it was not very likely that they would have agreed to any composition of the appellate body that would also have been acceptable to the Governors. It was suggested also that the hearing to be given to the appeals should be 'non-legalistic' in character. This, I think, must have been intended to mean that the proceedings were not to be judicial, but those of compromise by a mediator. This, of course, would have involved stepping outside the constitutional framework, and goes to the root of the conflict. On the one side was the view that, within the framework of the School's legalities, offences had been committed: the Director had given an order and the order had been disobeyed; this had within the framework been established. On the other side there was the desire to question the framework. Was the law just? Was the Director's order justified? Was it right that he should be able to give such orders? These are fair questions, but they could not be discussed within the framework, for they are, as I have indicated, questions about the validity of the framework itself. While I doubt whether agreement could have been reached upon them, they should have been discussed. It was a genuine conflict of principles: on the one hand, law and order; should not a university show by its example the type of positive commitment to law and order that is expected of the citizen? On the other hand, a critical attitude to law: what is the citizen to do if the law is unjust? Should he not disobey it? My own answer would be that he must seek first by reasoned argument and constitutional means to have it changed. The students chose force instead, and made discussion impossible. They said that they had exhausted all other means. When did they try them?

There was also a conflict of personal loyalties. The students felt an obligation to support Adelstein and Bloom. On the other side there were personal loyalties to Caine, the man who had had the responsibility on behalf of us all of taking difficult decisions, and whose honesty and scrupulousness in making them none who knew him could doubt; and there were personal loyalties to the members of the Board of Discipline, especially our two academic colleagues, Donnison and Wheatcroft. They had had on behalf of us all to carry a difficult and arduous burden, and to repudiate them was not acceptable—especially as they had heard the evidence and the rest had not.

Should the police have been called in to help remove the sitters? We dithered on the brink of this more than once. It was a course of action that would have commanded support from a large section of the public, and from many of our colleagues. There is on the other side a body of opinion that sees the incursion of the police into the buildings of a university as a kind of defilement. This view rests in my opinion on a gross confusion of mind. Clearly, if the police enter in order to prevent the university from exercising its proper functions, if they come to prevent free speech and free thought, then that is indeed a defilement; if, however, they come to enable the university to exercise its functions, and to remove those who are trying by force to prevent it from doing so, the case is altered. An ordered framework of society is a necessary condition of civilized life, and the police, in maintaining and restoring that framework, are the servants and agents of us all. London is not Chicago, and our police can, generally speaking, be trusted not to exceed their function.

There were, however, more genuine arguments against seeking their help. A forcible termination of the sit-in would have left the conflict un-resolved. We could not have had the students put out one day and then see them return on the next to resume the protest in even greater numbers. The identification of those who had been removed would have been diffi-cult or impossible, and selective re-admission was out of the question. The School would still have been at loggerheads with a large part of its student population, and it is difficult to see how normal life could have been resumed.

What was done was to adhere to constitutional arrangements and to wait for the appeal-hearing by the Standing Committee. Meanwhile we had, to use Caine's words, to live with the sit-in. In other words, we had come to rely upon passive resistance, which is not a bad way of maintaining one's principles against force of numbers.

8 The End of the Sit-in

While I was talking to Adelstein early on Thursday morning, a message had come to Sinclair, who was with me, asking him to go and speak to some Union officers. What they wished to tell him was that they were very worried about an impending incursion of supporters. Other students' unions all over the country had been invited to send delegations to join a public demonstration to be held on Friday. Hundreds or even thousands might arrive, and no preparations had been made for their reception or accommodation. There was a possibility of wholesale disorder, which might get out of hand to the serious embarrassment of us all. Sinclair agreed to help, and was able to arrange for members of the administrative staff to assist in controlling admission to the buildings of the School later on in the morning. These plans had to be abandoned, however, when militants among the students attacked as traitors those who had joined in making them. The problem fortunately proved to have been exaggerated, though from this time on there were apt to be considerable numbers of outsiders in the School, and some of them were suspected of swelling the militant vote at Union meetings. Their existence was used in sundry contexts, in Union debates and in discussion with the staff, as an additional reason for the urgency of ending the sit-in on whatever terms whoever happened to be speaking happened to favour. If it were not brought to an end, our students might lose control to the outsiders, and then what might happen?

On Thursday morning much attention was diverted to this problem and to the differences which it caused among our own students. In the afternoon the professorial members of the Standing Committee thought it might be useful to invite the Union Council to come and meet them. There was prolonged and heated debate in the Union on the question whether the Council should be allowed to accept the invitation. After two hours' debate they were permitted to do so, and were authorized 'to enter into negotiations with the Standing Committee of the Court of Governors or its representatives', provided that they took two additional students with them, and provided that any proposals that might be agreed upon were submitted to the Union for ratification. At the same time the Union reiterated its opposition to the suspensions and its determination to continue the sit-in until a settlement was reached.

The two students who were added to the Council for this purpose were Mr. Richard Atkinson and Mr. Richard Kuper. Atkinson, a Leeds graduate, reading for a Ph.D. degree, had been a member of the conciliation committee; Kuper was another of our South African *emigrés*, a graduate of the University of the Witwatersrand and then of Cambridge; a lively and attractive intellectual, he had been a graduate student at L.S.E. since 1964, and was also a lecturer at a College of Technology. Prominent in the Socialist Society, he had come to the fore among the militants, and was in the following year to be one of the founders of the Revolutionary Socialist Students' Federation.

That evening, therefore, the members of the Union Council, with Atkinson and Kuper, met Caine in company with Miss B. N. Seear and Roberts; MacRae, the third professorial member of the Standing Committee, was unable to be present. There has, as we shall see in due course, been some dispute about the status of this meeting. The Director and his two companions had no authority from the Standing Committee to negotiate, and were simply engaging on their own initiative in exploratory talks. They thought that the status of the students was similar, and that they too were present as well-intentioned individuals rather than as an authorized delegation. Repeated expressions of the students' anxiety to find a way of bringing the demonstrations to an end made a very favourable impression. Caine had to make clear that, even in return for a decision by the Union to terminate the sit-in and boycott, no kind of promise could possibly be made on behalf of the Standing Committee that would indicate any prospect of a favourable decision on the appeal by Adelstein and Bloom; that was not a subject for bargaining. The students asked him whether he would be prepared to ask the Standing Committee to exercise clemency. If he promised to do so, they might be able to get the sit-in ended. He could not: it would have put the Standing Committee under undue pressure. With his agreement, however, Miss Seear and Roberts told the students that they had a proposal to make, but one which must remain confidential unless it were adopted. The proposal was that if the students, acting as individuals, and acting entirely on good faith, could secure that night the calling-off of the sit-in and boycott, then they themselves, similarly acting as individuals, would do their best as individuals to persuade the other members of the Standing Committee, if they upheld the original verdict, nevertheless to mitigate the sentences by putting them into suspense, on the understanding that they would not be enforced unless the two students committed a further offence. Miss Seear and Roberts emphasized that they were in no position to enter into any bargain on behalf of the Standing Committee; but if the sit-in were at an end then conditions would be created in which they could state openly to the Standing Committee that it was their opinion that clemency would restore good relations between staff and students. After discussion the students withdrew, but returned very soon to say that they would be quite unable to secure an end of the demonstration without an actual agreement, which they could not be given, that the appeal would be upheld.

On other matters more progress was made. It was agreed that the suspensions imposed by Sinclair in Connaught House the previous day should be commuted to fines, which would be paid to charity; and a reasonably sympathetic hearing was given to a request that there should be an independent inquiry into the situation at the School. Kuper, who later presented to the Union a report on the discussions (except the Seear–Roberts proposal) added that he thought that the chances of a favourable verdict by the Standing Committee on the appeals would be improved if the students maintained good order during the march and public meeting in Lincoln's Inn Fields that had been arranged for the following day. The authorities, however, had refused to guarantee any change of attitude over the suspensions of Adelstein and Bloom; and the mood of the Union meeting suggested that without a favourable decision on their appeals the chance of a settlement was remote.

It had been my task during the day to make arrangements again with the police for eviction of the sitters-in. There was doubt, however, whether their help would be forthcoming or whether they would take the line that the removal of trespassers was the responsibility of the occupiers of the premises concerned, and that the most the police would do would be to stand by to prevent any breach of the peace. These doubts gave us a bad moment; it was not that we were desperately anxious to have the sit-in ended by the intervention of the police; but consciousness that their help was in the last resort available meant a good deal; if we were going to be deprived of it, we felt that we had come upon a gap in the framework of law and order. In fact, however, after further consultation our hopes of aid, if it were needed, were restored; but fortunately before the end of the day events at the School had, we felt, taken a distinct turn for the better, and that way of bringing the sit-in to an end was clearly inappropriate. All parties seemed to be cheered that night by the fact that the discussions in the early evening had been so friendly, and there was something of a feeling of truce. In the late evening I was asked by the students to come down to the entrance hall, where someone from outside was trying to harangue them and was distinctly unwelcome. They feared that he might be ill-used if he would not go. I went through the familiar process of first asking him and then directing him to leave as a trespasser, and then requested a small party of students to remove him, which they readily did, while the way was kept clear by Jefferys on one side and myself on the other. While we were all feeling bonhomous over this co-operative effort, Mr. Scott Moss, Academic Affairs Vice-President of the Union, came up to speak to me. It seemed likely, he said cheerfully, that we should have to have all the students removed by the police sooner or later; to make that possible he recognized that it would be necessary for them first to be suspended; would I, however, bear in mind that a mere twenty-four hours' suspension would be enough? I thanked him for his advice (which shows again no feeling that the intervention of the police would be an impropriety) and promised to bear it in mind.

Discussion among the academic staff had continued during the day, and Professor Peter Wiles, Professor of Russian Social and Economic Studies, had been invited by a group of his colleagues to take the chair at a meeting in the afternoon, which all members of the staff were invited to attend. He accepted the invitation, and by all accounts proved a firm and independent chairman. He began the meeting by announcing what he called the ground rules; the group, of about seventy, had no formal *locus standi*, and accordingly any votes taken would be no more than straw votes, to indicate the balance of opinion; no resolutions would be passed. A variety of points of view was represented, but the composition of the group did not necessarily reflect the views of the staff as a whole; for example, only one or two of the 'hawks' were there. Wiles later reported to the Director the passing of straw votes suggesting some modification of the membership of the appellate body, some partial mitigation of the sentences on Adelstein and Bloom, and the 'freezing' of the suspension of the Connaught House invaders. The Standing Committee of the Governors should meet the Union Council face to face, and their approach should combine conciliation with firmness. In the following morning's *Guardian*, Mr. Eric Silver reported 'There was strong support within the group . . . for a vote of no confidence in the administration if Sir Sydney and his advisers refused to adopt a more statesmanlike posture.' What had happened in fact did not go nearly as far as that. One of the informal votes taken at the meeting had indicated that fifty-five members of the staff present had taken the view, to which nine were opposed, that the situation had not been well handled. In the light of hindsight it was perhaps a mistake, in view of the group's self-selected composition and lack of status, to let any vote be taken on these lines. The most surprising thing about it was that as many as nine people present at the meeting were opposed to it. It made no positive proposal and its effect on the course of events was the reverse of conciliatory. It encouraged the students to hope for concessions, at the very same time as it diminished their chance of getting any, for the publication of Mr. Silver's report undoubtedly strengthened the resolve of the authorities to stand fast. Among the teaching staff there was also a hostile reaction; a number of them signed a letter to the Director, referring to Mr. Silver's report and continuing:

None of us has taken any part before in any concerted move of this kind, because we dislike the formation of staff pressure-groups, are not publicity seekers, and prefer to leave the government of the School to the free working of its properly constituted organs. In view of the attitude of so many of our colleagues, however, we think you may like to know that we, the under-signed, together (we are sure) with many others whose views we know, but who cannot be contacted at this late hour, believe that weakness towards the two main known culprits in this sad affair will mark, not the end, but only the beginning of the School's troubles. We do not ourselves propose to give copies of this letter to the press, but leave you to use it at your own discretion.

When Wiles's meeting reassembled on Friday afternoon, it was generally agreed that what had been said to *The Guardian* made things awkward. The Graduate Students' Association were holding a meeting and it was agreed that Wiles should go to tell them the true state of affairs. On his way a number of students stopped him to congratulate him on his initiative; he said that what they had been reading was not true. He told the Graduate Students' Association the same, and returned to his own meeting. He found that it had moved to the left and that he was alone in urging concessions by the students; the meeting had lost any representative character that it had ever had. He took his leave.

That afternoon, at two o'clock, the students' procession assembled for a protest march to Lincoln's Inn Fields. As they gathered, 'one banner stood out', said *The Church Times*, 'like a sore thumb. It was carried by a little old man who was handing out Bible literature. Instead of protesting about the suspension of students, or the appointment of a Principal, it warned in no uncertain terms: "The Lord rained brimstone and fire upon Sodom. Escape for your life."'

About two thousand students from L.S.E. and elsewhere took part in the march, all wearing daffodils as their emblem. As they marched they sang 'We shall overcome!' and some chanted 'Walter Adams out, student representation in!' When they arrived at Lincoln's Inn Fields Mr. Raphael Tuck, M.P., congratulated them on their orderly and dignified behaviour, condemned the composition of the appeal committee, and urged on the students a conciliatory approach.

Watherston read out a message that he had received from the Director:

1. I would like to make clear to the incoming President and Council of the Students' Union my views on a number of matters, including issues raised by the Union during the term of office of the past-President, on which I hope that real and rapid progress can be made when the present unhappy situation is terminated.

2. I know that there is widespread concern about the position of Marshall Bloom in relation to the University examinations which he would expect to take this summer. It is clearly impossible to say anything definitive on this until his appeal has been heard, but I can give an assurance of my own full sympathy with the view that the School should use its endeavours with the University of London to enable Mr. Bloom to sit.

3. There has already been discussion with the Students' Union on the principle of student representation. I hope very much to see established in the School in the near future a more efficient system of consultation, together with a wider representation of students on relevant School committees. I am sure that students have a constructive role to play in solving the many difficult problems which face us all at the present time.

4. There has already been much progress in the re-examination of our disciplinary procedures by a joint committee of staff and students. This should continue as quickly as possible. In particular, I welcome the idea that the student body has itself a role and a responsibility in the maintenance of order and discipline in the School and should be represented in the working of the School's own disciplinary procedure.

5. If student representation is to be as useful and effective as we would all wish it to be, it must fully reflect the interests of all sections of student opinion. I understand that there is already a widespread feeling among students that changes are necessary in the constitution and organization of the Union. I would like to see a joint effort by the School and student representatives to re-examine the structure and procedures of the Union.

6. I hope that next term we shall get down in earnest to the hard work that will have to be done if the principle of student representation is to be expressed really effectively in productive co-operation between staff and students.

Watherston said that he welcomed this message as a sign that the administration and the staff were moving in the right direction, but added that it had nothing to do with the immediate issue of the suspensions of Adelstein and Bloom.

The Standing Committee were meeting that afternoon to hear the appeals. Griffith and Zander represented the appellants. I was present and was represented by Mann; and the tutors of the appellants were again present. The defence began the proceedings by objecting formally to the composition of the Committee. It was not the fault, it was argued, of any member of this Committee who was present, but it was constitutionally very difficult for them, having been concerned in another and most direct way with the proceedings of these last few days, to sit also as a judicial body. The point had to be made in case proceedings had to be taken elsewhere. The objection was over-ruled; the committee were fully aware of the distinction between their administrative and their judicial functions. The facts were then outlined and the grounds of appeal stated. The ground covered was substantially the same as at the original hearing; the only new point made referred to the Board of Discipline's statement

if any student publicly puts a proposal to other students which, if accepted, involves a clear breach of an order of the Director, he is in our view guilty of disobedience of that order . . . It is no answer to say that the proposal is only put as an alternative to a lawful proposal. Nor is it an answer to say that the meeting was disorderly and might well have broken into the Old Theatre had they not spoken at all: it was their clear duty, if they did speak, to tell the students present that the order of the Director should be obeyed and to refuse to put to a vote any proposal involving disobedience of that order.

It was argued that this was to impose on student officers an inappropriate duty to act as a kind of police force, to act as the Director's deputies in enforcing his orders. Mann replied by drawing attention to the Board's words 'if they did speak'. It was not suggested that Adelstein and Bloom were under any duty to get up and persuade the crowd to obey the Director, but only that, if they did get up to speak, they should behave in the way that the Board had indicated. References to the sit-in were oblique. Griffith repeated the argument he had used to the Board about the danger of creating situations which the enemies of the School who were among us could exploit. It was his view that the penalties that had been imposed by the Board, whose hearing had been completely fair, were of such dimension as to create the present situation. His colleague reminded the Committee that the events of the previous few days must be disregarded and their decision as a judicial body must be based solely on the events of 31 January. Mann urged that the question of what was the right punishment should be answered without reference to extrinsic circumstances, in particular without reference to any extrinsic circumstances which might have arisen since the Board announced its decision. If pressure could be thought to lead to a reduction of penalty, it could also be thought to lead to an increase of penalty. That way was anarchy, and it was a way which would make a complete mockery of the judicial nature of the proceedings which all on both sides of the table had tried to observe throughout.

At the conclusion of the argument the committee retired. Meanwhile, by an odd coincidence, the students' Law Society were entertaining the Lord Chancellor at dinner downstairs—an indication of the way in which, just under the surface, much of normal life was continuing.

When the hearing was resumed, the findings of the Standing Committee were announced:

1. The Committee unanimously affirm the findings of the Board of Discipline that both Mr. Bloom and Mr. Adelstein were guilty of disobedience to an instruction given by the Director.

2. The Committee by a majority consider the charge against Mr. Adelstein of encouraging disobedience to an instruction given by the Director was not proved beyond reasonable doubt.

3. The Committee consider that the offence of disobedience merits the penalty of suspension imposed on both Mr. Bloom and Mr. Adelstein by the Board of Discipline, which they therefore confirm.

4. The Committee have requested the Director (subject to his being satisfied with the behaviour of Mr. Bloom and Mr. Adelstein and their full observance of the suspension order from today's date onwards) to arrange that as from 30 May, 1967, Mr. Bloom and Mr. Adelstein may have access to School premises for the purpose only of visiting their respective tutors to receive instruction under arrangements approved by the Director, and making use of the facilities of the Library.

5. The Committee understand that the Director will use his best endeavours to procure that the University of London will allow Mr. Bloom to sit for his proposed examination notwithstanding his suspension.

The Standing Committee did not explain the reasons for their decisions. Most important was the variation that they had made in the sentence. Although offering a reduction of penalty, it also had the effect of making enforcement of the suspensions much easier. Hitherto, if Adelstein or Bloom had continued, in defiance of the suspension, to come into the School, all that we could have done would have been either to bring him before the Board of Discipline as having committed a further offence, or to apply to the courts for an injunction to restrain him from coming in— both ponderous measures. The Standing Committee had now provided a device whereby the Director was able to say that, every time either of them came in while under suspension, the partial lifting of the suspension for which the Committee had provided would be delayed for a further day.

The Students' Union had been awaiting the result of the appeal in considerable confidence that the decision would be favourable. They found it hard to accept the fact that it had gone against them. They debated it until 2 a.m. in increasingly militant terms, Bloom in particular making an appeal for a continuation of the struggle. They agreed to meet again at one o'clock on Saturday. A meeting, subdued and quiet, of between sixty and a hundred members of the staff also discussed the Standing Committee's verdict that night. Their general conclusion was that if they intervened at all it should be to tell the students that there was nothing more that the staff could do, and that the demonstration should be called off.

Next morning I discussed the situation on the telephone with Lord Bridges and then went up to the School to talk to Caine. We were all in agreement that there should be no more concessions, or even discussion of them, while the sit-in continued. There should in any event be no question whatever of a bargain with the Union about the suspensions; that would make nonsense of the careful judicial procedure that had been followed. I suggested, however, that it would be as well to make all this perfectly clear, since otherwise the sit-in might go dragging on in the expectation of extracting further concessions. Watherston in Lincoln's Inn Fields had spoken of the Director's conciliatory statement as a sign of movement in the right direction, but had added that it had nothing to do with the main issue of the suspensions. The activities of the staff, however well-meaning some of them might be, and the way in which they had been reported in the press (especially the piece in Friday's *Guardian*) must inevitably be creating among the students an impression that they need only keep the pressure up and they would get all they wanted. (The conclusion of the meeting of members of the staff in the early hours of Saturday morning was not known to us.) The tenor of the Union debate on the previous night had seemed to be militant. If it was absolutely clear that the students would gain nothing by continuing the sit-in, it would be best to let them know. So, without mentioning the matter to anyone else, we agreed to make a statement and I was instructed to seek an opportunity of reading it to the Union when they met that afternoon. I made a de-

The clearance of Connaught House

The entrance hall during the sit-in

The march to Lincoln's Inn Fields

parture from the normal role of the official whose task it is merely to convey the views and decisions of others, and signed the statement myself. It was probably improper to do so, but I am not in the least degree penitent about it. It seemed to me to be time for a nailing of the colours to the mast, and I was very glad to lend a hand with a hammer. The statement read as follows:

We wish to state our views on the present situation at L.S.E.:

(a) Discussions must and will continue urgently of improvements in the School's system of government, in arrangements for consultation with students, and in disciplinary procedures;

(b) Urgently as this is needed, progress cannot be made until the School gets back to normal, and the sooner that happens the better; there will be no discussion under duress;

(c) The decisions of the Standing Committee on the suspension of Mr. Adelstein and Mr. Bloom will stand; they have never been, and will not be, a matter for negotiation.

We had not expected the statement to be popular, and it certainly was not; but that was not its purpose. Its purpose was to bring clarity and to help to end the sit-in; and it is my belief that it was successful. It was indeed, as we shall see, the basis for part of Watherston's argument when he moved on the following Monday that the sit-in should end at the end of term.

My reading of the statement was followed by a speech by Zander, who had come to urge the Union to end the demonstration. He felt that the statement made it unlikely that they would do so. He had throughout the week given no indication to any student that he sympathized with them; now in an impassioned oration he told them that their boycott and sit-in had been the best things to happen to L.S.E. for he did not know how long. Almost half the staff, he said, were committed to doing something about the situation. Just when progress looked like being possible my miserable little statement had put the whole thing in jeopardy. But he went on—and this part of his speech the newspapers failed to report—to urge them to call off the sit-in and get things back to normal so that negotiations could be conducted through proper constitutional channels. Atkinson then made an angry speech, proclaiming the last paragraph of the statement that I had read to be a lie. He felt it entitled him to reveal to the Union the tenor of the discussions with Miss Seear and Roberts on the previous Thursday evening. They had, he said, negotiated about the suspensions, and here was I saying that no negotiations had ever taken place!

The debate continued. There was a clear division of opinion between those who thought that no more was going to be gained by any further demonstrations, which would have no more than a symbolic importance, and that the important thing to be done was to get negotiations started; and on the other hand those who were in favour of battling on. A motion which would have suspended all direct action from the end of term until the

H

beginning of the Summer Term was defeated by 280 votes to 210; and it was agreed by 347 votes to 116 as follows:

1. Union considers that the present situation has not radically changed, and therefore proposes that the sit-in and boycott continue in solidarity with Messrs. Adelstein and Bloom in accordance with the principled decision of Union of Monday, 13th March, 1967, until some genuine concessions are made by the Administration or the Court of Governors.

2. A standing delegation of about thirty representatives will be selected at this meeting to organize the continuation of any action we decide to take, twelve of whom would form a sub-committee to start negotiations with the Administration.

3. Union urges individual members to write to their Local Education Authorities in order to acquaint them with the reason behind our stand.

At twenty past seven the Union adjourned.

Atkinson's charge that the last paragraph of the statement signed by the Chairman, the Director, and myself was a lie calls for comment. It is perhaps enough to say, first, that it is not at all clear that what had taken place on the Thursday night can be described with any precision as negotiation about the suspensions; and, second, that the statement that I read did not say that negotiations had not taken place. (When John Milton wrote 'Nothing is here for tears' he was not saying that no one was weeping.) I am sure, however, that none of us had Thursday evening's events much in mind: at the end of an exhausting week they were forgotten.

Sunday was a quiet day, but the students were active. A committee appointed for the purpose prepared a letter to all members of the staff, copies of which were also sent to the Governors, the press, and known sympathizers, stating their point of view at some length. It is a definitive statement of their case, and I have reproduced it as Appendix IV.[1] Others busied themselves with organizing a 'free university', in which teaching would be given by sympathetic members of the staff of the School and others; the enterprise did not take full shape for another fortnight.

During Sunday night two professors, who were on duty at the School as the Director's deputies, talked to Union officials on the question whether some kind of peace formula could be found before the end of term. The Union officials wanted two things: first, the suspension of the suspensions, about which the professors could do nothing; second, some provision for continuing meetings during the vacation. It was agreed that such meetings would be useful, but between whom should they take place? The Union was to meet on Monday and Tuesday, and could appoint representatives; but no meeting of the Academic Board, by which staff representatives might be appointed, was impending. The question was left for later discussion.

The Union met at half past seven on Monday evening. It was reported

[1] See p. 184.

that Watherston had seen Caine, and had obtained from him an undertaking that neither he nor I would institute disciplinary proceedings for anything done during the sit-in. The Union were told of steps that were being taken to secure the revocation of the suspensions by action of the courts. A report was made of the meetings with the two professors, and of the fact that a further meeting would be held next morning. In addition a student who had spoken to the porters reminded the Union of all the extra work they had been doing, and asked the Union on their behalf to suspend the sit-in over the Easter holiday (the following week-end).

There followed a debate on future policy. Watherston proposed, and Atkinson seconded, the motion:

Union

1. Continues its opposition to the vicious victimization of Messrs. Adelstein and Bloom;

2. Nevertheless temporarily suspends the sit-in from 5 p.m. on Tuesday, 21 March;

3. Insists that rooms of the School remain open for the purposes of free discussion and debate on immediate and general issues and invites all staff to participate in this experiment;

4. Reiterates its demands for an independent enquiry;

5. Insists that our grievances and demands concerning representation be given extreme urgency;

6. Demands that no disciplinary action should result from our legitimate and restrained demonstrations this week in full support of Messrs Adelstein and Bloom;

7. Will re-introduce our demonstrations next term should the Administration yet again prove itself intransigent on any of these issues.

In proposing the motion Watherston said that if the sit-in continued the power of decision would be left with the small minority of students remaining in the School during the vacation; but it would be better for all students to be able to participate in the decisions on any future action. The sit-in had been very effective so far. The Director, however, had indicated in the statement of Saturday that the School authorities would not budge while the sit-in continued, and it would be a test of their good faith to suspend the sit-in and see what the authorities did.

Atkinson seconded the motion. He said that it would in no way involve the Union in going back on the position it had taken up, especially as the right had been reserved to resume the sit-in at any time during the summer term. What was needed was a temporary de-escalation (in strategic metaphor, evidently all escalators go up). The demonstrations could be resumed next term, but only if the School remained as intransigent as it had been during the previous few weeks.

Other speakers urged delay. The debate was ill-timed. There was a great deal to be discussed, and the staff were ready for discussion; moves had been made by senior members of the staff that very day. The Union ought to show intransigence and exploit the situation fully by keeping the pressure up till the very last moment of term. It could consider the resolution again the following afternoon. Without the confrontation it was naïve to expect anything to come of the negotiations. It was doubtful, if the sit-in were suspended, how many students would resume it next term. On the other hand it was urged that it was important to know when to be hawkish and when to wait. The demonstration was coming apart at the seams because of the arrival of outsiders who did not have the same interests as the students; they might take the School over. Union could not meet during the vacation, and it should not, by letting the sit-in continue, leave the power of decision to the small number remaining at the School.

The motion was passed by 232 votes to 177 and the meeting adjourned at 11.25 p.m. The debate had been very acrimonious and bitter; the division was largely on political lines, between the Socialist Society and their followers on one side and the pragmatists on the other. When it ended someone shouted 'All who voted against Watherston's motion stay behind, and we will decide what to do.' There were enough of them to have continued the sit-in on their own. For a short time it looked as though that might happen, but Watherston went into the theatre and spoke again; there was perhaps not really so very much, he said, between the two sides; if the Union had another meeting next day it could state its position with greater precision on various issues, and satisfy all its members. His suggestion was accepted.

The staff-student committee on the disciplinary regulations had started work early in the term, as soon as the student representatives had been appointed. Proposals put forward by the students' representatives had been examined and it had been agreed to meet again on 21 March, when the staff members were to table proposals. Since, as we now heard, the Union had agreed to suspend the sit-in, the way was clear for the scheduled meeting to be held. The staff members met and drew up outline proposals providing:

1. for inclusion in the regulations of a guarantee of the rights of freedom of speech, assembly and association, these rights to be subject to such reasonable restrictions as might be imposed in the interests of the safety and good order of the School, the protection of the rights, freedoms and reputations of persons belonging to the School, or the carrying on of its educational functions;

2. a Board of Discipline containing two Governors, two members of the Academic Board, and two students;

3. a right of appeal to an independent body, perhaps a lawyer nominated by an external authority.

These proposals we presented to the students. They were read to the Union that afternoon, and greeted by the newspapers as 'a victory for the students'. The Union, however, did not think they went far enough: some members thought them worse than the existing regulations in the explicit limitation that they made of students' rights. It was announced that three student members of the committee would not be available during the vacation, and there were therefore three vacancies; they were filled by three new representatives, who were instructed to secure greater concessions.

Later in the Union meeting Atkinson moved, and Jefferys seconded, the following motion:

Union, wishing to clarify its position in regard to its present policies, states:
(a) that it is suspending the sit-in in the foyer because it considers the Open University to be the most effective and constructive form of protest during the vacation; and
(b) reaffirms its principled stand against the victimization of Messrs. Adelstein and Bloom, and pledges that it will continue the sit-in and boycott on the second day of the summer term unless genuine concessions on this issue have been made by the Administration.

The motion was the attempt, promised by Watherston the previous day, to please everybody, by papering over the cracks; the cracks nearly opened during the debate with a dispute whether or not the motion allowed for a sit-in to take place during the vacation, but the motion was carried by an overwhelming majority. Watherston then proposed:

Union agrees to the establishment of a committee comprising ten members of staff (to be appointed by the Ad Hoc Committee on Relations between the School and its Students) and ten students (to be elected from this Union meeting) to work throughout the vacation under the following terms of reference:
'To consider changes in the structure of the School, and related matters, which are necessary to create an academic community, to make recommendations to the Academic Board and the Students' Union, and to establish a relationship with the joint Staff-Governors Committee on the Machinery of Government of the School. Concrete proposals will be made by the first day of the Summer Term.'
Student members of this committee will discuss with, and take suggestions from, the Open University throughout this period, and no policy decisions will be taken by the Union before the first day of next term.

This motion was passed without opposition and the Union then adjourned in order to resume the sit-in for a quarter of an hour before dispersing at five o'clock.

The Open University began its proceedings on 3 April, made colourful by a gift of red balloons to all the participants from a revolutionary body, the Situationist International. A prominent place in the programme each day was a seminar on the subject 'L.S.E.: What it is, and how to fight it'. The programme, ranging from psychiatry to Tariq Ali on Vietnam, had a distinctly political flavour. It was no great success, partly because it was found that a critical approach was no substitute for a certain modicum of knowledge; 'we were not able', its organizer wrote later, 'to either plan or inform students of seminars well enough in advance for additional reading to be done. Nor had we fully developed our ideas of what "freeing education" was.' As a symbolic protest also the Open University soon lost its force as its organizers were pressed and persuaded with increasing success to conform to normal administrative arrangements for such mundane matters as the booking of lecture rooms, and to abandon their declared intention of keeping the School open for twenty-four hours a day.

9 The Settlement

At the end of the term, and in fact on the last day of the sit-in, the Ad Hoc Committee on Relationships with Students met and invited the Students' Union to send representatives to meet us on 4 April. Our purpose was to discuss with them the lines on which we intended to report to the Academic Board on the teaching relationship, and to begin discussion of organized consultation with students. When the meeting took place, however, there was some confusion, as the students were expecting an invitation to send ten representatives to meet ten representatives of the academic staff in accordance with their resolution of 21 March,[1] of which we had not been informed. They also objected to the inclusion of Roberts and myself in the body that they were to meet. Our number was eleven, but we agreed to reduce it to ten by appointing a sub-committee of that number, and I volunteered to drop out for the purpose, but to attend as secretary. We adhered firmly, however, to the principle that it was for us, not them, to decide the membership of our side in the discussions. They went formally on record as objecting to Roberts, first because of what they believed he had said at the press conference on 14 March,[2] secondly because of his participation in the Roberts–Seear 'negotiations', which they alleged, because of their interpretation of the statement that I had read on 18 March, had not been genuine,[3] and thirdly because he had withdrawn from addressing their Open University, after he had first accepted an invitation to do so but had subsequently discovered that it was part of their demonstration of protest. Their vendetta against Roberts was one of the most unfair things to happen in the whole of the conflict. Roberts's work in calling for, organizing, and reporting on the survey of student opinion was one of the best and most courageous things done for the benefit of students at the School for many years. He is a man who cares deeply for students, but he was forthright—as forthright in his comments on the sit-in as in his report on the survey—and loyal to his colleagues on the Board of Discipline. The students' objection to myself was, I found on subsequent

---

[1] See p. 105.
[2] See p. 84.
[3] See pp. 94, 101.

enquiry, more prosaic: I was an administrator, and they wished to meet academics, not administrators.

After these preliminary arguments, we made a start. The students asked that the first matter to be discussed should be the suspension of Adelstein and Bloom. Staff members replied at first that this was not a subject with which the Academic Board was competent to deal, and it was therefore outside the scope of the present committee of the board. The suspensions had been imposed after the prescribed processes had been carried out; for some members at least it was a matter of conscience to accept the decision of their colleagues, to whom they had committed responsibility in the matter, and who had heard the evidence, which they themselves had not. The students replied that this was the most important single issue affecting staff-student relations at the moment, and it must be discussed if a fruitful basis was to be established for wider discussions; this was accepted.

The students then proposed that the suspensions should be suspended from the beginning of the summer term in order to release tension and create a propitious atmosphere for discussion of other subjects. If this were done it would not, Watherston said, be treated as a grand victory for the students, but as ushering in a new era, and showing a constructive attitude to present differences. It had, others added, been suggested during the sit-in that it might be easier for the Standing Committee to reach a favourable decision if the sit-in were called off; the sit-in had been suspended, so that condition had been satisfied.

In further discussion it was agreed that the question now to be discussed was not whether the decision of the Standing Committee was just, but whether it would be right for the Court of Governors, acting in a capacity similar to that of the Home Secretary, to mitigate the penalty. A student suggested that the suspension of the suspensions could be probationary. Might not the Governors feel, the students were asked, that they were being asked to revoke the suspensions under the threat of a resumption of the sit-in at the beginning of next term? Was there any gesture that the students could make that would convince the Governors that the desired decision really would be the prelude to improved relationships? Watherston replied that if the Governors were to agree to the proposal he would be prepared to issue a statement saying that this action would usher in a new era of relations between staff and students in which they would hope to work amicably together, and that it should not be seen as a victory for 'student power'. Others added that the students were making an important concession in that they were not now asking, as all the Union resolutions on the subject had asked, for justice, but for clemency; they were no longer asking for a verdict of 'Not Guilty'. The Governors need not fear, it was argued, that the lifting of the suspensions would be seen as being granted under the threat of a continuation of the boycott, and so as establishing that other objects could be achieved by similar means. It was true that if the present conflict remained unresolved it was likely that even moderate students would insist on further action; but this was the only issue on which the whole student body was united. On the Adams issue, indeed on all other issues, student opinion was divided, and it was most unlikely that any new one would arise that could give occasion for a boycott, especially in the next six months, when students would first be concerned with examinations and then on vacation. In general, moreover, if discussions of the present kind were seen not to be effective, the propensity to direct action would be increased. It was in the end agreed that the Court of Governors should be told that the Students' Union wished to put forward a plea for clemency for Adelstein and Bloom, and should be asked to give a hearing on the subject to Watherston as President of the Union.

Next day, Thursday, 6 April, the Standing Committee met at 3.30 p.m., in preparation for a meeting of the Court at 5 p.m. Caine reported that he would be away for about a fortnight during the vacation and that arrangements would need to be made for the running of the School during his absence. (His holiday had been planned a long time in advance, and was needed. He had not only had the crisis at the School to deal with; on behalf of the Government he had, as Chairman of the Governors of the Reserve Bank of Rhodesia, conducted the world-wide search for the assets of the dissident regime in Rhodesia; and as Deputy Chairman of the Independent Television Authority he had been heavily engaged in preparation for re-assigning contracts amongst the television companies.) It was agreed that he was right to try to get away for a time. In accordance with custom, three professorial Governors, Professors Freedman, MacRae, and Roberts, were appointed to exercise his functions during his absence.

Caine then reported the recommendations that had been made by the joint sub-committee of staff and students. The Standing Committee were of opinion that it would be wrong for Watherston to be heard without adequate notice to the Court, but they recommended that arrangements should be made for him to appear in the near future before a special committee to be appointed for the purpose.

When the Court assembled they were told of this proposal. Caine explained carefully that the Students' Union were not questioning the judgment of the Board of Discipline as upheld by the Standing Committee, but were asking for an amnesty, which they hoped would be the basis for improving staff-student relationships for the future. The Standing Committee were not themselves asking the Governors to exercise clemency, but asking them to arrange for the appeal from the Union to be considered. The Standing Committee, it was explained, had thought it their duty to act in a purely judicial capacity when they had heard the appeals, and to determine them on the evidence before them, without considering any wider implications; they would see no objection to the proposed completely different appeal being heard.

In the course of discussion the question was raised whether a dangerous precedent would be set if the Court decided to withdraw or mitigate the sentences. In reply it was pointed out that new disciplinary machinery was to be set up, so that this was the last case that would have to be dealt with under present arrangements, and the danger of creating a difficult precedent was much reduced. Several members felt that, while it would be wrong for the Court to over-ride completely the decision of the Board of Discipline and the Standing Committee, some mitigation of sentence might be possible; but it was strongly urged that any suspension of the sentences should be in the nature of probation, conditional on good conduct.

From one quarter firm opposition was expressed to any act of clemency; a much stronger line should have been taken. It was unfortunate that the administration had become involved in pseudo-legal procedures and that the two students had been suspended rather than expelled. It was no argument to say that there were several people besides Adelstein and Bloom who were more culpable. There was widespread indignation that students who were subsidised from public funds should be involved in political demonstrations of this kind. The students apparently had every intention of continuing their demonstration next term and might make it quite impossible for Adams to take up his appointment. There was some support for these views, which accurately reflected a substantial section of public opinion. Others expressed a different view. Whatever could or could not have been achieved by stronger action earlier, it was necessary to consider the situation as it now existed. The charges on which the two students had been convicted were mild in comparison with the more serious events which had occurred and it might appear that they were being punished more severely than was appropriate. Very many students were deeply concerned with the present situation and the appeal ought to be heard.

Several Governors supported this view, and there was a strong body of opinion that Watherston ought to be heard by the whole Court and not by the committee. While they could not reasonably define the arguments that Watherston should put to them, it should be understood that there could not be any question of re-opening the case and reconsidering the decisions of the Board of Discipline and the Standing Committee. When the question whether he be heard was put to the vote it was decided in the affirmative by a substantial majority; and it was agreed to meet again on the following Monday, 10 April, for the purpose.

Meanwhile, the lawyers had been busy. A firm of solicitors had written to us on behalf of Adelstein and Bloom, to request that the invalidity of their suspension be admitted, and the suspension revoked. The grounds adduced were, first of all, a number of alleged irregularities in the proceedings of the Standing Committee and, secondly, that the decision of the Board of Discipline in finding Adelstein and Bloom guilty of disobedience was not supported by the findings of fact and constituted an error on the face of the record such as to enable the High Court to quash the decision. Counsel advised us that the procedural points should present no difficulty;

even if they were accepted, moreover, their only effect would be to wipe out the decision of the Standing Committee and restore that of the Board of Discipline, pending a re-hearing of the appeal by the Standing Committee. More difficult was the question of the definition of 'disobedience'. The courts could intervene if the conduct alleged could not constitute an offence against the School regulation. They might conceivably adopt a very strict definition of disobedience, under which it could be established that, since the forbidden meeting had not taken place, there could not have been disobedience. On the other hand, a much more robust view might be taken; and counsel settled for us a very firm reply to the students' solicitors.

On Friday, 7 April, the Director left for his holiday in Greece. Before he went some thought had been given to the question whether there were conditions upon which the Governors might be advised to accede to Watherston's plea. There must be an apology from Adelstein and Bloom, and an undertaking from them to abide by constitutional procedures and to collaborate with Adams. Was this enough? The complaint of victimization rested in part on the fact that no disciplinary proceedings had been instituted against the unidentified persons who had issued the inflammatory leaflets and had taken the lead in the violent assault on the doors of the Old Theatre on 31 January; might it be desirable to make it a condition of an amnesty that these persons should come forward, identify themselves, and apologize for their acts? This question was left for consideration.

Discussion continued during the week-end and Caine, who had arrived in Athens, was consulted by telephone. I think the situation can fairly be summed up as follows:

1. The sit-in. There was a chance that the sit-in would be renewed at the beginning of next term, but even if it did it was reasonably likely to fizzle out in view of the impending examinations. Even if it did not fizzle out, it might not be of serious dimensions.

2. The legal proceedings. Unless the dispute was settled an action against the School would be instituted within a week. The chances of success seemed to be, say, two to one in our favour. Even if we lost, it would be a defeat by due process, rather than by force, and so tolerable.

3. Isolating the extremists. The underlying policy of Caine and the Standing Committee throughout the year had been to try to remedy outstanding grievances quickly, so satisfying reasonable students and isolating the extremists. Now, however, a substantial number of ordinary sensible students had been persuaded to believe—and it made no difference that, according to our point of view, they believed it wrongly—that serious injustice had been done. It would be in accordance with the underlying policy to try to secure a settlement now in some form which did not involve the sacrifice of principles.

4. Apologies. An apology from Adelstein and Bloom would provide a perfectly reasonable ground for suspending the sentences, especially as the absence of any expression of regret from them had at the time been a factor in the decision to prosecute. That the fomenters of disorder and violence on 31 January might come forward, identify themselves, and apologize was a profoundly attractive idea, but there were two difficulties in the way. The students concerned were still unknown and unidentified; but we now had strong suspicions, and those whom we suspected would be most unlikely to come forward and apologize. The other objection rested on a point of principle. If Adelstein and Bloom were willing to apologize, then to make the acceptance of their apology conditional on the acts of others would be to run the risk of continuing to punish them because others would not apologize. This really would be victimization and would be wrong.

On Monday, 10 April, the Court of Governors met again. Watherston was invited in. He submitted to the Court as an aide-mémoire the following notes on the basis of which he proposed to speak:

Reasons for Student Action

1. Accumulated feeling about the growing remoteness of the academic staff and administration.
2. Shock at the fact that the Director had banned the meeting on 31 January 1967.
3. Resentment that the two student leaders who had exercised a moderating influence had been picked out for technical offences because of their office.
4. Feeling that the disciplinary procedure was outdated and biased.
5. Conciliation on the sentences had been tried and failed.

Amnesty

1. An amnesty would not be regarded as impugning the findings or sentences but as an act of grace on the part of the authorities.
2. The amnesty to be the suspension of the suspensions as from the first day of next term.

Reason for Amnesty

1. Student feelings about the sentences still very strong.
2. Relationships in the School have been soured by events.
3. Messrs. Adelstein and Bloom have already suffered considerably from anxiety, press publicity and the lack of Library facilities during the vacation.
4. Clear the air and make possible the restoration of harmonious staff–student relations.
5. Facilitate the transition from one Director to the next.
6. Victory for the School as a whole.

In his address Watherston spoke of the strain on the School of growing student numbers, their effect on the staff–student ratio, and the remoteness, in the student mind, of the academic staff and the administration, which they felt to be paternalist. In the Michaelmas Term of 1966 the appointment of Dr. Adams as Director had been seriously questioned. This had been a reflection of general uneasiness, but the appointment was not really a live issue any longer; it had been pushed into the background by the more recent difficulties, and he had himself been elected to the office of President of the Union on a programme which provided for co-operation with Dr. Adams.

Coming to the meeting of 31 January, Watherston said that students felt that it had been sponsored by the Students' Union Council, and did not regard it as out of the ordinary. They had been shocked at the ban, which seemed to them an impairment of the ordinary citizen's freedom of discussion. The Students' Union had, however, now no wish to dispute the findings of the Board of Discipline and the Standing Committee; but they felt that Adelstein and Bloom had been 'picked out' and that the charges on which they had been found guilty were of a technical nature. They had, he said, been a moderating influence on 31 January, when others had been committing a really serious breach of discipline by pushing their way into the Old Theatre, but had been granted an amnesty by the Director. It was therefore harsh to punish these two, who had been placed in a position of great difficulty. They had, Watherston admitted, a duty to the Director, but they also had a duty to other students who had wished to hold this meeting. The disciplinary procedure, moreover, was felt by many students to be out of date and biased. As the Court knew, a committee was considering a new procedure; the case of Adelstein and Bloom was likely to be the last under the present procedure, and could, therefore, be specially considered without risk of setting a precedent.

While the disciplinary proceedings were going on, he continued, the students had taken a moderate line, and the Union had resisted pressure to organize disorderly demonstrations. A conciliation committee had visited senior members of the staff asking for moderation in return, and the sentences, when announced, had been a shock. The students felt that they had tried all other means without success, and the demonstrations had been a last resort. They had been orderly demonstrations, and they had been supported by students of a wide range of political opinions.

The amnesty that he sought would, he said, be an act of grace, and the findings of the Board of Discipline would not be impugned. It would not be regarded by students as a victory, or as meaning that they could force decisions on the School by militant action. Students on the whole wanted to get on with their work and to co-operate with the School authorities. Extremist elements could arouse demonstrations of the type that had recently taken place only if they had support, on keenly felt issues, from more moderate elements in the School. Adelstein and Bloom had been considerably punished already; the charges had been hanging over their heads for a considerable time; they had been the subject of condemnation and vilification in the press, and this might affect their careers and their future social relationships. For his own part, Watherston concluded, he wished to see a new mood of co-operation, and his presidential campaign had been based on a programme of negotiation with the School authorities through constitutional channels. He hoped that the Court of Governors would make this possible.

In answer to questions, he said that Adelstein and Bloom knew what he was saying and had agreed to it; he also gave it as his view that a student officer should not be punished for carrying out any task entrusted to him by the students because he held his office; and confirmed his understanding that the suspension of the sentences would carry an implied condition of good conduct. Asked whether it was now accepted that the conclusions of the Board of Discipline were fair and reasonable, he said that it was not, but they were recognized as something that had happened and something that, if the amnesty were granted, the students would put up with. He was told that a decision would not be reached for two or three days, and then withdrew.

Discussion began with an agreement that whatever conclusion the Court might come to should not be given effect until the views of Caine and Adams had been obtained. A number of Governors then urged that no concession should be made; it would be an act of weakness, would seem to countenance the view—which was entirely unacceptable—that the disciplinary proceeds had been out of date and biased, and would appear to condone the failure of student leaders to accept their responsibilities. Others urged the importance of recognizing that the judicial proceedings were over: Watherston's mission had been essentially political, and the Court ought, perhaps, to consider reaching a settlement on a political basis. Many students, however wrongly, genuinely felt that the sentences imposed on Adelstein and Bloom had been harsh. It was in the interest of the School to make some concession to the students so as to ease tension and to introduce a better atmosphere into the discussions currently being conducted with the students.

Justice, it was urged, however, had been done by the School; those who were asking for clemency should apologize for their actions, and there should be no suggestion that the School was making a bargain with the students; but the School should not be too particular about how the tension was eased. There had been faults on both sides and the matter might even be settled on the basis of an expression of regret from the two students rather than an apology. Some, indeed, thought it very unlikely that an apology would be obtainable, and were inclined to favour simple suspension of the sentences subject to the good behaviour of Adelstein and Bloom.

The Chairman summed up, saying that there were three courses open to the Court—to make no concessions; to suspend the sentences subject to good behaviour; and to make such a suspension conditional upon an apology from Bloom and Adelstein. The Court decided not to vote immediately on these three possibilities, but that the Director and Adams should be consulted; they would themselves meet again three days later, on Thursday, 13 April.

The reception of Watherston's statement had been mixed. He had spoken very well, but he had certainly not come to offer the surrender of the Students' Union and to apologize for the sit-in. He abstained, however, from all polemics, and explained his point of view with clarity and firmness, but with restraint. It was perhaps a mistake for him to be asked—as he was—whether the conclusions of the Board of Discipline were now accepted as fair and reasonable, and it would have been impossible (and untruthful) for him to reply otherwise than as he did. He felt, as did his Union, which he was representing, that those conclusions had been wrong, and that the protest had been right. He had come to explain that the protest had been restrained and conscientious, but some of the Governors read this as an attempt to reopen the issues. This was, I think, unfair, though understandable. It took several days for Watherston's restrained and unemotional appeal to have full effect, and I doubt whether even now he has the credit that he undoubtedly deserves for the success of his pacificatory mission, and for his achievements as President in the twelve months that were to follow.

After the meeting of the Court there were further informal consultations with Caine, Adams, and others. Watherston's statement, it was clear, had not moved the Court to the desired conclusion; more was needed by way of commitment to future co-operation. The minimum pre-requisite for an amnesty was an expression of regret and a public statement by Watherston, Adelstein, and Bloom of their intention to act constructively and to collaborate with the academic staff and the new Director in the improvement of staff-student relationships. If such a statement were forthcoming there would be hope for the future. The task of obtaining it if possible was given to me; but I was to wait for the first approach to come, as I was sure it would, from the other side, and I was not to make any kind of offer or bargain; there were to be no negotiations.

When opportunity offered next morning, therefore, I told one of Adelstein and Bloom's advisers that the Governors had not yet reached a decision on Watherston's plea, which, while most ably presented, had failed to convince them. I took the opportunity to state the official point of view, and I was heard with patience. I suggested that it was not too late even now for the Governors to be persuaded. Three things seemed to me, I explained, to be necessary: acceptance of the disciplinary proceedings (which was not the same as agreeing with them); real personal regret at the chain of events; and a real commitment on the part of Adelstein, Bloom, and Watherston to work with the present administration, with Adams, and with the academic staff in improving staff-student relationships. This, I said, might be enough to move the Governors, but I could not be sure; I had no authority to treat on their behalf. The time, moreover, for anything of the sort was very short, and I felt sure that the Governors would no longer be willing to entertain the notion of clemency when once any proceedings were begun in the courts.

There were comings and goings in the next few days. I was in touch with Caine in Athens, with the Chairman and other Governors. On Thursday 13 April, I was brought a statement signed by Adelstein and Bloom, and a message from Watherston, saying that he felt he was in a somewhat different category and also that he had made his statement. He did, however, wish it to be known that he associated himself with Adelstein and Bloom's statement, which was submitted on the understanding that it would not be published unless an amnesty was granted.

Informal soundings that I made suggested that the form of statement submitted would not be acceptable to the Governors, and this was confirmed when they met that afternoon at half past four. The words used in it suggested that part of the responsibility for what had occurred rested with the Governors, and this was not acceptable in this context. There were other possible implications that were also unacceptable, and the commitment to co-operation that was offered seemed too conditional. It did not take long to discover that the Court of Governors were agreed that with some amendments the statement would be sufficient to make the grant of the proposed amnesty possible; but that they were also agreed that without it (and without those amendments) there could be no amnesty. On both points they were now unanimous, hawks and doves being in whole-hearted agreement.

I was sent off to see the students' adviser again with this message. I asked him to do all that he could to secure the signature of a revised statement, and said that I thought we ought to be prepared to go on all night if necessary—for we were now fairly sure that the legal proceedings were due to begin next afternoon, and once that happened there was not going to be any settlement. I waited half an hour for an answer and, none having come, returned to the Court of Governors. I told them what I had said, and added that I hoped that they would be willing that a quorum (four members) of the Court should remain in session for as long as necessary to wait for the answer and to deal with any drafting point that might arise. They agreed to this, and the meeting was breaking up when word was brought that the students' adviser wished to address the Court. It was agreed that he should be heard and that two of the leading doves should reply on behalf of the Court. What he had to say was that he expected great difficulty in securing the amendments desired by the Court. In reply, he was told of the inadequacies of the statement as it at present stood; it showed no commitment to constitutional methods of seeking change. The refusal by those who sought amnesty to commit themselves to an undertaking to work with Caine, Adams, and the School authorities through constitutional processes would be sinister and unacceptable. It was essential to have an explicit commitment to work with Adams, because it was out of objection to his appointment that the trouble had all arisen; and the statement must not be in a form which suggested conditions or might seem to be preparing for them to be introduced later. He left, to see what he could do.

A small number of Governors remained and had dinner with myself and the other officers in attendance. At nine o'clock those who were left came up to my office, prepared to sit as long as might be necessary. There were comings and goings, but the quorum was maintained at all times. Exchanges with the advisers of Adelstein and Bloom continued until about midnight, when the students and their advisers went home. After brief discussion the quorum of the Court adjourned at one a.m. on Friday 14 April, agreeing to call as many members of the Court as possible to meet again at 11.45 a.m.

As we were breaking up, we heard that the press were asking questions outside. There was some fear lest the impression might be given that discussion had been broken off by the Court, and I was instructed to issue a statement that the Court had adjourned, but that Watherston's plea was still under consideration. This had one odd side-effect. At least one prominent Governor was distinctly irritated that the public should be given the impression that the Court were so ineffectual that they had been locked in debate from half past four to one o'clock in the morning without being able to reach a conclusion!

Next morning I had a further conversation with the adviser of Adelstein and Bloom about the form of statement that the previous night's quorum had in the end agreed would be acceptable. Just before noon, the Court duly met and approved its terms. Two professorial governors volunteered to go to see the students' adviser and to convey to him the views of the Court. Meanwhile I got into touch with Adams and asked him to come to the School as soon as he could. While we waited for him, and for the return of the two Governors, I was set to work preparing two alternative statements for the press, one for use if it proved possible to grant an amnesty, and the other for use if it did not.

When the two Governors returned, they brought the statement duly signed by Adelstein and Bloom with one small amendment. Adams, who had arrived meanwhile, found it satisfactory and the Court were confident, in the light of my telephone conversations with Caine, that he too would accept it. It was proposed, and the Court agreed, that the amnesty should be granted on the basis of the document now signed. Watherston was invited in and informed of the decision, and reiterated his willingness to work with the Governors in the best interests of the School. The statement issued to the press, after referring to Watherston's plea for the suspension of the penalties, continued by quoting the form of words signed by Adelstein and Bloom:

We sincerely regret that events have arisen which have led to conflict within the School and we hope that this conflict can now be ended. We, for our part, take full responsibility for our share in these events. We are intent on working with the School authorities through constitutional processes. We hope to see the re-establishment of good relations in L.S.E., and we will

I

use our best endeavours to bring this about on the basis of co-operation and mutual respect between all sections of the School.

                                        (Signed)   D. L. ADELSTEIN
                                                   M. J. BLOOM

'In the light of the undertakings given,' the announcement concluded, 'the Court of Governors have decided on an act of clemency, and have accordingly, during the good behaviour of Mr. Adelstein and Mr. Bloom, suspended the penalty imposed on them.'

The reception of the settlement thus arrived at was mixed. Some of my colleagues and some of the public regarded it as a victory for the militants. The militants, indeed, forgetting what Watherston had undertaken on their behalf, claimed it as such. Even while they claimed it, however, they were at a loss to explain how they had won it. 'There is only one possible explanation,' said the Socialist Society.[1] 'The vacation had destroyed the continuity of the sit-in, and there were likely to be difficulties in restarting it. But returning students, refreshed by the vacation, might be prepared to stage "guerilla" sit-ins at short notice.' That is to say, what a full-scale sit-in, lasting more than a week, had failed to achieve was secured by a mere possibility, not spoken of at the time, of an occasional little sit-in.[2]

In fact the failure of the sit-in was a necessary condition of any settlement of the kind that had been achieved. It was a cardinal point of policy not to yield to force or the present threat of force. The sit-in had begun as a demonstration of protest. The attempted blockade of the School and the invasion of Connaught House, with the object of 'paralyzing' the School, introduced the element of force. Neither attempt at its use was successful. A group of buildings, inter-connected by bridges, and possessing as many entrances as the School (ten, if I am not mistaken) is very difficult to blockade with success; and the attack on Connaught House had been met by a determined counter-attack. What the use of force did achieve, however, was to obscure the element of moral protest, already diminished by the prominence of the Socialist Society, which had given the sit-in a political appearance. It was only when the passage of time had dimmed the memory of these aspects of the sit-in, and when the use of force was no longer present or seriously threatened, that the persuasive effect of the moral protest could be felt. Its effect was then strengthened greatly by the careful moderation of Watherston's appeal, with its implicit distinction of the majority of students from the militants, and its explicit acceptance of

[1] *LSE: what it is: and how we fought it*, London, 1967, p. 15.

[2] An alternative way of accounting for 'victory' has been found by Mr. Richard Atkinson. Writing as Assistant Lecturer in Sociology at Birmingham University in *The Times* of 1 October 1968 he says that the fellow students of Adelstein and Bloom 'sat-in until their two colleagues were reinstated'. It is much neater and easier to miss out the awkward interval between the end of the sit-in and the settlement than to account for it—to say nothing—as he says nothing—of the statement by Adelstein and Bloom.

constitutional methods of negotiation for the future. What still remained necessary to make a settlement possible was the explicit commitment of Adelstein and Bloom also to the use for the future of constitutional methods of seeking change, and of their best endeavours for the re-establishment of good relations in the School. By patience and determination that commitment also was secured, and the way laid open to a settlement which, as Watherston said, involved neither party in the compromise of either conscience or principle. With that settlement this chapter in the history of the School was ended.

The summer term was perhaps no more than an interlude. Caine was on the point of retirement, Adams not yet in office. The students were heavily engaged with work and examinations. The staff were painfully divided, counting the cost and licking their wounds. For my part, I was ceasing to be a close observer of events at the School, with my mind turning to a new range of problems that were waiting for me elsewhere. The next chapter of the School's history, beginning with the peaceful arrival of Adams in the autumn, belongs to another volume, to be written, I hope, but by another hand.

10 Reflections

Explanations of our conflict were not wanting. We were told, for example, that it was all due to the fact that we were overcrowded. 'That crowding increases the propensity to aggressive behaviour,' as Lorenz says, 'has long been known and demonstrated by sociological research.'[1] If only, it was suggested, we had more elbow-room, we should be able to live together in peace. It was not an entirely unwelcome explanation. It cast the blame for our troubles on our circumstances rather than ourselves, and there was always the possibility that, if due notice were taken of it in the appropriate quarters, our claims for new buildings might be given higher priority. It was, however, no more than a partial explanation. The conflict was new; the intensity with which our buildings were used, the fact that they were crowded, was not. Indeed, we had been growing less crowded; in the few years before 1966–7 there had been considerable improvements in our buildings, and additions to them. To take an example, a frequent ground of complaint was not only the alleged difficulty of getting books in the library, but also the difficulty of finding a vacant place in the reading-rooms. Yet in its field our library was one of the richest not simply in the United Kingdom but in the world; special arrangements had been made, when the post-Robbins expansion began, to increase the number of copies of the books most needed by undergraduates, and the ratio of reading-room places to full-time students was better than the average for the universities of this country.

What may well have been significant, however, was the high-minded utilitarianism that characterized our use of space: every teacher had his own room; the lecture-rooms were adequate to the need, if no more than adequate; but we badly needed more common-rooms, more places where people could stand or sit when they were not working. Envious comparisons with the new 'plate-glass universities' that were being built, and especially with their resplendent students' union buildings, were a new factor; and the number of our American students made comparisons with the wealthier universities of the U.S.A. perhaps another natural ground for discontent. Even more significant may have been the fact that, as I have

[1] K. Lorenz, *On Aggression*, London, 1963.

shown in my first chapter, there had been a sharp rise in student numbers in the autumn of 1966, and a temporary set-back in the trend of improvement. Things were suddenly and perceptibly worse. Tempers were perhaps a little raised, flash-points a little lowered.

Another popular explanation was that our students were being led astray by foreigners. Oddly enough, the advocates of this view did not appear to notice one or two small facts which they might have taken as supporting evidence. A number of students who had been born in South Africa—Adelstein, Kuper, Ross, for example—played a prominent part in our troubles; and it is interesting to note that, of the students brought before the Board of Discipline, two had been born in South Africa, two were Americans, one a Pakistani, and one only a native of these islands. Yet I find it almost impossible to see this as more than an interesting co-incidence. There was, however, a group of foreign students that could be felt to be influential as a group—the Americans. There were in 1966-7 four hundred students from the United States, an increase of twenty-five per cent over the previous year, and even more in excess, as it happens, of the number in the following year. Why were they so numerous? One reason was, no doubt, the U.S. draft regulations, which allowed post-ponement of military service to graduate students. Another was the recent introduction of the 'taught Master's degree', which incidentally tended to attract a less committedly academic graduate than the old-style research degree, and tended also, because it could be taken in one year, to attract birds of passage whose commitment to the School and understanding of it were slight.

Those who came to the School from America included a number, like Bloom, who had practical experience of the methods of protest used in the civil rights movement and in the universities of their own country. Graduate students had not in the recent past taken much part, or even interest, in the Students' Union, but in the autumn of 1966, as one of the participants told Caine later, a deliberate attempt was made by a group of the Americans to encourage the Union to greater militancy.

Finally, there is the effect of imitation to be reckoned with. Militants at the School, themselves to be imitated later elsewhere, were ready, if not anxious, to imitate what had been done in America. (Is a university a real twentieth-century university, are its students up to the mark, they may have asked themselves, if there has not been a sit-in?) There are one or two slight pieces of evidence, by way of conversations overheard and the like, that some students were waiting to have a sit-in before they could decide what to sit-in about; it will indeed be remembered that the banned meeting of 31 January was at one stage conceived as 'a teach-in on sit-ins'.

The American influence was clearly strong, and it is not surprising that a Member of Parliament, listening to a Union debate during the sit-in, noticed that most of the speakers seemed to have an American accent. Nevertheless, the influence must not be exaggerated. The Americans were, so to speak, the old soldiers, with experience of campaigns elsewhere, knowledgeable about tactics and fluent users of the jargon of protest. They could help to make grievances more articulate and could help to exploit them, but they could not invent them.

There were also those who proclaimed that our students had been led astray by political agitators. Of orthodox Communists there was no perceptible trace; but a regular, card-carrying member of the party would have been a familiar, old-fashioned figure in contrast with the colourful views of the Socialist Society. The explicitly revolutionary movement among students was in its earliest days then, but the rejection of the present organization of society was already clear enough as a primary doctrine of the Socialist Society's members; and their rejection was of both root and branch. The 'power structure' of the School was seen as a branch of the structure of British society. The School was seen as serving the needs of capitalism by providing its technocrats and its theoretical apologists. Resistance, therefore, to authority in the School was part of the sacred duty of resistance to the ruling class everywhere.

The members of the Socialist Society, who espoused these doctrines, were, it is true, then comparatively few; not many more, I believe, than a hundred. To argue from this, however, that their part in the troubles at L.S.E. was negligible is to overlook the role of leadership. One could, as Lewis Feuer says of a similar context at Berkeley, use the same argument to show that the Bolsheviks had little to do with the October Revolution because there were so few of them in the groups that stormed the Winter Palace.[1]

We have noted the populist strain of thought in the Students' Union, in Adelstein's conception of his own role, and in the rejection of the notion of leadership. This, however, merely left the way open for informal, unofficial leadership. In any large body, leadership occurs, whether one likes it or not. Those who have a clear conception of their purposes, energy, ability and determination lead: others follow. In the weeks that led up to the sit-in prominent members of the Socialist Society, writing pamphlets, speaking in the Union, competed for leadership with the more moderate and achieved considerable success. The tussle for control of the student body continued during the sit-in. Gradually the moderates strengthened their position, and it is to them that one must look if one wishes to find the motives of the protest amongst the greater number of its supporters. They lacked pamphleteers, and a clear and permanent record of their views and feelings is not easy to discover. They made their contribution, however, to the statement issued by a committee of thirty-four members on behalf of the Union on Sunday 19 March 1967.[2] That statement is almost devoid of political content; and it does not mention the name of Adams once, so

[1] 'Rebellion at Berkeley II—A Reply', *The New Leader*, vol. XLVIII, no. 1, p. 17.
[2] Reproduced as Appendix IV, p. 184.

that any notion that the whole protest was against his appointment is clearly implausible.

There never was a single really widespread act or expression of protest against that appointment during the whole year. The significance of the anti-Adams movement was not, I suggest, that it had in itself any importance but the fact that it led to two important chains of events. One of these culminated in the refusal of permission to Adelstein to write to *The Times*, the other in the denial of the Old Theatre for the meeting on 31 January. Both these decisions left other channels of expression open. They imposed limitations of time, place, and manner only; but they were portrayed as denials of freedom of expression to the student body, and that portrayal won wide acceptance. Both chains of events also led to disciplinary proceedings. In the proceedings of the Michaelmas Term Adelstein was portrayed as being deprived of the basic rights of natural justice. In the following term he and Bloom were portrayed as being 'victimized' and subjected to trial by a body which was 'structurally biased', that is to say, by a body which included no students but only persons who would not question the rightness of the Director's order. In consequence it was alleged that the proceedings and conclusions of the Board of Discipline were outrageous and unjust. This in turn led to what may have been most important of all, a sense that the views of the student body generally were being totally ignored.

The conflict, therefore, that culminated in the 'sit-in' arose in part simply from an increased readiness of students to question administrative decisions that appeared to them (mistakenly, I believe) to involve an abridgement of their rights; in part from their rejection (equally mistaken) of the disciplinary proceedings as unjust; and in part from their demand that their own views be taken into account by the authorities. Other factors lent colour and noise to the protests, lowered flash-points, helped to give impetus and direction, but were, I am sure, less significant.

Events at the School provided encouragement and a model for protests elsewhere. They helped to make the new movement among students articulate, but they did not cause it. The wave of conflict would before long have begun somewhere else (at the University of Essex perhaps) if it had not begun at L.S.E. In explanations of it, sociologists, amateur and professional, have been prolific enough. It is no part of my present purpose to study those explanations. I am content to leave sociology to the sociologists; my own concern is with the nature of the changes that have occurred in the attitudes of students and with the response that the universities should make. There have been considerable changes, most clearly apparent perhaps in the students of the social sciences; and the greatly increased interest in those branches of learning is itself in all probability a related phenomenon. Not long ago it was dispiriting to see how many students seemed completely uninterested in political questions, conformist in outlook, and aspiring to nothing more than a good degree, a good job, and

—the one evidence of far-sightedness—a good pension scheme. Now the pendulum has swung the other way. It may be salutary for some of us to recall how gladly we were at first inclined to welcome the stirrings at Berkeley as a long overdue emergence of dissent in what had seemed the suffocating conformity of American life.

Whatever the causes and the explanations, it is a fact that a considerable proportion of our young people are now deeply concerned with major political problems—war (no matter how distant), poverty, and racial discrimination; and they are as deeply dissatisfied with the progress made towards the solution of political and social problems by existing agencies of change, especially the principal political parties. They combine with their concerns a remarkable appearance of self-confidence. They proclaim a confident awareness of their adulthood, and of their independence and the civic rights that should accompany it. They tend to be more likely to reject authority than to accept it. They are also confidently aware of their collective strength as a substantial and influential class of persons. Propaganda for the enlargement of the universities, laying perhaps exaggerated stress on society's need for more graduates, has persuaded many students, if no others, of their own importance, if not indispensability; that they confer a benefit on society by being students.

There is much here that is clearly good: an unselfish concern with the problems of others, a large charity (even if it does not extend to vice-chancellors and politicians), a renewed idealism and a passionate desire for the improvement of the lot of the poor and the oppressed. There is also much that is very dangerous. There is a rejection of the patient, practical, virtues of pragmatism and compromise as hypocritical. There is a belief that blind adherence to 'principles' is in all circumstances right, as if sincerity (the quintessence of which is fanaticism) were the one political virtue; as if principles were never in conflict; as if it were better to do much harm for good motives than to be realistically content with doing some modest good. There is a readiness to deny freedom of speech and expression to those who hold unpopular views, while claiming it in its fullest and widest form for one's own. There is a readiness to reject the citizen's commitment to law and order if it stands in the way of immediate demonstration of one's own state of mind. There are, in short, all the ingredients necessary for submission to manipulation by political extremists. Fortunately the extremists are as yet a comparatively small number, the revolutionaries who reject both the present organization of society and the customary framework of political thought, which they regard as corrupted by the capitalist system and all that goes with it. United as they are in what they reject, it is not at all clear what they would prefer; if the world were unfortunate enough to see them succeed in their destructive purposes it would soon enough see them quarrel among themselves about what to set in the place of what they had destroyed. Some of them, indeed, would be for setting nothing at all in its place, believing that all organization becomes inevitably corrupt, so that the only hope of perfection lies in perpetual revolution. They all appear to share a quasi-religious fanaticism, seeing themselves as the saving remnant, to whom truth has been revealed, while the majority of their fellow-men are conditioned and manipulated by the mass media in the interest of those who govern through 'the military-industrial complex'. Since the thought of the majority is, they believe, manipulated and standardized, the majority is no longer fit to govern. Tolerance has been slanted and corrupted, and freedom can be restored only by slanting it the other way. Censorship must be introduced, and must be operated by the few who have seen the light, and who alone are fit to govern. The cure for manipulation of the masses, in short, is to install a new set of manipulators. It is easy to see why political discussion with the revolutionaries is so baffling and difficult; there is no common ground. Everything as it now is is, for them, corrupt, including the universities, which instead of serving as nuclear breeding grounds of revolution are simply producing the supply of skilled brain-workers that the present system needs to serve and perpetuate it. The university must be perverted to revolutionary ends, or destroyed.

The number of the extremists is, as I have said, comparatively small, but a number of factors exaggerate their strength and attract disproportionate attention to them. Important among these factors is the limited range of vision of the mass media. It is the abnormal, not the normal, that is news—and the more abnormal and colourful, the more newsworthy. A hundred noisy and high-spirited 'revolutionaries', if they deploy themselves at the right place and at the right time (or, according to the point of view, the wrong place and the wrong time) attract disproportionate attention and cause disproportionate concern; their thousand colleagues who are going about their normal business in their normal way are unreported and in danger of being forgotten. This peculiarity of the mass media has, indeed, created for the extremists one of their most useful instruments, the 'pseudo-event', an occurrence which would not have taken place if the mass media had not been there to report it.

If they play their cards right, the extremists can increase their influence on the course of events by bringing into play the force of generational solidarity and what I might call 'the Voltaire effect'. By this I mean (alluding to the words 'I disapprove of what you say, but I will defend to the death your right to say it') the readiness of large numbers of students, however little they may agree with the minority, to protest strongly against any infringement of its rights—rights to which the widest interpretation is given—to express its thoughts in words and action, when, where, and however it thinks fit. In particular, students are very reluctant indeed to accept any intervention of an older generation in curtailment of those rights. The force of generational solidarity in face of authority is very strong, going down, I suspect, to the instinctual level. Students of animal behaviour may see in a student sit-in an example of 'mobbing', the device adopted by weak and defenceless creatures of huddling together in large numbers as a means of defence against predators. The extremists have also been helped by fashion, and by the entertainment value of protest. A sit-in is in some respects simply a new form of rag, and a 'demo' is a new kind of popular sport.

The initial reactions of the public, middle-aged or older, have been varied. At one extreme there has been the panic-stricken desire for the reimposition of iron control—large numbers of expulsions, for example, which would not be just and could not be enforced; or the extraordinary argument that because students are in receipt of public funds they should be required to abstain from public controversy. (Would the same criterion be applied to pensioned Admirals?). At the other extreme has been worship of the young just because they are young, of fanatics just because they are sincere—as if fanatics were ever anything else. Alternatively, there has been simple despair, which might be summed up in the thought 'We are old and on the way out. They are young and on the way up. They are bound to prevail, so I must either climb on their band-wagon, or grin and bear it.' It would be no less (and no more) reasonable to say 'We have only to wait. They too will before long be middle-aged. Experience and responsibility will teach them a thing or two.' The 'problem of young people' is also a problem of middle-aged people. Sociologists who are endeavouring to find an explanation of the present intergenerational conflict by studying the young, should not neglect the possibility that the study of the other side in the conflict might also be illuminating.

Why has there been so great a loss of confidence among the middle-aged, showing itself sometimes in rigidity and sometimes in timidity? One of the reasons is certainly that the wave of protest has come at a bad moment. The older generations are baffled and a little weary of well-doing. Our defeat of fascism cost us, as we are slowly learning, most of the military and economic power on which our past freedom of action so largely depended. We are discovering that it does not really make so very much difference what is the policy of the British Government; circumstances are stronger than we are. The lesson that we need to live within our national means is being learned with difficulty. Politicians have made promises that governments cannot keep and are discredited. Loss of confidence is proclaimed as a national problem. Is it surprising that the middle-aged lack confidence in the handling of the young?

Similarly in the universities, the movement among students comes at a bad moment. A very great expansion of the universities has been achieved in the last two decades in spite of great difficulty; but there has followed an uncertainty of purpose. The rapid growth of university staffs has weakened the transmission of the traditional academic values and the professional ethics of the teacher. The university itself has been so anxious to respond to contemporary needs and to limited views of its own function that it has lost its firm grasp of its own values. At the same time increasing involvement with government, increasing detailed governmental control and decreasing governmental sympathy for the university's problems—or even understanding of them—have had their effect. The University Grants Committee, once seen, when funds were reasonably plentiful, as a brilliant device for bringing government money to the universities without governmental interference, tends to be restricted to a negative role now that funds are short. It continues to serve as a 'buffer' between the universities and the government, but a buffer now which protects the government from having any positive responsibility for the well-being of the universities. It is not altogether surprising that morale is low among university administrators and senior teachers.

It is, therefore, at what would even otherwise have been a time of difficulty that those who are responsible for our universities have to bear a heavy and unaccustomed burden. They face an unusually sensitive student body, unusually conscious of its strength. It contains a minority, hostile to the essential purposes of the university, which seeks to disrupt its life and prevent it from doing its work. That minority attracts support from the majority whenever a mistake is made in handling the situation that it creates, and may attract the support even if no mistake is made. What precautions can be taken?

Clearly, the possibilities of conflict will be reduced if its occasions can be avoided. Disciplinary machinery, for example, is the most serious potential cause of conflict, and should be carefully reconsidered in the light of contemporary social changes. There should be no rules that cannot be justified and no rules that cannot or will not be enforced. When rules have to be enforced the method of enforcement must be clearly fair. To this subject I turn in my final chapter. Care should also be taken to remove legitimate grounds of complaint; the university must attend constantly to its own imperfections, expose its arrangements to the criticisms of its students, and take careful account of those criticisms. To the mechanisms needed for this purpose I shall also turn later. With the best will in the world, however, conflict cannot always be avoided, especially if there are some who will seek it for its own sake. To the forms that it may take, to tactics and strategy, attention needs to be given in advance.

More important than all this, however, is the general attitude to be taken to the lines of thought likely to be encountered among the student body. The challenge to be faced is that of those who say, or hope, or fear, or suspect that desirable change is not possible within the existing system, so that that system must be broken. What must be shown in reply is that desirable change is in fact possible within the system, that those who wield authority do not have closed minds, and that they are prepared to admit error when they have fallen into it.

It is as well to bear in mind that some of the young may have a clearer vision than some of their elders of some of the failings of contemporary society and of the contemporary university. For the rest of us, it is important not to be so repelled by their exaggeration that we fail to take advantage of their possible insights. Even the young revolutionary may have something of importance to say, if only we can teach him to say it quietly enough to be heard. He must be taught that there are quicker, easier, and more efficient ways of reform than destroying all that is and starting again. Sir Eric Ashby wrote a few years ago in a moving passage, of which we should all have done well to take more notice, about what he called the rebel scholar:

> He is impatient of what may appear to be compromise or appeasement. The tortuous diplomacy which leads to academic decision-making he regards as sheer weakness. He is not prepared to play a subtle game of chess with the establishment; he would rather pick up the chess-board and bang the establishment over the head with it. Never mind. If he is a genuine rebel he is worth his weight in gold. He must be taught the techniques of successful dissent. Above all he must be persuaded not to abdicate from the society of Masters and Scholars. This means that his ideas—raw and repetitive as they may seem to old men—must be nurtured, and gently disciplined by drawing them into the channels of administrative action.[1]

Not all of those who greeted these words with the warmth that they deserve have apprehended their full meaning. The rebel is not taught the techniques of successful dissent by having the game conceded to him as soon as he waves the chess-board in the air. He is not taught the techniques of successful dissent if he is allowed to achieve a momentary success by the use of the wrong techniques. Equally, however, he will not be taught by those who would refuse to speak to him after he has broken the rules of the game.

What has to be done is to teach him how to promote change within established systems, and especially the system of constitutional action, rational discussion, and law and order—a smug phrase, 'law and order', but it stands for the basis of any worthwhile, civilized life (including the freedom from midnight arrest by the secret police). We have to show that even the system itself can be changed within the system; constitutional change, if it is necessary, can be constitutionally arrived at. We have to show the value and the power of critical discussion.

Part of the task clearly belongs to the teaching function of the university. The first necessity is the critical study of the political and social ideas that are apparently prevalent amongst the young themselves, and the prophets that they follow. As the world now is, to dismiss Mao or Marcuse as no more worthy of attention that Joanna Southcott is impossible. The task must be undertaken. This is the concern of sociologists and political philosophers. It is in fact already among their students that the rebels are most numerous, and one cannot but have an uneasy suspicion that the teaching provided them has sometimes been inadequate. Listening to the

[1] E. Ashby, . . . *And Scholars*, London, 1965.

rebels, or reading what they have written, one cannot dismiss entirely from one's mind Mr. Melvin Lasky's Czech student, who said:

I know nothing really about Columbia, or the L.S.E., or the Sorbonne, or any of the institutions of higher learning in the West. But they *must* truly be as bad as your students say they are—for they have apparently produced a youth that is so disoriented and uneducated, so incapable of reading books critically and thinking intelligently as to be a screaming indictment of themselves.[1]

I should not wish to claim that this indictment is anything but wildly exaggerated; but the number of teachers of the social sciences has increased so rapidly and so greatly in recent years that it could hardly be a matter for surprise if there had been some fall in quality. Discussion is apt to be confused by the fact that revolutionaries sometimes talk as if the social sciences were the only object of University study. We must not fall into the same error, but when issues of political philosophy are now engaging the interest of students of all subjects, it is desirable to see that those issues are rationally and carefully examined—brought, in fact, within the ambit of the University's teaching.

A notable, though unusual, example of what can be done was provided, after the disorders in the summer of 1968 at the University of Essex, by the attempt of the Commission of Enquiry, in consultation with all members of the University, to arrive at an acceptable statement of the principle of free speech and of some at least of the limitations to which it is subject. (In a similar way, at a famous American university, a sit-in was avoided by holding a teach-in on the issues concerned.) There are a number of similar questions which could be the subject of similar critical study and enquiry; questions, for example, about the justification of protest and about its forms, legitimate or illegitimate. Most public discussion of them has been superficial, one side arguing that protest takes illegal forms, the other that they are effective. Both contentions are true, but neither is necessarily a complete answer to the question whether it is morally justified. The indirect effects of demonstrations of protest also need to be studied: some protests against racial discrimination, for example, show so little understanding that, while enforcing compliance in the individual case, they may encourage intolerance elsewhere.

The questions that so deeply concern the young must be submitted to dispassionate academic examination; but it is also by example that the universities have to teach. They are themselves in need of reform. In the last quarter of a century they have grown rapidly in size and number. The rate and extent of their growth have made a qualitative as well as a quantitative difference, and have made corresponding changes desirable in their systems of government and, still more important, of communication. It is distressing that they have only recently begun to regard their own internal

[1] *Encounter*, August 1968, p. 89.

workings as proper subjects for careful study and experiment. A beginning has been made, though not in all respects too promising a beginning; the approach has been too mechanistic, in terms of engineering rather than of biology. Attention is being paid, for example, to 'decision-making', when what matters more is the study of opinion-formation, of methods of assisting the emergence within the university of informed opinion about its problems.

We have in the universities our fair share of unexamined mythology, so fervently accepted that its intellectual basis must be suspect. To take the most obvious example, it is said that no one can teach well unless he is actively engaged in research.[1] This belief is evidently the basis of systems of appointment and promotion. Whatever the rules may say about regard being had to teaching ability, it is evaluation of research that determines who is promoted. Yet no evidence has ever to my knowledge been produced of the necessity and precise nature of the alleged connection of the two activities, and there have been good teachers who did little or no research. Some of them have complained to me, with cheerful ruefulness rather than bitterness, of the difference between their prospects and those of colleagues who confined their teaching and their attendance to one day a week, spending the rest of their time on the research which would win them promotion; they themselves stayed as long and as often as their students might need them, and expected their chances of advancement to pass them by.

The advancement of learning is a primary task of the University; of that task research is an important part, but so also is the thoughtful organization and consolidation of knowledge. One way or another, the good teacher must be engaged in thinking about his subject; but that research is necessary for all, and that it should be the sole basis for promotion, I doubt. I would indeed urge that careful attention be given to the relationships between some types of teaching and some types of research. Elementary and general teaching, for example, are particularly difficult because they call for the mature powers of an outstanding teacher, thinking actively about his subject as a whole, without being distracted by the latest (and passing) fashions in methodology or border-line research. In practice, because elementary teaching has low prestige, it is too often left to the teachers who are least qualified to undertake it, the graduate assistants and junior lecturers, who have not yet learned to see the wood for the trees.

Perhaps also in need of examination is the nature of the teacher's contract. He enjoys the freedom of the professional man, but combines with it the security of the salaried employee. As Professor Richard Titmuss has put it: 'Even during term-time, the academic (at least in Britain) has no

---

[1] If so, why is a proposal to reward good teaching hailed as a discouragement to research?

regular hours of daily attendance that he must keep; there is none to say to him "Go" and he goeth; "Come" and he cometh; in the way he does his work he is free from almost all explicit control.'[1] Professor Titmuss continues by asserting his belief that these freedoms are to a great degree essential to the job as we know it, but that the personal possession of them seems to militate against institutional self-criticism. In the latter contention I whole-heartedly concur; in the former with less certainty. The teacher must be exempt from any constraint over his originality and his freedom of thought, I agree. It may be that this cannot be achieved without his being left a remarkable degree of freedom to be idle if he prefers. Most university teachers do all that could reasonably be expected of them, and many do far more. The idle minority is relatively small, but it is a minority, nevertheless, that does disproportionate harm. One teacher who neglects his students or shows contempt for them by his slip-shod performance does harm that ten active colleagues cannot undo. There was once among university teachers an unwritten, indeed unformulated, code of professional ethics, to which most subscribed, whether consciously or unconsciously; and most complied with it. It was handed down by oral tradition and by example. These processes of communication have failed in face of the large and rapid increase of the size of the profession, to say nothing of the increasing claims made upon its time for purposes external to the university. Sir Eric Ashby has suggested that the code of conduct should be restored and made explicit, and I believe there are few reforms so likely to be beneficial to the university. Such a code is one of the distinguishing marks of what we call a profession, and if the profession is large the code needs to be reduced to writing. Its enforcement should, if at all possible, be left, I suggest, primarily in the hands of the profession itself; who else could be more careful of its good name?

The universities, then, have their imperfections, which have gone unremedied, largely unrecognized, and hardly spoken of, largely because of the lack, to which Professor Titmuss draws attention, of any adequate provision for institutional self-criticism. It has become a common place that a university is a self-governing community of scholars. Adam Smith would, I am sure, remind us that a community of teachers governed by the teachers is all too likely to become a community governed for the benefit of the teachers. A built-in critical element is highly desirable. In part only the teachers can provide it; but there is a substantial contribution that the students could make. They should be asked to make it; not allowed to make it, to keep them quiet; but asked to make it, because the university needs their criticism. An incidental advantage will be that an opportunity will be given for the university to show, in a way in which it has not always shown it, that change can be sought with success within the existing constitutional framework. If, however, the views of students are to be as

---

[1] *Commitment to Welfare*, London, 1968, p. 28.

carefully considered as they should be, the manner in which they are to be obtained needs thought. I propose to examine it in the next chapter.

It has to be remembered again, however, that there are students whose clear purpose is not to reform the university but to destroy it, because it is part of 'the system', or to use it as a base for the preparation of revolution. Their prospects of ultimate success are slight, but they may nevertheless do considerable harm. Their purpose is wholly inconsistent with the disinterested pursuit and dissemination of truth, which is the function of the university. Unless, therefore, they soon become—as they may—no more serious than a rather tiresome joke, they will need to be resisted. Resistance to them must be firm but also resourceful, and must be consistent with the proper maintenance of their rights as citizens and as members of the university. If they try to make continuance of the university's work impossible they will present serious problems. A sit-in or similar demonstration may be no more than a way of expressing an opinion. If so, note should of course be taken of that opinion and it may be that it should be answered. As a way of expressing an opinion it may be awkward and tiresome, but that is insufficient ground for stopping it; and any attempt to stop it would very possibly bring into play the Voltaire reaction and attract wider support to the protest.

If, however, it goes beyond the expression of opinion and becomes an attempt to make the continuance of normal life and work impossible, what is to be done? I would hope that it can be circumvented—literally circumvented. With luck or forethought, if one way is blocked by a sit-in, there should be another way round. It may be possible to keep the protest to a limited area and encapsulate it, while normal life flows around it. In Caine's phrase, 'to learn to live with the sit-in' may not be comfortable, but it has been shown to be sometimes possible. If circumstances make that impossible, however, what is to be done? One possibility, surrender, will usually have its short-sighted advocates, believing that nothing can be worse than public conflict, and that peace is worth any price. If what is to be defended is right, however, it should not be surrendered in response to militancy: that would be to teach the wrong lesson, the lesson that force is the best argument. If what is to be defended is wrong, should it be surrendered? It should, of course, have been conceded before the protest. If it has not been, then I fear that to defend the indefensible may be a lesser evil than to give way, at least until the protest is over. Any concession, however reasonable, that is made in face of militancy, or even at a time when militant action is being taken, will be greeted as a concession to militancy and a victory for it, as proving that militant action achieves what negotiation does not. This has been proved true too often, and every time it is, a step is taken away from reasonable methods of settling differences. Militancy must not be allowed to pay; and only authorities who are justifiably very confident of their strength can afford even to let it seem to pay. Nor will surrender necessarily bring peace. It will not satisfy those whose purpose is the perpetuation of conflict.

If surrender is ruled out, and if the continuance of normal work becomes impossible, two alternatives remain. One is to abandon the attempt to continue normal work, accepting as inevitable the damage that will be done to the interests of innocent parties, and to close the institution until matters take a turn for the better, or until opinion is prepared for the alternative. The alternative is to meet force with force, and restore law and order. This may well be repugnant, but it is better than allowing a minority to frustrate the purposes of the majority. Repugnant or not, however, can it be done? If the demonstrators have been deprived by proper processes of their right to be present on the premises, then the occupier of the premises—that is, the university—has the right to use reasonable force to remove them if they will not move voluntarily. The university does not usually, however, have a 'strong-arm squad' able to remove any significant number. In such circumstances I should myself see no objection of principle to the calling-in of the police, at least in this country, where we have a civilized police-force. The fact has to be faced, however, that the intervention of the police would be regarded by many academic people and by still more students with dismay or even horror. That reaction, as I have said in an earlier chapter, I believe to be irrational. Law and order form an essential basis for civilized life, and their maintenance and restoration are a decent, honourable task. Nevertheless, the reaction of which I have spoken, irrational or not, is to be expected and must be reckoned with; those who live and work in the universities are not necessarily any more rational than their fellow-men. There is, moreover, another, more practical, difficulty: even if called, the police may not come. It is no part of their duty in this country, where trespass is not a criminal offence, to remove trespassers from private property, unless there is risk of harm being done to persons or property. The university may in consequence be at the mercy of those who wish to prevent its work from continuing. This is a gap in the system of law and order. In the long run the gap may need to be filled by legislation, so that the police can be called in. This does not mean that I think it will often be wise to call them in but the possibility should be there. There cannot be lawless vacuums in society.

K

11 Students and University Government: Representation or Consultation?

In the preceding chapter I have written of the part that students can play in the process of institutional self-criticism which is as necessary to the well-being of the universities as to that of any other organization. More generally, the channels of communication between the university and its students need improvement and I doubt whether there would be many to deny it. There would be much less agreement how it is to be achieved. Among students, some ask simply that they be more fully consulted in the affairs of their universities; others go further, asking for representation, for student members to be appointed to the bodies that take the decisions.

It tends to be assumed that these demands are for alternative forms of arrangement: that if consultation is arranged, representation will not be granted; and that if representation is granted, consultation will be un-necessary. This is not, however, to be taken for granted. The purpose of student representation would be to enable student opinion to be taken into account in the making of decisions. The assumption that the addition of, say, two or three students to a committee would enable that com-mittee to be informed of student opinion would be sound enough if student opinion were uniform; but it is not, and there is no reason to expect it to be. There is not always, indeed, any such thing as the opinion of students; there are the opinions of students, many and various—first year, second year, third year; undergraduate and graduate; mediocre and brilliant; conventional and unconventional; left-wing and right-wing, arts and science; rich and poor; British and foreign; men and women; married and single. All these differences, and many others, are in various contexts relevant. It would be a matter of pure chance whether the one, two, or half a dozen students on a committee represented the relevant differences. It would only be if they had adequate means of consulting the views of other students that they could do efficiently their work of representation; and only if they consulted the views of other students regularly and con-stantly that they could be sure that they would not miss relevant varieties of opinion. Representation of students, therefore, could not function effectively without sufficient means of consultation. The choice is between a system in which the consultation is carried out by student representatives and one in which it is carried out by others; but consultation is common to both, and I therefore propose to consider means of consultation before considering the case for representation.

Some suppose that it will be sufficient provision for consultation if the questions for consideration are submitted to a meeting of the students' union or to its officers; but experience has shown that neither union meetings nor union members are necessarily representative in the relevant sense. They are, of course, formally representative. The officers are chosen by an electoral process in which all students can vote, but it is in practice a minority who do so. The officers cannot be relied upon to reflect the views of the majority. As Caine points out in a forthcoming work, 'students' union officers are entirely free of the sanction by which elected representatives are normally controlled, the desire to stand for re-election and the consequent need to retain the confidence of the electorate'.[1]

Nor is it any safer to accept as conclusive evidence of student opinion the resolutions of a union meeting. The proportion of members who attend is generally small. At L.S.E., which I do not suppose to be untypical in this respect, attendance by twenty per cent of the membership strains the accommodation to the limit, and is regarded as a sign of overwhelming interest in the subject that is being discussed. Attendance during my years at the school was normally less than a tenth of the membership.

In circumstances of this kind, well-organized and determined minorities are much too powerful. Since there is nothing that resembles or corresponds to a party system, a cohesive group of, say, a hundred begins with the advantage that it is a hundred times larger than the normal group, which consists of the individual unorganized member. It can be said that the majority have only themselves to blame if resolutions are passed with which they do not agree. They need only to organize to defeat the minority: indeed, they need not even do that; it is enough if they attend regularly. The average student, however, and especially the academically inclined student, does not want to have to give up an hour or two every week to attending the union meeting in order to make sure that minority views do not prevail. What he wants is to elect sensible fellow-students who can be relied upon to represent his views and interests in a responsible and reliable manner: he wishes to leave them to get on with it, and he wishes them to leave him free to be, in students' union jargon, 'apathetic'; that is, to devote his time to other matters. I see nothing wrong with this attitude; on the contrary, it seems entirely reasonable. Life has much to offer to the student, and there are many who do not find students' union politics (even when they concern major questions of university policy) among the most attractive pastimes.

[1] S. Caine, *British Universities: Purpose and Prospects*, London, 1969.

The ordinary student asks then for an organization that he can rely upon to forward his interests and reflect his views without making heavy demands on his time and without serious risk of his finding himself committed to policies and actions that he may disapprove. Can such an organization be provided? I believe that it can, but only, I suggest, by the establishment of a consultative system with a structure carefully devised to represent—and represent, as it were, automatically—as many important varieties of student opinion as possible: undergraduates and graduates; students of this faculty and students of that, students of the first year, the second year, the third year, and so forth. What is needed, in short, is a students' representative council, with members elected by constituencies of relevantly various kinds. It will clearly need to be a body of substantial size, delegating to committees responsibility, subject to its own general control, for particular topics and areas of concern, including in particular consultative committees for each academic department or faculty. Their work is going to make heavy demands on the time and efforts of a substantial number (even though a comparatively small minority) of students; but consultation is important, and must be genuine and careful; slipshod and haphazard consultation could easily be far worse than no consultation at all.

A students' representative council of the kind that I have described should, I suggest, form part of the normal structure of the university, and it should have its secretarial services provided by the staff of the university registry like any other important university body. This will in part be a mark of its status; but what is more important is that it is only in this way that it can be effectively tied into the main structure of the university, with officials responsible to the university for seeing that it is consulted when it should be, that its views are satisfactorily recorded and communicated. For some students it may come hard to trust professional administrators, as it comes hard to some teachers, but come it must if the students' representative council is to be able to do its work effectively.

The committees of the council must be available for consultation by the bodies charged with the goverment of the university. Much of the communication between them will be in written form, as communication normally is between university bodies; but it will also need to be supplemented at times—as is also normal—by oral consultation between chairmen, joint meetings of representatives, and so forth.

Through such a system the views of the students should ordinarily be available to those who govern the university. Is this enough? As I have said, some students say that consultation is not enough, and ask for representation. Their principal arguments may be classified as follows:

1. the argument for effective consultation;
2. the argument for environmental control;
3. the argument for consumer control;
4. the argument of community in scholarship.

The force of some of these arguments differs in relation to the context; they may be more persuasive in relation to the physical context, for example —buildings, residential provision, refectories, and the like—than in the intellectual context—decisions about courses of study, academic appointments, and the like. This distinction will need to be kept in mind as we examine them in turn.

The argument for effective consultation, as I have chosen to call it, maintains that it is only if students participate in the government of the university that they can be sure that their views will be taken into account. If they are not present when the decisions are made, who will remember to consult them? Only if they themselves are there will they know what is being discussed and have a chance to make their contribution to its discussion.

This argument assumes the unaltered continuance of present patterns of behaviour in university government. If, however, as is highly desirable, the patterns change and, for example, information about what is going on, about the problems that face the university, and about possible solutions to them is much more freely spread; if more attention is paid to making members of the university knowledgeable about its affairs so that informed opinion can emerge as a result of wider discussion; if more attention is paid to democracy at the grass-roots, in the individual academic departments; if these things—which are needed as part of the adjustment of universities to changes in their size and circumstances—are done, then there is no reason why students too should not be better-informed than they are now, with the result that they will not have to wait to be consulted, but will have early knowledge of important questions that are coming up for decision. If, moreover, as I have suggested, the secretariat of the students' representative council is provided by the university registry, it will be part of the regular duties of the registry to see that that council is consulted, as it is part of its regular duties to see that all relevant bodies are consulted. In these circumstances I see no reason for assuming that consultation cannot be made to work without representation.

The argument for environmental control maintains that as a matter of principle we should all, other things being equal, expect to participate in decisions affecting our own lives; and that the student, whose life is affected by the decisions taken in his university, should therefore expect to participate in those decisions. The general principle thus stated is not, however, absolute. It must yield to the establishment of the fact that there is another person, or class of persons, whose qualifications for making the decisions are stronger, or whose entitlement to make them is stronger because the effect of them on him or them is greater.

In respect of some aspects of the physical environment the students' argument is persuasive. They are more affected by, for example, the quality of the refectory than are their teachers, and it is hard to say that their teachers, because they have high academic qualifications in, say,

Greek or sociology or international law are necessarily better qualified than the students to govern a catering establishment. In academic matters, however, the case is altered; the relationship of teacher and pupil implies greater knowledge on the part of the teacher, carrying with it greater qualification to make decisions about the curriculum. It is he who knows the content, as it were, of the next chapter, which the student has not read; and he knows what preparation is necessary—however irrelevant it may seem at the moment—to the understanding of it.

It can also reasonably be argued that the student is in the university for a comparatively brief period, and that decisions made in its management will have far more effect on the lives of the teachers, who will be there much longer, than on his. Some students will, however, ingeniously reply to this that they 'are undergoing a particularly formative period in their lives. Not only are their careers at stake but their future attitudes, beliefs, responses to life etc. are all in the melting pot. For the staff these vital issues are more or less decided. It therefore follows that students have even greater interest than the staff in their education and they therefore ought to have a predominant say'.[1]

It is true that these years have a very great influence on the student's life; but for more than one reason this does not establish any claim to make decisions about the curriculum. The argument overlooks the ordinary time-lag in giving effect to such decisions. Many of the students who claim the right to participate in them will have finished their courses and gone away before decisions take effect, for curricular changes are not made overnight. More important is the fact that the argument does nothing to establish the student's qualification to make the decisions. A surgical operation has far more importance for the patient than for the surgeon; but that does not entitle the patient to direct how it shall be performed; what it does do is to entitle him to decide whether to undergo the operation or not; and the students' argument establishes, I would contend, their entitlement (which is not in question) to decide whether to accept a place at a university or not, but not their entitlement to decide how they are to be taught. Of course they must be free to comment and criticize, and their opinions should be heard; but they should not be decisive.

The argument for consumer control contends that, just as we are taking more and more account of the wishes of the consumer in other contexts, we should allow the student as consumer of what the university has to offer to control the provision made for him. To the extent that the argument is based on analogy, it is misleading to suggest that it tends to establish a case for more than consultation. If consumers are dissatisfied, taking over the shop is not their usual remedy. The argument is open, however, to more serious objections than that. It is a form of the contention that he who pays the piper should call the tune, that if I pay for something I have a right to regulate it. This is a sound enough principle if it is well under-

[1] D. Adelstein, *Teach Yourself Student Power*, London, 1968, p. 21.

stood; but if what I am paying for is the application of skill, judgment, and knowledge that I do not myself possess, I shall defeat my object if I seek to regulate their exercise. It is largely on this reservation that academic autonomy rests. University teachers are paid to exercise independence of mind, to be original. Independence and originality are not at command; nobody can tell anyone else how to be original. This is the reason why the student-consumer cannot reasonably expect to call their tune; if it were not so, they would be open to direction from the real payer of the pipers—the state. Dr. Imre Lakatos of L.S.E. says in an unpublished open letter:

There are no arguments for Student Power that would not be arguments also for Government Power. Students may be part of the academic community in an important sense in which the Government are not; but they receive their education at considerable expense to the taxpayers, whose representatives may therefore be said to have more right to interfere with University life than the students whose education they finance. Militant students frequently use the analogy that the consumer ought to be able to influence the production of the goods he buys: they do not notice that in this analogy the real consumer is the State—*they* are the goods to be delivered. It is the thin wall of academic autonomy and nothing else that protects students from political interference in the age of State-financed education.

Dr. Lakatos continues:

This is perhaps the most important reason why we should resist student power while accepting student freedom to criticize: because we resist government power while accepting government freedom to criticize. Of course there will be people both among students and politicians who believe that freedom of criticism is useless without power. But the history of universities is full of evidence to the contrary. Indeed, the main danger is that academics, fully aware that academic autonomy has no real power basis, are too quick rather than too slow in yielding to outside criticism and pressure.

I would sum up by saying that the argument for consumer control rests on no sound principle of general application; that it is clearly excluded by the nature of the task of the university teacher, who knows what he is about better than does the 'consumer'; and that if the principle were accepted, the state's claim as consumer—and paymaster—would take precedence over that of the student.

The argument of community in scholarship maintains that the university is a community of scholars, in which students as well as teachers are included. They are merely at different stages of their scholarly careers. The teacher goes on learning all his life, from his research and from his students. He goes on, that is to say, being a student. The students learn not only from him but from each other; that is to say, they also teach. No real distinction can be drawn between students and teachers: though some are further advanced than others, they are all scholars alike, and all alike entitled to participate in the government of the scholarly community of which they are members. Most of us would, I think, say at once that it is absurd to say that there is no real difference between the first-year student and the senior professor; the difference is obvious, and the professor, because he knows about his subject, is clearly qualified to take decisions about its teaching in a way that the student is not. Mr. Adelstein, however, has a reply to give us:[1]

We are told that students are ignorant and unenlightened in contrast to teaching staff, who are not. But enlightenment is gradual and relative. At no specific point does one suddenly enter into enlightenment as Buddhists do into nirvana. Yet the system operates as though this were the case. The point at which the lecturer is appointed is, in effect, his admission into the guild of the knowing. Before this he was wholly incompetent to make any academic decisions. Now he is, suddenly, totally able.

Mr. Adelstein's argument illustrates a difficulty familiar in practical life, that of drawing a line in any single position that is in itself defensible, though we can be sure that the line has to be drawn somewhere. On no particular day can we say that the man who was a mere novice yesterday is an accomplished scholar today. On no single day is he significantly different from what he was on the day before: so, it is argued, he is not significantly different from what he was twenty years ago. This form of argument is a device of great antiquity. By its use, passing through a great number of gradations of shades of grey, not one of which is significantly different from the next, one can show that black is not significantly different from white; one can show, a hair at a time, that a luxurious head of hair is no different from a bald pate; or one can show that a man should draw the old-age pension at the age of two. But we all know that it is not so; a line can be drawn, has to be drawn somewhere; black is not white; and the scholar who has completed his apprenticeship is better qualified than the one who has not. Even if every apprentice were destined to become a scholar, the apprentice would still not yet be a full member of the scholarly community; and, of course, very few of the apprentices ever will be. Most never will meet the requirements; even of those who might, many do not so desire; and even those who can and will have not yet done so.

In the passage from which I have quoted, however, Mr. Adelstein goes on to develop a more sophisticated form of the argument:

A more important consideration is the nature of the knowledge the student is supposed to be absorbing. The key purpose of higher education is not, after all, to instill a series of facts and techniques into the student ... the function of higher education is essentially that of teaching an approach, methodology, the 'ways' of a particular discipline. It is not the facts but the surrounding culture that are important. The technocratic society demands not a stereotyped response to expected situations but an innovatory one to new problems ... Productive intellectual work involves critical enquiry and students, uninitiated in accepted disciplinary thinking, are admirably suited to this purpose.

[1] *Teach Yourself Student Power*, London, 1968, p. 22.

Uncorrupted by facts, his techniques unblunted by experience, one is tempted to ask, who could do better? In similar vein, perhaps, though in a political context, it was interesting to note some militant students in *The Times* of 18 March 1968 quoting with approval Sir Eric Ashby as writing 'The main purpose of a university education is to teach students a critical approach to facts and theories.' Sir Eric commented a few days later 'I did indeed write this. But my next sentence, not quoted . . . [by the students], runs: "A pre-requisite, of course, is a mastery of the facts and theories to be criticized". The first step in the art of dissent is to understand what one is dissenting from. And the second step is to learn to dissent with intelligence and wit.' Mr. Adelstein appears to think that a critical attitude is best secured by being 'uninitiated in' (i.e. ignorant of?) 'accepted disciplinary thinking'; but, as Ashby indicates, mastery of accepted thinking is a pre-requisite to competent criticism. It is true enough, in the vivid analogy that Professor Robert K. Merton[1] has traced back to Bernard of Chartres, that we can see further than the great scholars who were our predecessors; but we achieve it not by our own powers of vision but by climbing up and sitting like dwarfs on their shoulders. It is the climb that Mr. Adelstein has failed to take into account.

There is an anti-academic strand in current student thought. One sometimes comes across a crude notion that education consists of the communication of a mass of factual information—and perhaps the more facts the better the education—and that the purpose of examiners is to see how many facts the candidate can remember. I doubt whether anyone who is personally concerned with education really holds this view: it is an Aunt Sally erected to be demolished, especially by those who wish to attack the examination system. Some of the militant students seem to have recoiled to the other extreme and to think of real education as intelligent thought unencumbered by facts; it is as if all truth were discoverable by sitting down and thinking in the abstract (a method of proceeding tried by Descartes, whom it led so far as the knowledge of his own existence!). Knowledge, however, is no more the mere exercise of pure intelligence than it is an assembly of crude facts. It is an ordered system of information and mental techniques. The facts without methodology are useless, but the methodology cannot be developed without the facts. Knowledge does not come without time and labour; we have to absorb our heritage, climb to the giant's shoulders. The scholars are those that have made a substantial part of the ascent; the apprentices are little above ground level. They are not yet of the community of scholars, nor qualified to share in its government.

The arguments in favour of student participation in the control of their intellectual environment, in the determination, that is to say, of academic policy, are inadequate. There are, moreover, positive arguments against. Some of them we have touched on already: the shortness of the time for

[1] *On the Shoulders of Giants*, New York, 1965.

which the student is at the university, his lack of permanent commitment to it, his relative ignorance. In addition there is the disruptive effect that his participation could have. A committee of teachers is a body of men sharing, for all their differences, a certain habit of mind, a common approach to the problems. They are used to working together, aiming always at reaching a consensus rather than a majority decision, for a vote is a comparatively uncommon phenomenon in most academic bodies. They share a common assumption that when the majority view emerges the minority will yield. Include among them a different group, however small, not sharing their habit of mind, lacking experience of the work of the committee and not staying long enough to acquire it, nor yet to share the consequences of the decisions; the result will almost certainly be some initial loss of efficiency. It might or might not be restored as mutual confidence developed. If that were all, it would perhaps be no serious matter. The fact has to be allowed for, however, that the number of students who would be prepared to give up time to committee work, much of which lacks excitement and interest, is unlikely to be great; but the militants would be willing to give time to it, and to engineer their own election. The disruption that they could achieve would be considerable, simply by not being prepared to take no for an answer. Their values and their purposes are not academic. They have other ideas about the function of a university. They may be a transient phenomenon, but one can never be sure that it will not recur.

I quote Dr. Lakatos again, speaking of the principle that students as well as teachers should determine academic policy:

This principle is clearly inconsistent with the principle of *academic autonomy*, according to which the determination of academic policy is exclusively the business of academics of some seniority. The implementation of this latter principle has been achieved—and sustained—in a long historical process. I came from a part of the world where this principle has never been completely implemented and where during the last 30–40 years it has been tragically eroded, first under Nazi and then under Stalinist pressure. As an undergraduate I witnessed the demands of Nazi students at my University to suppress 'Jewish-liberal-marxist influence' expressed in the syllabuses. I saw how they, in concord with outside political forces, tried for many years—not without some success—to influence appointments and have teachers sacked who resisted their bandwagon. Later I was a graduate student at Moscow University when resolutions of the Central Committee of the Communist Party determined syllabuses in genetics and sent the dissenters to death. I also remember when students demanded that Einstein's 'bourgeois relativism' (i.e. his relativity theory) should not be taught, and that those who taught such courses should confess their crimes in public. There can be little doubt that it was little more than coincidence that the Central Committee stopped this particular campaign against relativity and diverted the students' attention to mathematical logic and mathematical economics where, as we know, they succeeded in thwarting the development of these subjects for many years. (I am fortunate that I did not have to witness the humiliation of University Professors by the students of Peking University during their 'cultural revolution'.)

Invoking these ghastly memories [he continues] may seem out of place in this country. It will be said that here there is no political force or motivation behind students' demands. Unlike the demands of Hitler's, Stalin's and Mao's youth, their aim is to improve rather than erode the university tradition of informed research and competent teaching.

But is this so? The 'Minority Report', which the L.S.E. Students' Union adopted, has an underlying philosophy which may have been taken directly from the posters of Mao's 'Cultural Revolution'. As Adelstein, one of its authors, put it (*The Times*, 18 March 1968):

Student representation on governing bodies is only the *beginning*, and representation can be good or bad—it can give a false sense of unity. The *next thing* is for students to begin to run their own courses, initially through their own societies, and then to demand that they should run a particular part of a course: its content, how it is taught, and who teaches it.

The *next step* is for students to appoint their own teachers and to do some teaching themselves. *Ultimately*, students should work for a certain amount of the time. Academic and intellectual problems become meaningful if they are associated with practical life ...

I accept the word militancy, but it means for me that one is prepared to consider any action that will achieve one's end, which is in accordance with one's ends. One would not rule out any mode of action because it has not been accepted in the past ... We do initiate unconstitutional action. We do not accept constitutional limits because they are undemocratic. When democracy fails, this is the only way of doing it ... [Dr. Lakato's italics]

'Should one', asks Dr. Lakatos, 'leave such an extremist manifesto ... without comment? Can one accept the "beginning" stage of this programme without argument, without having to fear that it is only the thin end of the wedge?'

Mr. Adelstein is not alone in regarding representation as no more than a first step, though he may be more prepared than most to state his programme fully. There are hints, or straws in the wind, elsewhere. The *New Left Review* editorial article 'Student Power: What is to be Done?'[1] refers repeatedly to the students' demand for control over the content of education, and urges the socialist student to make control over the university his first concern. At Oxford, Mr. Trevor Munroe, a prominent activist, has said:[2]

'student power will mean what it means elsewhere. Freedom, no more nor less than other citizens, for students in their extra-academic activity. Control, proportional to their significance in the university, over their academic lives. That this might go against some interpretations of the

[1] *New Left Review*, No. 43, pp. 3 et seq.
[2] *Isis*, 12 June 1986.

'spirit of scholarly enquiry' suggests the obsolence of that spirit rather than the illegitimacy of that demand'.

Even the National Union of Students proclaims with dangerous vagueness that 'all academic courses must reflect the needs of society'.

We have been warned; and the danger has already been illustrated in an attempt to prevent a lecture at the University of Essex by a scientist from a governmental defence establishment; and in the attempt, prominent in some American university troubles, and occurring here at the University of Sussex, to prevent members of the staff of the university from researching in fields that students consider unfit for academic investigation—a usurpation of a decision that belongs to their teachers and to them only.

It would be as well to heed these warnings. The principle of academic autonomy has no world-wide recognition or assured foundation. The universities of this country have enjoyed it for so long that they may forget how easily and gradually it could be eroded, and how hard it might be to restore it. It should not be imperilled in a fit of sentimental pseudo-liberalism; not indeed should academic people be compelled to give up hours of their time to battle constantly against its erosion. The determination of academic questions must be reserved for academic persons alone.

This is not to say, however, that students are not to be consulted on such matters. Their comments and criticisms should be heard and carefully considered. It is also desirable that they should have greater freedom to exercise informed choice of courses of study. Information about the differences between the universities and what they have to offer should be more carefully made available; the ignorance in which many students now make their choice is alarming, and must lead to disappointments that could have been avoided. Within the universities, too, opportunity of informed choice can be increased by the offering of new combinations of subjects, by enlarging the range of options, and by making it easier than it sometimes is for a student to change his mind. A number of important academic subjects are not taught at schools; the student cannot really know what they are like until he has tried them at the university. If he has made the wrong choice it is most desirable that he should be able to change to another subject, and perhaps even to another university, without excessive loss of time.

So much for academic matters, amongst which, by the way, I include the management of the library. The physical conditions of student life, however —bed, board, and recreation—are a matter on which it is easier to argue the claim of the students to a share in management, and perhaps even to a predominant share. In some countries of Europe the provision of residential accommodation for students has not been regarded as part of the responsibilities of the university, but as within the domain of student bodies. Given that they make use of competent administrative help, this arrangement has much to commend it. The student, while spending his leisure hours in the company of his own kind, spends them out of the presence of the university, a presence which in this country is too nearly all-pervasive. As an incidental advantage, the continental system reduces the range of the administrative burden carried by the university and its staff, a range which under our system is apt to be excessively wide.

There is no reason of principle why men and women of student age, with such help as they may seek from their seniors, and with the help of an adequate staff, cannot manage refectories and halls of residence. It is, however, probably no longer possible for us to adopt the continental system, much as I for one should prefer it. The conditions on which halls of residence have been founded by benefactors are one obstacle in the way. Another, even more serious, is that university money is involved. If the hall of residence or the refectory makes a loss, it is the university that meets it, and the university must therefore retain ultimate financial control. I should nevertheless argue that the case for reducing the extent of paternalist control and for giving students a large share in the management is a strong one. It would, of course, be wrong to involve them in detailed and time-consuming administrative work: the tendency sometimes found among students of trying to reduce expenditure by employing themselves as what one might call volunteer slave-labour, to the detriment of their academic work, should be resisted. Employees should be engaged to do employees' work. Other areas in which the management of policy should rest largely with students might be the control of lodgings, the appointments board, and the control of athletic grounds, for example.

Finally, there is the Students' Union's own building, where complete autonomy is demanded. Complete autonomy is enjoyed by few if any human institutions, and the Students' Union can hardly be an exception. Its buildings and its income are provided for defined purposes, and the students can hardly be free to change the purposes and retain the property. Suppose that the students of a university decide that their Students' Union building should be thrown open to the townsfolk. As the townsfolk vastly outnumber the students the result of adopting the proposal would simply be that the university would have no Students' Union building, and the purpose of the public authorities who paid for it would be frustrated. Clearly, then, there are limits to the degree of autonomy that can be allowed. The defined purposes must be maintained; and the auditors must report to some public authority—and what public authority can it be but the university?—that the funds provided have been put to the proper use. Subject to such over-riding controls the union must remain, but it should, I would agree, enjoy as much freedom to determine its own affairs as is consistent with them.

If, however, as I have suggested, a students' representative council is formed that can undertake the representative function more efficiently, is the Students' Union in the traditional form necessary with membership embracing all students whether they wish for it or not? A voluntary body, depending on voluntary subscriptions, could enjoy more substantial autonomy, even though the scale of its activities would be reduced.

The policy at which we have arrived in this chapter may seem tangled and confused, but the principles underlying it are, I suggest, clear enough. There should be full information available to students on the great majority of the affairs of the university, and they should be fully consulted. On a range of questions concerned with the physical environment there is every argument for giving the students, subject to suitable financial safeguards, a substantial share in the management of their universities. In academic matters, however, while student opinion should be freely sought and carefully considered, the decisions must be reserved to the academic staff, who have no right in a fit of enthusiasm to surrender or impair their own autonomy and that of their successors. In this context, academic decisions must be understood to include decisions on the allocation of resources if those decisions have academic implications.

12 Discipline

For the fifteen years preceding November 1966 L.S.E. had continued without formal disciplinary proceedings—without expulsions, suspensions, or even the imposition of a fine. This does not mean that for fifteen years the School was undisciplined; it means that for that time discipline was near to perfection in that there was a reasonable coincidence between the behaviour of students, the behaviour that the rules stated to be required, and the behaviour that they expected to be required of them. It is when expectations change and the rules do not that difficulty arises; it is, indeed, in matters of discipline that the greatest embarrassment can be caused by the failure of a university to adapt its organization and procedures to its own growth, changes in the social background, and changes in the expectations of its students.

As institutions grow in size, systems may have to bear burdens that personalities can no longer sustain. When an institution is small, its disciplinary authorities are people known and, all being well, trusted by those over whom they exercise authority. As the institution grows larger, the authorities become more remote and less known; the confidence which they can no longer personally win must instead be earned by the system within which they operate—the rules that they enforce and the procedure of enforcement. In smaller institutions—the small Oxbridge college for example, if there are any small ones left—it may still be possible for discipline to be administered informally, as within the family, at least until some occasion arises when the assumptions of the two generations concerned are markedly at variance; but in larger institutions it can be so no longer, though it may be possible to offer the accused student the choice—as is done at some American universities—between trial by quasi-judicial process, and the more familiar, old-fashioned and paternal type of procedure. Not all would choose the former.

Changes in the social background have also to be taken into account. The conception of the authorities as standing *in loco parentis*, and entitled to discipline their pupils with as unquestioned authority as a parent, is no longer accepted. Parents themselves no longer act in this manner; they neither expect nor desire submission from their children. Even if they did, it is no longer accepted that the university, a large, cold, inevitably bureau-cratic organization, stands in their place.

The greatest change perhaps is in the attitude and expectation of the students themselves. All discipline depends ultimately on consent, and the attitude of the governed has to be taken into account if that consent is to be retained. Students are now more conscious of adulthood. 'We want', Sir Eric Ashby quotes some of them as saying to the University Grants Committee, 'to be treated as much like ordinary citizens as possible.'[1] The student, moreover, no longer thinks of himself as one of a privileged minority, lucky to be at a university and ready to do what his elders and betters say, or to go elsewhere. He has, as he sees it, by his own work and merit won himself a right to higher education and he will stand on his rights. We are in a more litigious society than we once were. Patients readily sue hospitals, workers even sue their trade unions; is it to be wondered at that students grow more conscious of their rights in and against their universities, and expect to see those rights set down and safe-guarded in black and white?

Social change has also made the consequences of the disciplinary acts of a university much more serious than they once were. To be sent down from the university may never have been a cachet of distinction leading to certain success in politics or the City, but it was in the past no grave dis-ability. Nowadays, however, it can easily mean that a man's chosen career is closed to him—that of medicine, for example, or teaching. Even where it is not essential, a university education is a highly desirable qualification for success in a constantly widening range of careers, and, incidentally, especially perhaps for the first-generation university student, a vehicle of social mobility. To be sent down from a university is, therefore, in the long run, possibly a more severe penalty than, say, six months' imprisonment. Not unreasonably the student expects to have the same kind of safeguards against the one as he would have against the other.

In face of all these changes it is not surprising that change has brought conflict on the subject of discipline. About discipline in academic matters there has as yet, it is true, been surprisingly little dispute. The right of the university to decide that a student is not satisfying its academic require-ments and should withdraw has not as yet been much questioned; but questioning will grow with the increasingly articulate discontent with the pattern of examinations that students are now evincing. The universities must prepare their answer to it. In non-academic matters, however, there has been conflict enough about the requirements of discipline and the pro-cedure for their enforcement, and the conflict has sometimes been funda-mental. The most extreme student demand appears to be that there should be no rules at all. 'The fact is', Mr. Adelstein, for example, writes, 'that students ought to come neither above nor below the ordinary law of the land—there is no ounce of justification for academic authorities to have

[1] ... *And Scholars*, London, 1965, p. 17.

non-academic disciplinary powers.'[1] This conclusion is not argued nor explained, and one is left wondering whether Mr. Adelstein really can mean that there should be no disciplinary regulation of non-curricular matters. This position would be hard to sustain. The maintenance of any community for a common purpose calls for some regulation of activity, for rules which state the behaviour expected of one member towards another. In a university there must, for example, be rules governing the use of the library, and some way of dealing with those who do not conform to them. If a student insists on switching on his wireless set in the reading room, it would be useless to send for a policeman; the student is committing no offence against 'the ordinary law of the land'. No more would he be doing so if he insisted on holding a political meeting or a bingo session in a room where a lecture was due to be given, but his activities must clearly be controlled. As the Latey Committee on the Age of Majority say in their Report (Cmnd. 3342),

Any collective body, whether it is an iron-foundry or an old people's home, has to have arrangements to make sure, first, that people do what they are there to do—in this case, study; and second, that they do not make each other's lives unbearable by an unreasonable exercise of individual freedom. Colleges will go on demanding that students read books, go to lectures, write essays and stay in a fit state to do so; they will continue to require that the young people do not enjoy themselves with trumpets and strumpets to the point where it keeps other people awake.

The rooms and corridors of a university building, moreover, are not, for many purposes, within the definition of a public place, and sundry forms of objectionable conduct therein are not matters of which the law would take cognizance. It is the responsibility of the occupier of premises— and a university is the occupier of its premises—to regulate the conduct of those whom it permits to enter them. It may, indeed, be subject to pains and penalties if it fails to do so. If the students made a great noise, for example, or otherwise annoyed the neighbours, it is against the university as occupier of the premises that those neighbours would have to seek redress by legal proceedings; and if the students were known to take drugs on the premises, those who were concerned in the management of the premises might be liable to prosecution.[2] The university, then, must regulate students' conduct on the campus, prevent interference with its own purposes, and prevent the students from being a nuisance to one another or to the neighbours. What of conduct off the campus? A traditional view is that the university is entitled to protect its good name by regulating its students' conduct. Concern for the good name of the university is natural enough, but it is a vague term. Conceptions of what is reputable conduct differ, and can easily be felt by the elderly and conventional to justify a repression of unconventionality or of political views

---

[1] *Teach Yourself Student Power*, London, 1968, p. 21.
[2] At the time when I write, the question is uncertain.

L

which they regard as reprehensible. What one generation considers to damage the university's good name another may think enhances it. It is essential to a reasonable code of discipline that those who are subject to it should be reasonably clear what is allowed and what is forbidden. Rules vaguely forbidding conduct injurious to the reputation of the university fail to satisfy this requirement and can reasonably be regarded in consequence as unjust.[1] In the last resort, moreover, and in the long run, the good name of the university depends on matters other than the conduct of its junior members in the street. What a student does as an ordinary member of the public is, for the most part, no concern of the university. If he breaks the speed-limit, knocks off a policeman's helmet, or throws a brick through the Prime Minister's window, it is as a man in the street that he misbehaves, and as a man in the street that he is punished by the courts. Sensitive as its authorities may be, it is not by such acts as these that the reputation of the university with sensible people is impaired.

More persuasive, perhaps, at first sight is the argument that the university, by bringing large numbers of young people together in one place contracts a special responsibility to the neighbouring public, and especially the public authorities; but the argument appears on closer examination to rest on some equation of a collection of young people with, say, an explosives factory or a menagerie. I find it questionable whether the analogy holds and whether the responsibility is more than shadowy. The presence of a university brings advantages by way, for example, of enhancement of cultural activities, of trade, and of employment for the surrounding community, which can reasonably be expected to take some rough with the smooth. In particular, any use of this shadowy responsibility as a ground for restriction of political activity of students places far more weight upon it than it will bear.

It is as well to recognize, however, that in some such matters opinion is in a transitional phase, and there are in consequence possibilities of misunderstanding. The control of organized ragging in public places is something for which the police may leave the responsibility to the university and the university to the police, or, worse still, both the criminal courts and the university may punish a man for the same offence. To avoid such misunderstanding, a university should make clear what bounds it sets to its responsibilities. It may be more important that the boundary should be clearly understood than that it should be here rather than there; but it would probably be best, so far as possible, that the police and the public authorities should be left to exercise their proper responsibilities, and the university should not exercise a paternalistic discipline, creating unnecessary possibilities of conflict and treating its students as specially privileged or as subject to special control. The concept of the university as pervasive, all-embracing, regulating every aspect of the lives of its charges

---

[1] My argument does not necessarily imply, however, that no general rules are permissible, merely that they must be reasonably precise in meaning.

—all, of course, for their own good—is essentially paternalist, depending on the notion of authority as the all-wise father-corporation, and repulsive to modern ways of thought. It is also wasteful of administrative effort; the university has enough to do to regulate its own more domestic concerns.

In drawing the boundaries to which I have referred there are, however, awkward border-line cases. A student, let us say, misbehaves in his lodgings and upsets his landlady, or refuses to pay his bill. In the ordinary way I would suggest that this is a dispute between two citizens, to be brought, if appropriate, before the courts, but not of concern to the university. These circumstances may present themselves, however, in a town where lodgings are registered by the university, and the university may regard itself as responsible for maintaining an adequate supply of lodgings, and have difficulty in doing so. One student's bad behaviour in lodgings this year and the university's failure to protect the landlady may mean that some students have nowhere to live next year. In these circumstances the interests of the university are directly affected, and it would be hard to deny its right to take disciplinary action. I would, however, urge that the delineation of the university's rights and responsibilities in such a border-line area should be discussed with students. (The solution might, of course, be for the student body to have some responsibilities in this matter.)

To sum up the position that we have reached so far, it is that a university may in general, and indeed must, make regulations governing the conduct of students on its campus, and impose penalties for their breach; it may also in some circumstances—which should be carefully defined—impose penalties for objectionable conduct off the campus directly affecting its own interests, provided that such conduct is not the subject of a charge before the courts.

The overlapping jurisdiction of the courts of law and the disciplinary authorities of the university can give rise to the question whether a man who has committed a crime which is also an offence against the regulations of the university should be punished by the courts, the university, or both. The principle that it is morally repugnant that someone should be twice punished for one offence (the 'principle of double jeopardy', as the Americans call it) provides some help but not a complete and conclusive answer. If a medical practitioner or a solicitor, for example, is found guilty of a serious and relevant criminal offence, then he may, besides being punished by the courts, also be found unfit for the continued practice of his profession and may be excluded from it, and this is not regarded as double punishment. Similarly, a man's criminal conviction may make it doubtful whether he should remain a member of his university. For example, if he is convicted and sent to prison for peddling dangerous drugs can he when released safely be allowed to return to his university? Again, if in a university the property of some of its members is at risk, say, in its cloakrooms, is the university failing in its duty to protect that property if it allows someone to continue as a student who has been convicted—perhaps more than once—of shoplifting? Clearly it must be open to the university to terminate the membership of such a student; but not for the purpose of punishment, which has already been inflicted by the courts. If the offender is expelled it is not as a penalty but as a protection for other members of the university. The decision depends not on his degree of guilt but on the risk to them; the only question at issue is to expel or not to expel. Suspension cannot be appropriate, for it is not possible to say 'This man is a danger to others now, but will be no danger in two years' time.' The right course, if he is such a danger, is to expel him, but to let him apply for readmission when he can satisfy the university that the danger has passed.

A more difficult question is whether a university may properly take disciplinary action against a student for an offence of which he has been acquitted by the courts, or for which he has not been prosecuted for lack of evidence. It is tempting to answer it with an immediate negative, and ninety-nine times out of a hundred this would be right. Suppose, however, that evidence is available to the university—as has been known to happen—that is not available to the courts: a witness, for example, who is prepared to speak in the privacy of disciplinary proceedings, but not to the police or the courts; and suppose the alleged offence to be a serious one. Or suppose again that the evidence is nearly conclusive but fails—perhaps for technical reasons—to come up to the standards of the law of evidence. Society at large can say 'Better that ten guilty go free, than one innocent man be punished.' Can a small community accept as readily the presence in its midst of, say, a proselytizing drug-taker whose guilt is reasonably certain but could not by legal standards be proved in court? I find it very hard to say that it should.

There is another possibility of overlapping jurisdiction—with the civil courts; for example, would it be proper to bring disciplinary proceedings against a student for libelling a member of the staff? One's first inclination may be to say that the protection of reputations can safely be left to the courts. On second thoughts, however, is this answer so clearly right? Our universities put it in the power of students to publish, for example, a students' union newspaper and other magazines and pamphlets. If they are used to abuse a member of the staff, is his only redress to be in the courts? Ordinary people are naturally reluctant to have recourse to the courts. The student journalist is likely to be without means, and the plaintiff, so far from being able to recover any damages awarded to him, could not rely even on recovering his own costs, unless the circumstances were such as to allow him to sue the students' union also. The university put the means of disseminating the libel at the student's disposal—very possibly at the taxpayers' ultimate expense, since most student publications are subsidized. Should the university not then provide some measure of protection through its disciplinary machinery, especially if the libel is uttered by the defendant as a student rather than as a citizen and directed at the plaintiff more as a member of the university than as a citizen? I would hope that disciplinary action in this context would be infrequent; but the mere possibility of its being taken would serve to make the student journal a little more cautious and responsible and more ready to publish an apology when appropriate, just as the possibility of a libel action or reference to the Press Council makes national newspapers more cautious and also ready to apologize and retract when they have gone astray.

There remains, finally, the question whether it is right for students to be punished by their universities for acts which have little or no relevance to their academic work, and are not offences against the law, but transgress against conventional standards of morality. In practice this question arises most often in respect of sexual acts, and is more likely to trouble residential institutions than non-residential. The standards of conventional morality do not command anything like universal consent among the young, who have the right in these private matters to order their own lives as they think fit so long as their studies are not adversely affected (a condition which the increased availability of contraceptive advice does much to satisfy). On the other hand, the dissenting young have to bear in mind that there is no need to flaunt their dissent in such a manner as to upset those among their elders and their contemporaries whose standards are more conventional. A respect for the beliefs and even prejudices of those among whom we have to live is part of the code of civilized conduct. If a young man or woman in a residential institution cannot comply with this code, then he or she had better be required to live off the campus; but there should not ordinarily be any occasion for further disciplinary action than that. Private morality is a private matter.

Having established the necessity of having rules, and having given some general indication of their area of operation, I suggest that the following general principles should be taken into account in framing or reviewing those rules:

1. the rules must have legal authority;
2. they must be necessary;
3. they must be acceptable to the community at large and to those to whom they are to apply.

I take these principles in turn.

1. *Legal Basis.* It should hardly be necessary to say that the rules should have a proper legal basis, that is to say, that the person or persons by whom they are made must be properly authorized to make them; if this is not so, then any decisions based upon them, and in particular the imposition of penalties for failure to comply with them, may in some circumstances successfully be called in question in the courts.

The legal basis may at the present time be either or both of the following:

(a) a contract, express or implied, into which the student has entered with the university, one term of the contract being, say, that he will comply with the statutes of the university and all regulations or orders made under them; but it is necessary that the contract shall include that term and that the statute shall in fact authorize the making of the regulations—common sense is not enough.

(b) the fact—if it is a fact—that the university stands in *loco parentis*, as deputy, that is to say, for his parents and so entitled to exercise over him disciplinary control of the same kind within the same range as might a parent. As I have already indicated, this doctrine is distinctly flyblown; and it can hardly apply to students who have attained the age of legal majority, that is to say twenty-one years, soon to be reduced to eighteen when legislative effect is given (perhaps before these words appear in print) to the recommendations of the Latey Committee on the Age of Majority. Universities would be well advised, therefore, to make sure of the contractual-statutory basis described in the previous paragraph.

2. *Necessity*. I take it as axiomatic that it is in principle undesirable that the actions of one human being should be regulated by another, unless there is good reason to the contrary. It follows that it is desirable as a matter of principle that the regulations of a university be as few as possible. This is also, of course, a matter of practical convenience. The fewer the rules the less the labour of administering them, and the less the friction to which they may lead. A rule should not be made or retained unless it is necessary for the reasonably efficient and economical conduct of the affairs of the university, the carrying out of its purposes, and the protection of the rights of its members and servants in the pursuit of those purposes.

3. *Acceptability*. In broad and general terms, government in a university as elsewhere depends upon the consent of the governed. If the rules to which they are subject are in their opinion unreasonable, the enforcement of the rules is likely to be a matter of increasing difficulty. This does not mean that they must be accepted by every student all the time. It may be enough that they are, in cooler moments, and after due explanation, accepted by most; or even accepted last year and next year but not this; habits of mind change, and not always in the same direction. What seems at a time of controversy to be intolerable can be seen when passions have abated to have, after all, a good deal to be said for it.

What is acceptable, then, is not to be determined by, say, a plebiscite or a mass vote but is a matter of judgment. Whose is to be that judgment? Should the student voice be heard and should it be dominant? That it should be heard is clearly essential. Not merely will it serve as an indication whether or not the rule is here and now accepted (which will give at least some indication whether it is acceptable in the sense that I have suggested), but it will also serve as a constant reminder of the need for making sure that the rule is necessary. Consultation with students there must, therefore, certainly be; but it must be careful consultation, designed to ascertain the reflective judgment of the majority; and dominant the student voice should not be. The student's view is short, he will soon be gone, his responsibility is limited, and it is not for long that he is required to comply with the rules. It is the authorities and the staff of the university who will have to endure or enjoy the results of the decisions; it is their future working conditions, and perhaps their careers, that are in the longer term at stake; it is they who will be held accountable if things go wrong, to them that society looks to keep their own house in order. The dominant voice must be theirs.

We have now dealt with the areas in which the rules may operate and the principles that should govern their making, and have to consider their enforcement. There is a tendency to make heavy weather of this. The National Union of Students in their *Code of Discipline*, for example (which with their permission, I reproduce in Appendix V[1]), propose that no punishment should be imposed save by 'a properly constituted disciplinary committee', which they suggest should consist of eight members, from which there should be a right of appeal to an external appeals committee. Such a procedure seems excessively cumbrous for a good many minor offences; for example, misbehaviour in the library, or the type of thoughtless anti-social conduct which occurs in residential institutions—trumpets at midnight. In cases of this kind there will usually be no dispute as to the facts and no dispute whether they constitute an offence. The imposition of a penalty may not be necessary, but if it is it would be an absurd waste of labour that the time of eight people should be occupied. (One does not expect to appeal to the House of Lords against a fine of forty shillings for a car-parking offence.) Similarly, it should be possible if necessary for wardens, deans, tutors and the like to impose small penalties with no formal right of appeal. Intermediate types of offence, rather more serious, that might incur penalties of suspension for not more than a term, might also reasonably be disposed of by a warden, dean, or tutor, but against such penalties the student might reasonably be allowed to appeal to a disciplinary committee of the type that I shall discuss in a moment. In case of disorder, moreover, it may well be necessary for the disciplinary authorities to impose provisionally immediate penalties of suspension, for review by a disciplinary committee.

Major offences which may justify interruption of a man's studies by suspension or their termination by expulsion should be rare, but the disciplinary machinery cannot be hurriedly improvised or amended if a case of special difficulty occurs, and it needs to be so devised as to be capable of bearing the strain of the most difficult case that can conceivably

[1] See p. 190.

be brought before it. It may be, for example, a case of serious and repeated disruption of a university's work by way of protest on political or moral grounds against the inclusion in its research programme of branches of science closely related to particular forms of warfare. It is not for students to decide what research should be done, and in the last resort the authority of the teachers may need to be maintained by disciplinary action, which is likely to be unpopular. A disciplinary mechanism which can stand such a strain must also be capable of handling less complex or controversial cases with reasonable humanity, speed and economy of labour. The mechanism must

1. satisfy any relevant requirements of the law;
2. command confidence, not only among students but also among the staff and the authorities of the university;
3. be reasonably humane, swift, and economical of labour.

What are the relevant requirements of the law? It is the practice of the courts to intervene and review the decisions of persons in authority who exercise judicial functions if they fail to comply with the requirements of what is called 'natural justice'. Those requirements are, firstly, the impartiality of the adjudicating authority; and, secondly, the opportunity for each party to know what issues are at stake, to know the opponent's case and to have the opportunity of answering it.

The courts do not require any particular method of satisfying these requirements. It is a question of fact whether the procedure followed in a particular instance is satisfactory or not.

The tribunal or disciplinary committee before which cases are to be heard must be clearly impartial and must command confidence. The National Union of Students in their *Code* propose that it should consist of eight members, five drawn from the staff and three from the students, none of whom shall be an interested party, and that they shall be assisted by a legal adviser. They also propose that the vice-chancellor or other head of the institution should not be a member. It may reasonably be felt that a body of eight is too large: the objection is not only that the time of too many people will be taken up (and that it will be harder to assemble them at a time convenient to all), but still more that a smaller committee would be likely to do its work better. The smaller the committee the more intense the sense of responsibility that each member feels for its work and the greater the care that he will devote to it. It seems probable, however, that the N.U.S. are led to propose a committee of eight by their adoption of the principle that the committee should contain students, but in a minority, and a fear that the responsibility would be too heavy to place on a single student, or even on two of them. This means that the committee must have at least seven members. It is therefore probably best to consider first the question whether students should serve on the committee.

The arguments in favour of student membership are comparable to those for student representation generally. In something of the way in which the jury, though nominally confined to questions of fact, has at times compelled revision of the law to bring into accord with public opinion, student membership of the disciplinary committee will help to keep it in closer touch with the standards of conduct observed by the generality of students. I do not say that those standards must simply be accepted in their entirety—even a disciplinary committee has some educational function—but they must be taken fully into account.

On the other hand, it may be argued that the burden of membership of a disciplinary committee is too heavy to impose on students, since it might involve them in the imposition of sanctions, including that of expulsion, on other students. This argument runs the risk of paternalism, of treating students as not fully grown up. If they are themselves prepared to see the responsibility accepted by some of their number, and ask that it should be accepted, can they reasonably be deprived of the safeguard that its acceptance will undoubtedly provide? It is as well to remember that, if the Latey Committee's recommendations are accepted, persons of student age may be required to accept the responsibility entailed by service on a jury, which is comparable in magnitude.

The decision whether students are to serve may reasonably vary from institution to institution; not all universities have to make the same experiment at the same time. Something must depend on the views of the students themselves, and something on the size of the institution. In a small community the students may be able to have greater confidence in the staff, and may also feel that it would be harder for the accused and his student judges to live comfortably together cheek by jowl afterwards. If a compromise is desired, perhaps it may be sometimes found by permitting a student to attend as an assessor with the right to participate in the committee's deliberations, but not to vote, or students might elect one or two of the staff members of the committee, or elect a recent graduate as a member. In large institutions, however, it is likely to be found desirable that there should be student members of the committee itself. How many should serve? If, as I would urge, it is accepted as undesirable that the disciplinary committee should consist of more than five members and accepted that student members must be in the minority, then they must be limited in number to two at the most.

Should the vice-chancellor or other head of the institution serve on the disciplinary committee? The N.U.S. propose, without giving any reasons, that he should not. It has been argued[1] that this is a mistake; that if the vice-chancellor is dissociated from the disciplinary decision he loses direct contact with the students at a vital stage in staff-student relations; and there is considerable force in this argument. It is particularly desirable that a disciplinary committee should contain among its members at least one

[1] As, for example, by the Principal of the University of London in his Annual Report for 1966–7, p. 46.

who has continuing responsibility for the well-being of the institution, as opposed to members who will return to their normal pursuits at the end of the hearing, and will have no further responsibility for the consequences. This need can, however, be met by providing for staff members of the committee to serve for a substantial period—say five years—and the need for the presence of the vice-chancellor is diminished. Vice-chancellors have too many heavy responsibilities, some of which they must delegate.

It is, furthermore, desirable when possible that the vice-chancellor should be a little above the battle, and that the supreme authority in the University should not be engaged at too early a stage of any potentially controversial but, in the long run, comparatively minor matter; and there are advantages in separating the judiciary from the executive and avoiding the notion of the monolithic monster 'the Administration'.

Finally, the disciplinary committee must include members of the academic staff; and if the membership includes no lawyer then one should be appointed as adviser.

I have sought to outline the constitution of a disciplinary committee that could hope to command general confidence in its justice and impartiality. In times of stress and conflict, however, when the sympathies and emotions of all members of a University must inevitably be engaged, it might be better, as Lord Robbins has suggested to me, that, at least for major offences, the disciplinary authority should if possible be recruited from outside the institution concerned. An eminent lawyer, for example, aided by assessors from the staff and the student body, who would have the right to proffer to him advice and comment but not to vote or participate in his ultimate decision, would seem more likely to reach a just and impartial decision— to do justice and be seen to do justice—than any body constituted from within the university.

It has been noted above that the courts do not require any particular method of satisfying the requirements of natural justice; and it is not necessary to accept lock, stock, and barrel the procedures of the courts of this country, which have no monopoly of justice, and do not always achieve it. It is not to be taken for granted that our accusatorial procedure, involving the examination and cross-examination of witnesses by each side in turn, is more just than the inquisitorial method under which there is not necessarily a separate prosecutor, but the court enquires into the matter and itself undertakes the examination of witnesses. The accusatorial procedure has, however, in this country the very great advantage of familiarity. We know how it works and how to operate it; the man in the street, and the judge who may be called upon to review it, both regard it as fair. It commands confidence, that is to say, and satisfies the requirements of natural justice. There is much to command its acceptance.

There is an objection of some weight which may be summed up by describing such a procedure as 'legalistic', by which I think may be conveyed various of the allegations that it is pompous, long-winded, slow, over-elaborate, over-precise, disproportionate to the issues involved, and a sort of field-day for barrack-room lawyers. This objection is not without foundation. An attempt by laymen to follow and operate the procedures of the courts is in very great danger of degenerating into a mock trial; it is an attempt by amateurs to adopt the practices and techniques of the legal profession, and like all such attempts runs the risk of grasping at their more superficially obvious features while failing to grasp what underlies them—the risk, that is to say, of producing a mere caricature. The answer to the objection, however, may not be to abandon the attempt, but to improve it by calling in the professionals to do the job properly.

There are other considerations leading in the same direction. It would, I think, generally be conceded that, in any matter in which he may suffer serious penalties, whose effect, as we have seen, may be more serious for him than a sentence of imprisonment, a student should have the help of someone older and more experienced. It is natural to consider first the possibility that he be defended by his tutor. He may, however, have no confidence in his tutor, either because of their temperamental incompatibility or because, let us say, his tutor is an unworldly scholar of some remote discipline, more likely, he feels, to be a hindrance than a help to his defence. To meet this difficulty the natural next step of the university is to provide that he may be represented by any member of the academic staff of his choice. In any university which has a law faculty, it is more than likely that it will be from that faculty that the defendant will then seek aid. So the lawyer arrives on one side. It is desirable that prosecution and defence should understand one another—speak the same language, make the same practical assumptions, and the like. If this is accepted, then the prosecution had better be conducted by a lawyer; as a general rule, it is probably best to have lawyers on both sides or on neither.

What of the university that has no law faculty? Should its students have the right to professional legal representation, or must they make the most of such amateur talent as the academic staff possesses? Having regard to the weight of the possible penalties, the case for permitting professional legal representation is very strong.

We are then, however, taken inevitably a step further. If the student at a university that has no law faculty is to be allowed professional representation, should not the same opportunity be open to the student at a university that has such a faculty? The student might reasonably prefer the help of an experienced practitioner in the criminal courts to the services of a scholar, however eminent, in, say, international law, or the law of copyright. Who, however, is to bear the cost of obtaining professional services for the defence? I can see no justification for suggesting that the costs should be met directly by the university, and think that it must fall upon the students. There is no reason, however, why, like professional associations of various kinds—or even the Royal Automobile Club—the students' union should not add to its responsibilities that of providing the cost of legal aid. And in all this, let it not be forgotten that I have urged that there be as little discipline as possible. We shall not have capital trials every day.

The procedural matters that remain for discussion are comparatively minor. For the most part the proposals of the N.U.S. are fair and reasonable. Clearly the accused must be informed in writing, and in sufficiently specific terms, of the charge against him, and allowed enough time to prepare his defence; the burden of proof must rest on the prosecution; the defendant must be made aware of all the evidence against him; it is desirable that he be allowed to cross-examine adverse witnesses; and he must be allowed to present his own case and his own witnesses.

That it is necessary, however, to provide for a formal appeal seems less certain than is generally assumed. The analogy with the legal system may conceivably be misleading. That system does indeed generally provide for a right of appeal, but always to a more skilled and experienced body. A more skilled and experienced judicial body than its disciplinary committee a university cannot provide within its own walls. An external appellate authority may be more skilled and experienced in the administration of the law, but that is not what is needed. Unless a group of universities can combine to form some kind of common appellate body, I wonder whether it might not in fact be better to provide for the possibility of a review by the appropriate authorities of the university, perhaps the vice-chancellor alone, or a joint committee of Council and Senate, exercising a kind of prerogative of mercy, acting in a political rather than a judicial manner. This would be likely to provide better opportunity for the correction of error, and a greater safeguard for the accused; yet I doubt whether it would be generally acceptable.

The arrangements that are suggested above make ample provision for fair and impartial hearing of disciplinary charges against students, and it is to be hoped that, if treated as adults, students will accept the obligations that go with that status. It nevertheless remains possible that in times of difficulty small numbers of students who are sufficiently determined may make it impossible for a disciplinary committee to meet, or may, by obstructing witnesses, make it impossible for it to do its work. Their purpose may be either to compel the acquittal of the accused, or—if, for example, he is a member of an unpopular minority—to secure his condign punishment. The civil courts have means of protecting themselves against interference of this sort, but a university disciplinary committee has not, and some safeguard must be provided. The first and last duty of those who are appointed to govern an institution is to govern it, to enable its ordered life to continue, and they must be given means to do so. A university should not so tie itself up in legal knots that it cannot impose disciplinary sanctions without a formal hearing, but may be prevented from conducting that formal hearing. I would suggest that provision be made whereby, if it appears to the vice-chancellor that a disciplinary committee (or appellate body if there is one) cannot, because of actual or threatened disorder or obstruction, conveniently hear any charge, he may direct that the hearing be postponed or adjourned until in his opinion it can do so; and that he have power to direct that the accused be suspended until the hearing takes place. If provision of this kind is made, its existence may make it unnecessary ever to use it.

Appendix I

THE LONDON SCHOOL OF ECONOMICS AND POLITICAL SCIENCE

REGULATIONS FOR STUDENTS

1. All students shall obey all rules made and instructions given by the Director of the School or under his authority, and shall refrain from conduct derogatory to the character or welfare of the School.

2. The Director may at his discretion refuse to any applicant admission to a course of study at the School or continuance in a course beyond the normal period required for its completion. He may refuse to allow any student to renew his attendance at the School as from the beginning of any term, on the ground of the student's lack of ability or of industry, or for any other good cause.

3. Fees shall not be returnable, save that applications for their partial return may be considered in exceptional circumstances.

4. The copyright in lectures delivered in the School is vested in the lecturers, and notes taken at lectures shall be used only for purposes of private study.

5. Students introducing visitors to School premises shall be held responsible for their conduct.

6. The School premises shall not, without permission from the Director or Secretary, be used for the sale or organized distribution of books, papers or other articles, or for the making of collections for charitable or other purposes.

7. Save as provided in regulations 8 and 9, no student shall, without the permission of the Director, use the name or address of the School, or the title of any body if that title includes the name of the School, when communicating to any person or organization outside the School the text or sense of any resolution considered by any group or organization of students.

8. Notwithstanding regulation 7, the Students' Union may communicate the text or sense of any such resolution, if strictly limited to matters of concern to students as such, to any organization of students outside the School.

9. Notwithstanding regulations 7 and 10, where membership of any society is voluntary and that society is recognized by the Students' Union, a resolution of that society may be communicated to any person if (a) the communication also shows the numbers of members of the society voting for and against the resolution and (b) the terms of the resolution do not constitute an offence against any other regulation.

10. Save as provided in regulation 9, no student shall without the permission of the Director use the name or address of the School, or the title of any body if that title includes the name of the School, when sending any letter or other communication to the Press (other than a student publication)

or when distributing any document outside the School for any purpose; save that this regulation shall not preclude any graduate student from using the address of the School when sending to persons outside the School any communication whose terms have been approved by his supervisor for the purpose of eliciting information required for his research.

11. No student shall without the permission of the Director use the name or address of the School when making to any public authority in the United Kingdom or elsewhere any representations on behalf of any other student or group of students of the School.

12. Any student or body of students who may appeal for funds to sources external to the School must make clear by whom the appeal is made and that it is not made by or on behalf of the School itself.

13. The address of the University must not be used when making communications to the Press, except by those to whom the University has given special permission.

14. Representatives of the Press (other than representatives of student publications) shall not, without the permission of the Director, be admitted to any meeting held in the School, or to any meeting held outside the School by a body whose title includes the name of the School; nor may any arrangement be made without his permission for any part of the proceedings of such a meeting to be reported or recorded by any broadcasting or television corporation or authority.

15. No student shall, without permission given by the Director or under his authority, bring or cause to be brought into any of the School premises (including Passfield Hall and the athletic ground at Malden) any alcoholic liquor.

16. Bags, coats and other possessions of students must not be left in School premises in any place in which they may cause obstruction or danger. Cloakrooms, lockers, and, in some cases, special racks are provided for the convenience of students, but the School does not accept liability for any loss of personal property of students or damage to it.

17. No gambling or betting may take place on School premises.

18. Only those games may be played on School premises for which a student society or club has been approved.

19. The playing of cards on School premises is prohibited save:
(a) in any room which may from time to time be assigned for the purpose to a student society or club, and
(b) in accordance with the rules of that society or club.

20. If any offence shall be committed against any of these regulations it shall not be excused by the fact that the offender may have acted on behalf of any group or organization of students.

21. For any breach of these regulations a student may be fined any sum not exceeding £5, be suspended either from all use of the School or from any particular privileges, or be expelled from the School.

22. The penalties of expulsion and of suspension for more than three months may be inflicted only by the Board of Discipline constituted by the Governors, and students subjected to these penalties shall have the right of appeal from the Board to the Standing Committee of the Governors. The other penalties may be inflicted by the Director or under his authority.

BOARD OF DISCIPLINE

The Board of Discipline consists of the Director, and two members of the Court of Governors and two Professors, appointed by the Court of Governors and the Academic Board respectively at their last ordinary meetings of each session for the session following. Three members form a quorum.

STUDENT ACTIVITIES

The particular attention of all officers of student societies is drawn to the Rules Relating to Student Activities, with which all students are required to comply. A copy of those rules is posted outside the offices of the Students' Union in the St. Clements Building.

Appendix II

The Director's Letter to all Students, 7 January 1967

Dear Student

The events of last term have left me with the strong impression that most of our students have too little information about the way the School is run, its problems and its policies. You are no doubt aware of some of the ways in which the School's problems bear on you personally, but I suspect that you will know little of what has been done, or what is planned, to meet those problems. I have therefore prepared the following memorandum to put before you a number of things about the School's organization and activities which I think all students should know.

Our affairs are complex and they cannot be described in a few sentences or in dramatic form. I hope that nonetheless you will study the memorandum carefully.

As well as setting out the present structure of the School's organization the memorandum refers to the consideration which is now being given to changes in that organization which may affect students, including suggestions for change which have been put forward by the Students' Union. I want to make two general comments on the review which is in progress. First, the School unreservedly accepts that there are wide areas of policy and administration in which the ascertainment of student opinion is desirable and is anxious to find the best means of achieving that end. Secondly, consideration of these matters will be hindered, not helped, if proposals are put forward with an accompaniment of threats of boycotts or similar pressure. Such action interrupts and impedes the processes of discussion and persuasion by which the School always tries to solve its internal problems. I hope that the fuller understanding of the existing situation which my memorandum is designed to provide will help students to join more effectively in those processes of rational discussion.

Yours sincerely,
SYDNEY CAINE

To all students of the School.

1. The Character of the School as a University institution
To begin with the obvious: the position of L.S.E. is ambiguous. It is a larger body than many of the Universities in Britain. It has a unique concentration of graduate students. It is famous throughout the world. It is both a university in terms of teaching, research and administration, and a part of a larger whole, the University of London. Although the range of scholarly concern at L.S.E. is great, it is only a fraction of the totality of university subjects. The enduring reputation of the School is founded on its

M

scholarly production—the quality and number of its students scattered throughout all countries and the merit of the researches, influence and publications of its staff.

In such an enterprise as L.S.E. there are inevitably tensions and compromises. A university exists today to perform those tasks for which the first universities came into being. It teaches, and thus transmits both knowledge and a certain kind of imagination and competence about the practical world. It extends knowledge and technique by study and research. It preserves both a body of knowledge and a spirit of enquiry and criticism. To transmit, extend, and preserve learning, a university has to be both an orderly part of the ongoing world without its confines and a retreat, for both students and teachers, from certain pressing urgencies of life. It is this that makes membership of this voluntary society of a university both a privilege and the acceptance of a duty to the community one has joined.

The teachers and administrators of this School are involved by the fame, the physical situation, and the nature of the School in a relationship of duty to the larger society. They must heed its just needs, and be as widely and well available as they can. What is learned from research, public contacts and committees is fed back to our community. Teachers and administrators are not separate species. They have a common concern and a university in whose administration its teachers are not involved rapidly degenerates. Administrators cannot serve their functions without a lively concern in the problems of teaching and study. The student must therefore expect to find tensions, competing interests and obligations, and inevitable compromises in L.S.E. Without them the School would not be a part of the community of learning. Without them it would neither change nor progress.

2. Current problems of the School

At the end of the last war the School was not only by far the largest centre of the social studies in this country, but was also virtually the only place where many subjects in that field could be studied. The School felt, therefore, a special responsibility to the many would-be students of the social sciences, and strained itself to the limit to take them in. The staff willingly accepted the burden of an unfavourable student-staff ratio; the School's buildings were allowed to become more crowded; because if L.S.E. did not take the students they would be left out altogether. Staff and students alike thought it better that students should be crowded in here under less than ideal conditions than not be in a university reading the social sciences. Things gradually improved, and our resources were being considerably enlarged, when in 1963 the Robbins Report faced the School with the same problem all over again. Although the number of places in the social sciences elsewhere had considerably increased, it was clear that a serious overall shortage of university places was imminent. After a long and anxious debate, the academic staff of the School concluded that they would go on putting up with unfavourable conditions rather than see good candidates for places excluded altogether, and accepted a postponement of their hopes of improving our situation.

If it had not been for these decisions, many of the School's students would not be here now, and perhaps not at a university at all. The School has made strenuous efforts to get additional resources, but has had great disappointments. When we committed ourselves to the increase of student numbers we made clear what additional resources we should need: but we did not receive them. In spite of disappointments, in spite of the overcrowding, great efforts have been made to minimize our various shortages and difficulties. Much has been, and is being, achieved. To take an example or two, the Students' Union office seven years ago consisted only of rooms in the attic of an old building on the corner of Clements Inn Passage and Houghton Street; the Three Tuns Bar was only a small ground-floor room in the same building; and the only common room available to students apart from the Founders' Room was half of the area now occupied by the third-floor snack bar in the Old Building. Three years ago the Teaching Library was represented simply by a much smaller lending library. Five years ago there was no Robinson Room, and little more than a year ago the refectory was a gloomy place filled with worn-out furniture, and some five hundred square feet smaller in area than it is today. Over the last ten years, in fact, the amount of space available to the School has been doubled, and more is on the way—a new building is due to be started before the end of March on the vacant site next to St. Clement's Building.

Over the last few years the School has put much time and energy into the effort to find a much more satisfactory home for the library; this is a large and expensive enterprise, to which the national economic situation is as unfavourable as it could be. Meanwhile, improvements are being constantly made; for example, the library will have at least sixty more reading places in the term which is just beginning. Let there be no misunderstanding, however. Even if the plans for a new library succeed, present students are unlikely to see their result. With the best will in the world some years will inevitably be spent in architectural planning, negotiating with public authorities, getting the money, going out to tender and so on, as well as in the actual building work, before any new building can come into use.

Carr-Saunders Hall, a new hall of residence for men, is now nearing completion—the result not only of a most generous benefaction, but also of several years' hard work by the administration—from the Chairman of the Court and other Governors (who played a large part in finding a site) downwards. There are many other enlargements and improvements that the School would like to undertake, but not many of today's students are likely to see them brought to fruition, not only because of the time that it takes to get building work done, but still more because of the national economic situation and the many other claims on the taxpayers' money.

3. The financial background

The average student costs the School a great deal more than he brings it in fees. Those fees bring in a fraction over ten per cent of the School's income; endowment income and miscellaneous receipts another fifteen per cent; the remaining seventy-five per cent comes from the government grant, received through the University of London. For this money the School competes with the other London colleges, the other universities, and, ultimately, the other claimants on the taxpayers' money—the rest of the educational system, hospitals, roads, defence, and so on. Like everyone else, the School does not think it gets its fair share. More money is needed to improve the student–staff ratio, to buy more library books, keep the library open longer, improve amenities for students, and so on. Without more money more cannot be done: it is as simple as that.

So much for day-to-day expenditure: for capital expenditure the School is even more completely dependent on the government for specific *ad hoc* grants for the purchase of particular sites and the cost of particular new buildings. Our situation is especially difficult because sites in this locality are as expensive as anywhere in the world, and I think we are almost certain soon to have to decide whether to put up with continued overcrowding or to reduce it by having fewer students.

4. The government of the School
The School, like all universities, is a society of scholars engaged in the enlargement and spreading of knowledge, and cannot function healthily without much internal consultation. Moreover, the subjects the School teaches, the whole range of the social sciences, have become very much more complex than they were. The School has to cover many specialities and teach for a wide range of degrees. Maintaining a balance between these varied academic interests again requires wide consultation. The School is dependent on outside authorities for many things. It is a part of the University of London, and receives through the University the State assistance which forms three-quarters of its income. The degrees for which it teaches are London degrees, and the regulations which govern those degrees and the examinations connected with them are still largely controlled by the University. On capital grants (for new sites and buildings) the School has to discuss its needs with the University Grants Committee as well as with the University of London, and when new building is required it is subject to close and detailed control both by the University Grants Committee and by the local planning authority. The requirements of these bodies may conflict, and much time may be spent in reconciling and satisfying them. On other matters discussion and negotiation may be necessary with Government departments, the Social Science Research Council, the big educational foundations in the United Kingdom and in America, and account must be taken of all manner of special requirements laid down by such bodies. All these things make what at first sight seem straightforward issues complicated.

The ultimate governing body of the School is the Court of Governors. The Court has a maximum membership of a hundred, and a normal membership of seventy to eighty; its members are people of distinction in public life and, apart from a small number who are elected from among the teaching staff, are primarily occupied in work outside the School. The Court has delegated most of its executive powers to a committee of a dozen or so of its own members (including three members of the academic staff), known as the Standing Committee, or to the Director. The Court, however, receives regularly reports on the School's work and development, and is fully consulted on major issues of policy.

The Standing Committee takes decisions in major matters of finance and administrative policy, and has final responsibility for the making of appointments to the staff; but it in turn looks for guidance to a number of committees consisting partly or wholly of academics. Two of these are especially important, the Academic Board and the Appointments Committee. All teachers on the permanent staff are members of the Academic Board, which, broadly, controls academic affairs in the School; it approves, for example, the syllabuses of diplomas granted by the School, and expresses the School's point of view on University regulations on degrees. It is advised by a series of committees on admissions, the Graduate School, teaching arrangements, scholarships and prizes, halls of residence, and so forth. The Board also considers the broader aspects of academic policy arising from the reports of the Library Committee, the Accommodation Committee (which is concerned with the allocation of existing space), and the Building Committee (which is concerned with the design of new buildings or conversions). Finally, the Board is systematically consulted on major issues of long-term policy.

The Appointments Committee consists of all Professors, and is concerned with the creation of new academic posts, selections for appointment, promotions, and terms of service of academic staff. Through its control over new posts, the Appointments Committee exercises great influence on the academic development of the School.

An indication has been given of the main fields where there is need for a committee to concentrate discussion and consultation—on the Library, or new buildings, or the regulations for a new degree—but of course many decisions involve several such areas of consultation. A decision to start teaching in a new field of learning may involve additional academic appointments, changes in the pattern of admissions of students, the allocation of rooms, the provision of special equipment, and the buying of a new range of books for the Library, as well as raising academic issues about relationships to existing courses. It is therefore inevitable that some proposals have to be considered by a number of committees if they are to be fitted into the School's scheme of things.

5. Possible changes affecting students

The L.S.E. has never been static in its internal organization, and it is as willing as ever today to consider changes. Wide-ranging possible changes at present under consideration include:

(i) discussions which have been going on for more than a year on the improvement of the main structure of committees so as to make it more efficient; in these discussions the interests of students will be taken into account;

(ii) last summer the Academic Board set up a special committee to examine generally the relations between the School and its students. The immediate occasion for this was a feeling expressed by members of the Board, when they were asked to advise on the Students' Union proposal for an automatic 'sabbatical year' for the President of the Students' Union, that the whole role of the Students' Union needed re-assessment; but it was due also to a more general concern about relationships with the students as individuals in the rapidly-changing conditions of today. A sample survey of student opinion suggested that the problems of greatest concern to individual students are those concerned with teaching arrangements, and the Committee has therefore already promoted further enquiry in that field as described below. The Committee has since had long discussions with members of the Students' Council, and hopes to report soon on outstanding issues, including the role of the Union, the question of student representation on the School's committees, and the 'sabbatical year' proposal;

(iii) a number of aspects of our teaching programme are now being reconsidered. Academic departments are reviewing their arrangements for consultation with students. The fundamental structure of our first-degree courses is being examined by a committee appointed for the purpose. So is the tutorial system for the B.Sc.(Econ.), and we shall seek to ensure that students, tutors, and class-teachers all understand what their respective roles are, that part-time teachers are sufficiently briefed to take their place in the system, and that the student who is at a loss has always someone to whom he can go for advice. On a number of these matters further ascertainment of student opinion is to be arranged;

(iv) at the end of last term, the Academic Board agreed that a review of the disciplinary regulations should be undertaken by a joint committee of staff and students: the staff representatives have been appointed, and the committee will start its work as soon as the student representatives have been selected.

These various discussions will ensure that full consideration is given to a number of proposals put forward by the Students' Union in the last year, as well as alternative methods of dealing with the basic problems underlying them.

Appendix III

Decision of the Board of Discipline of the London School of Economics and Political Science (Lord Bridges, Professor Donnison, Dr. Farrer-Brown, and Professor Wheatcroft) delivered on 13 March 1967

What I am about to read is the unanimous decision of the Board.

This Board of Discipline was convened to hear 12 complaints of breach of discipline which were preferred by the Secretary of the School against six students of the School, namely, Mr. D. L. Adelstein, Mr. M. I. Bloom, Mr. M. S. K. Malik, Mr. S. J. Moss, Miss P. G. Jones and Mr. A. P. Ross. All the complaints alleged a breach of Regulation 1 for students which is in the following terms:

'All students shall obey all rules made and instructions given by the Director of the School or under his authority, and shall refrain from conduct derogatory to the character or welfare of the School.'

Each student on arrival at the School signs a slip as follows:

'I acknowledge receipt of a copy of the Regulations for Students. I accept them as binding upon me, and I undertake to comply with them.'

Regulation 1 is in two parts: one part requires students to obey the orders of the Director, the other requires them to refrain from conduct derogatory to the School. Originally the complaints alleged breaches under both heads but they were amended in the course of the proceedings so as to omit any reference to derogatory conduct. Hence we are only concerned to determine whether any or all of these six students disobeyed an order of the Director.

No rules have been laid down for the conduct of proceedings before a Board of Discipline of the School and we considered carefully how we should conduct these proceedings. Disobedience of an order of the Director is an extremely serious matter, both for the student concerned and the School, and we decided that any student charged with such a serious offence should be given full facilities to defend himself and that we ought not to find such an offence proved unless we were satisfied of it beyond reasonable doubt.

Hence we thought it right to permit each student to be represented before us by a member of the staff of his or her choice and they were in fact represented by three members of the staff of the Law Department. In view of this we later agreed to the Secretary being represented by another member of that Department. We are most grateful to these four members of the staff for the care and attention which they gave to the matter before us and for the assistance we obtained from their questions and arguments.

We also thought it right to require the Secretary to commence by producing the evidence in support of his complaints and we then heard the evidence of the persons complained against and of any witnesses they wished to call. All witnesses were examined and cross-examined and such questions as we put to the witnesses related to the evidence they had already given.

After the evidence was finished each of the representatives made submissions to us on behalf of the persons they represented. Finally, although we sat in private with the parties and their representatives, we permitted six students, nominated by the Students' Union, to attend the proceedings as observers.

We also arranged for a shorthand note of the proceedings to be taken and when the evidence and speeches were finished we all read carefully the transcripts of the shorthand note which totalled some 200 pages before meeting to arrive at our conclusions.

We were asked by the representatives of the students to give our reasons for any decision we arrived at and we agreed to this also.

In consequence of this procedure these proceedings have taken some time to complete but we considered that this was necessary to enable us to perform our task properly in dealing with a complex and difficult case.

Before dealing with the particular complaints preferred before us it is convenient to state first the background to the matters before us together with our findings on the main facts, as to which there is little conflict of evidence.

Last summer term it was announced that Dr. Adams had been appointed as Director of the School to succeed Sir Sydney Caine at the commencement of the 1967–8 academic session. This appointment was viewed with disfavour by a number of students of the School and during the Michaelmas Term a number of meetings and incidents took place which expressed the opposition of some students to this appointment.

In the early part of the Lent Term Mr. Bloom thought it proper to bring this issue to the attention of the students again and he made preparations to hold a meeting for this purpose in the Old Theatre of the School on Tuesday 31 January. He was the President of the Graduate Students' Association and he booked the Old Theatre from 4 to 6.30 p.m. that afternoon in the name of that association. Under the normal procedure such a booking would not be, and was not, queried by the clerk in charge of timetables and rooms. Mr. Bloom told us that the proposed meeting had been authorized by the committee of the Graduate Students' Association but no minute of any meeting of that committee was produced, and Mr. Bloom's subsequent actions indicated strongly that the meeting was his idea and had little to do with the Graduate Students' Association.

Mr. Bloom, however, did consult the Council of the Students' Union with regard to the meeting and the minutes of their meeting were produced to us. A minute of a meeting of Union Council on 25 January read 'Council agreed to Marshall Bloom arranging a Teach-In on sit-ins on Tuesday 31 January to which outside speakers would be invited'. Some witnesses suggested to us that there was some doubt what 'a Teach-In on sit-ins' meant, but we have no doubt from the evidence that from its inception this meeting was intended by its promoters to discuss ways of stopping Dr. Adams from taking up his appointment as Director. This is made clear in the minute of the Union Council's meeting on 30 January which reads 'Council agreed that the meeting organized by Marshall Bloom on ways of opposing Dr. Adams would be held on Tuesday afternoon'.

Mr. Bloom told us that no notices of the meeting were sent out by the

Graduate Students' Association, but that a Xerox copy of an article in the *New Statesman* endorsed with a notice 'Come to a discussion at the Old Theatre at 4 p.m. on Tuesday' or in some similar words was circulated within the School. Further at a meeting of the Union on 20 January the External Affairs Vice-President of the Union (Mr. Malik) announced 'that there would be a meeting on Tuesday at 4 p.m. on Dr. Adams'.

At some time not later than midday on Tuesday 31 January further notices of the meeting were circulating in the students' Refectory and were observed there by the Secretary. One, which he brought away, and was produced to us, was in the following terms:

STOP ADAMS   STOP ADAMS   STOP ADAMS   STOP ADAMS

Soon a man who is an inefficient administrator, a man who considers it no part of his duty to protect his staff and students against intimidation, censorship, imprisonment and deportation by an illegal regime, a man who has had a vote of no confidence passed against him by his own teaching staff, will become *your* Director.

The basic facts are not controversial: all the reports on University College, Rhodesia, whether written by a headmaster of Eton, Amnesty International, the International Students Conference, or fifty-five lecturers at the college, have strongly criticized Adams.

The selection of this man as L.S.E.'s new director is symbolic of a host of problems including the place of the students in their college, and there is no better place to begin work for a different L.S.E. than by opposing the appointment of Adams. Although the selection committee itself is unlikely to reverse its decision, given his own health, Adams might resign if it were clear that enough students did not want him.

We must make it clear that we still don't want Adams and are prepared to take direct action to prevent his becoming our Director. Come to a meeting on Tuesday, at 4.0 p.m., in the Old Theatre, to discuss what can be done to stop him.

We should make it clear that the Secretary did not seek to prove that Mr. Bloom or any of the other persons complained against were responsible for this particular notice.

The Secretary brought this notice to the Director who decided that it would be improper for such a meeting to be held in the Old Theatre. He accordingly instructed the Secretary to cancel the booking of the Old Theatre and sent for Mr. Bloom. He saw Mr. Bloom at or shortly after 2.30 p.m.

Both Mr. Bloom and the Director gave evidence as to what took place at that meeting between them, which was a short meeting.

Mr. Bloom said:

The Director first asked me a question to make sure that he seemed to be speaking to the right person, I gather, namely who was responsible for this meeting, to which I answered, 'The GSA Committee and the Union Council'. He then proceeded to say that the meeting had been banned, namely that the booking of the Old Theatre had been cancelled. He then submitted to me document C and said because this leaflet had mentioned 'direct action' the meeting had been banned. I did not understand exactly what had been banned or why, but I did not ask any questions other than to say, 'I understand your position'. I also asked one thing, if we did not discuss the direct action, could the meeting be allowed to continue, since we had speakers invited and since the entire plans for the afternoon had been to have a discussion and nothing else. The Director replied that he did not feel any meeting could take place at this time, but the Union might hold at some future date a meeting on Dr. Adams. After that I left his office.

The Director's evidence was shorter but did not differ materially from what Mr. Bloom said. The Director agreed to confirm his decision in writing and shortly after Mr. Bloom had left a letter was prepared and approved by the Director in the following terms:

Dear Mr. Bloom,

When I saw you this afternoon to tell you that I had cancelled the booking of the Old Theatre for your meeting at 4.0 p.m. today, I told you that I would confirm my decision by letter.

When I learned yesterday of the nature of the meeting for which the Theatre had been booked, I took it that its purpose was further discussion of Dr. Adams's appointment, possibly leading to some kind of reasoned representations to the School. Last night I saw that certain of the notices of the meeting were undoubtedly defamatory, and I removed those but let the remainder stay. Today, however, on seeing the leaflet that was distributed in the refectory, I felt bound to take a different view. That leaflet concludes with the following paragraph:

'We must make it clear that we still don't want Adams and are prepared to take direct action to prevent his becoming our Director. Come to a meeting on Tuesday, at 4.0 p.m., in the Old Theatre, to discuss what can be done to stop him.'

It would be wrong on my part, injurious to the reputation of the School, and dangerous to the academic freedom of its staff, if I were to allow facilities to be provided for the discussion by students of 'direct action' to prevent my designated successor (or for that matter any other senior member of the staff) from taking up his appointment. I have, therefore, as I have told you, cancelled the booking of the Theatre, and posted a notice of which I enclose a copy.

I indicated earlier in this letter that I was prepared to allow facilities for a meeting at which, in effect, the possibility of reasoned representations against the appointment of my successor might be discussed. I ought to say that I now doubt whether I should again take that view; the reference to 'direct action' once made in the way that it has been made seems to me to alter the whole situation.

This letter was not, however, sent until some time later and is only relevant to show the reasons for banning the meeting which the Director gave to Mr. Bloom.

Shortly after this meeting with Mr. Bloom the Director gave instructions for notices to be posted on the doors of the Old Theatre in the following terms:

I AM NOT PREPARED TO PROVIDE FACILITIES FOR THE PURPOSES FOR WHICH THE MEETING FIXED FOR 4 P.M. IN THE OLD THEATRE TODAY WAS INTENDED.
THE BOOKING OF THE OLD THEATRE HAS THEREFORE BEEN CANCELLED.

S. CAINE
DIRECTOR

31.1.67

At some time in the afternoon some of these notices were pulled down and removed but duplicates were replaced by the porters. As a further precaution, on the Secretary's instructions the main fuses of the lights in the Old Theatre were removed.

After seeing the Director Mr. Bloom went to the Student Union offices and told a number of students that the Director had banned the meeting. An emergency meeting of the Council of the Union was held about 3 p.m. at which the six persons complained against were present. No minutes of that meeting were produced to us but in an official statement issued by the Union a few days later it was said that 'at 3 p.m. on Tuesday 31 January a meeting of five members of Union Council was held and it was felt that the 4 p.m. meeting should continue'. The 'five members' presumably excluded Mr. Bloom who told us that he was not then an official member of the Union Council although they permitted him to attend Council meetings.

Exactly what took place at that meeting was the subject of much evidence before us and we deal with this in detail later. It is, however, relevant here to record that Mr. Adelstein, the President of the Union, left the meeting for a short time when he endeavoured to speak to the Director on the telephone but was unable to get in touch with him as the number was engaged: he told us that after the meeting he again endeavoured to speak to the Director by telephone but with the same result as the Director was not then in his office.

After the Council meeting Mr. Malik, with the approval of Mr. Bloom and Mr. Adelstein, made arrangements for the students' bar—known as 'the Three Tuns' bar—to be fitted with loud speaker equipment so that a meeting could be held there.

Between 3 and 4 p.m. some new notices were circulating of which samples were obtained by the Secretary and produced to us. These notices ran as follows:

AT 2 P.M. THIS AFTERNOON SIR SYDNEY CAINE SAW MARSHALL BLOOM, CHAIRMAN OF THE GRADUATE STUDENTS' ASSOCIATION TO HIS OFFICE AND TOLD HIM THAT THE 'STOP ADAMS' MEETING SCHEDULED FOR THIS AFTERNOON AT 4 P.M. WAS BANNED.

THIS MEETING WAS SPONSORED BY THE STUDENTS' UNION COUNCIL AND THE GRADUATE STUDENTS' ASSOCIATION.

THIS IS AN ATTACK ON FREE SPEECH—IT MUST BE OPPOSED.

THIS MEETING SHALL TAKE PLACE

4 p.m.   In the OLD THEATRE!

On one that we saw there was written in large letters 'Caine bans Adams Meeting': on another 'Caine bans free speech'. Here again the Secretary did not seek to prove that any of the six persons complained against were responsible for these notices.

Some time before 4 p.m. Mr. Bloom was present in the entrance hall of the School, together with some of the other persons complained against: he took up a position in the centre of the hall and a number of persons, including Miss Jones, sat down near him. A crowd rapidly collected consisting, no doubt, of persons who had intended to come to the meeting and had not heard of the ban, those who had heard of the ban and were indignant about it, and other persons passing through the hall on their way to other parts of the School who stopped to see what was going on. The crowd was noisy and disorderly and this attracted further persons: fairly soon the entrance hall and adjacent corridors were full of people as were the stairs leading to the entrance hall with a further crowd on the Mezzanine floor above.

At this point it is material to record that on the instructions of the Director a number of porters were standing at the doors of the Old Theatre with instructions to prevent access to the Theatre.

At some time about 4 p.m. Mr. Bloom made an attempt to bring the crowd to order and spoke to them. He did so from behind a large black banner on which was written in white letters 'Students Rights'. A photograph of him with the banner appeared in a newspaper. He told us that the banner was brought to the School by two other persons and was not his.

He told us that he informed those present of the Director's ban on the meeting and that the Three Tuns' bar had been fitted with microphones so that the meeting could be held there, but that no one went there.

At no stage did he suggest that as the meeting had been banned by the Director, it could not be held and that the crowd should all go away.

Quite soon afterwards the Secretary told Mr. Bloom that the Director would be willing to come down to speak to them: Mr. Bloom, who at that time was still attempting to control the crowd, put the proposal to a show of hands which was apparently in favour of hearing the Director.

Some few minutes later the Director arrived on the scene: he was heard with difficulty owing to interruptions and general noise but made it clear that he had banned the use of the Old Theatre for the meeting and refused to alter that decision. At one point he was asked 'What about our rights' and replied 'You have no rights in the Old Theatre'; the last few words were apparently not heard by many of those present who heard it as 'You have no rights' and this led to further noise and angry questions to the Director.

Various members of the crowd then spoke including Mr. Bloom. He told us that he tried to put to the vote the question whether they should all stay where they were or go to the bar, but half-a-dozen students interrupted him saying, 'we should vote on the Old Theatre or the Bar': he then changed the wording to that desired by these students and took a vote on 'Old Theatre or the Bar' and 'the Old Theatre' won.

It is now necessary to refer to Mr. Adelstein's part in the proceedings. He arrived after 4 p.m. at the main entrance of the School and was unable to obtain entry. He then went to the East Wing door, came over the bridge to the main building and descended the stairs through the crowd to the bottom of the stairs: he was apparently not then aware of the porters being on the doors of the Old Theatre.

His first intervention was to suggest that they should all go to the Three Tuns' bar: this apparently was not acceptable to the crowd and no one went there. A little later he came into the main body of the crowd and made a speech to which we refer in detail later. Mr. Adelstein told us that at this stage he thought the Director was prepared to listen to argument and might be willing to reconsider his decision; and he (Mr. Adelstein) was not then aware that porters were barring the doors of the Old Theatre. After this speech he discovered that the porters were on the doors and he then told the crowd that they could not get into the Old Theatre as the porters were there. He also appealed to the Director to alter his decision but the Director refused to do so.

Subsequently Mr. Adelstein made a second speech in which he put three possible courses to the crowd (a) to go to the Three Tuns, or (b) to stay where they were, or (c) to storm the Old Theatre. Apparently the majority of persons present were in favour of the third course and attempts were made to push past the porters into the Old Theatre. The gathering was by now quite out of hand and a number of students succeeded in entering the Old Theatre. Someone had provided candles which were lit in the Old Theatre as the lights did not work.

Whilst these events were going on one of the porters who had not been detailed for duty on the doors was present in the hall and went to the assistance of his colleagues. He suffered from heart disease and in the disturbance he had a heart attack and collapsed: he died shortly afterwards. There is no evidence that he was assaulted and the heart attack could easily have occurred on another occasion: no one concerned should regard themselves as responsible for his death.

On hearing about the porter the Director went into the Old Theatre and told those present that the porter had died and asked them to go: they then left the Theatre. That evening a joint statement was issued by the School and the Students' Union in the following terms:

> The School and its Students' Union deeply regret that, in the course of an attempt by students to gain admission to the School's main lecture theatre for the purpose of holding a meeting for which the Director had refused permission, one of the School porters had a heart attack and died. The porter's state of health was known to the School authorities and he had not been detailed to take any part but came to join his colleagues at the doors of the theatre.
>
> The School and the Students' Union share the deepest regret that the chain of events should have had this tragic end.

It is clear to us that a serious breach of discipline occurred on 31 January in that a number of students disobeyed the Director's order by breaking into the Old Theatre. It was not suggested, however, that any of the six students complained against before us actually broke in themselves, although they were all present at the gathering in the entrance hall. It is also clear from the Director's evidence that he did not at any time order that gathering to disperse and the only order which these six persons are charged with disobeying is the Director's original order to ban the meeting called for 4 p.m. in the Old Theatre, which he refused to withdraw although he was repeatedly pressed to do so during the gathering.

It is now convenient to refer to the terms of the complaints preferred by the Secretary.

Six of the complaints (Nos. 2–7) are in the same terms and are made against each of the six students in the following terms:

> That, when the Director had forbidden the use of the Old Theatre for a meeting on 31 January 1967 at 4.0 p.m. and had by necessary implication indicated his refusal to permit that meeting to take place at that time on any other part of the premises of the School under the Director's jurisdiction, he nevertheless joined with other persons in deciding that that meeting be held on those premises, and that this conduct was in disobedience to an instruction given by the Director or under his authority; contrary to Regulation 1 for students.

In the closing speech on behalf of the Secretary it was made clear that this complaint only referred to the acts of those six students when present at the Union Council meeting at 3 p.m. on 31 January and did not refer to their later actions in the entrance hall. It is not surprising that this complaint was made in view of the terms of the statement authorized by the Union Council which said that at 3 p.m. on Tuesday, 31 January a meeting of five members of the Union Council was held and 'it was felt that the 4 p.m. meeting should continue'. It is clear in that document that the 4 p.m. meeting was to be a meeting on ways of opposing Dr. Adams.

One witness told us of a conversation he had held with Mr. Adelstein immediately after the Council meeting when Mr. Adelstein told him that they had decided to go on with the meeting and asked him to get as many people as possible there by 4 p.m. This witness was not cross-examined on this evidence and Mr. Adelstein did not give any evidence regarding the conversation: we must therefore assume that this evidence of that witness was substantially true.

The five members referred to in the Union statement were the persons complained against, other than Mr. Bloom, who was also present at the meeting, and they all told us their versions of what happened at the meeting. It was not a long meeting and, as we have said, for a short time Mr. Adelstein was absent when he tried to telephone the Director.

We also had evidence from other students who were present in the room where the meeting was held. Although the various accounts of the meeting differ in some respects, they all agreed in saying that the meeting was a confused one and that no definite decision was taken as to their future action. Some of them said they did not understand why the Director had banned the 4 p.m. meeting; others thought the Director did not know that the Union had sponsored the 4 p.m. meeting and that if he did know he might change his mind: some thought it might be possible to hold the 4 p.m. meeting with the Director's permission on other premises such as the Three Tuns' bar. It is, however, quite clear that everyone present wanted the meeting to be held somehow and none of them suggested that the meeting should be called off.

We believe it to be true that many of those present were in a state of some confusion. The blame for this appears to us to rest mainly on Mr. Bloom: had he given them the same account of his meeting with the Director as he gave to us, they would have seen much more clearly why the Director had banned the meeting and that it was unlikely, to say the least, that the Director would alter his decision.

We consider that those present at this meeting acted irresponsibly in failing to appreciate, and in disregarding, the effect and consequences of the Director's ban and that they committed a grave error of judgment in not taking immediate action to call the meeting off. However, they are not charged with an error of judgment but with taking a decision together to hold the 4 p.m. meeting in defiance of the Director's ban and to support such a charge we think it is necessary to establish that they not only each separately formed an intention to defy the ban, but also together took some overt act, such as a formal resolution, which was contrary to the Director's order. It is important to state in this context that none of the observers present at the meeting appear to have thought that a resolution of this kind had been passed and it does not appear that when the crowd later collected outside the Old Theatre that anyone suggested that the Union Council had passed any such resolution.

After full consideration of all the evidence relating to this meeting we feel that there is an element of doubt whether the actions of those present at the meeting did constitute disobedience of the Director's order. They are entitled to the benefit of our doubt.

We accordingly come to the conclusion that complaints numbered 2 to 7 inclusive are not proved to our satisfaction beyond reasonable doubt and that they should accordingly be dismissed.

It is convenient here to mention complaints Nos. 8 and 12 against Mr. Malik. Complaint No. 12 was withdrawn at the hearing before us and when Mr. Malik had given his explanation of the conduct referred to in complaint No. 8 Mr. Mann, for the Secretary, admitted that he could not dispute that explanation and this complaint was also withdrawn.

There remain for consideration complaints 1 and 11 against Mr. Adelstein and complaints 9 and 10 against Mr. Bloom. Nos. 1 and 9 were in the same terms (after amendment) as follows:

> That, when the Director had forbidden the use of the Old Theatre for a meeting on 31 January 1967 at 4.0 p.m., he nevertheless caused or permitted a gathering of students in the entrance hall of the Old Building to vote upon a proposal that they transfer their meeting to the Old Theatre; and that this conduct was in disobedience to an instruction given by the Director or under his authority; contrary to Regulation 1 for students.

Complaint No. 10 against Mr. Bloom was as follows:

That, when the Director had forbidden the use of the Old Theatre for a meeting on 31 January 1967 at 4.0 p.m. and had by necessary implication indicated his refusal to permit that meeting to take place at that time on any other part of the premises of the School under the Director's jurisdiction, he nevertheless convened and presided over that meeting in the entrance hall of the Old Building at that time; and that this conduct was in disobedience to an instruction given by the Director or under his authority; contrary to Regulation 1 for students.

Complaint 11 against Mr. Adelstein was as follows:

That, when the Director had forbidden the use of the Old Theatre for a meeting on 31 January 1967 at 4 p.m., he did nevertheless encourage a gathering of students in the entrance hall of the Old Building to demand admission to the Old Theatre; and that this conduct was in disobedience to an instruction given by the Director or under his authority; contrary to Regulation 1 for students.

It was admitted by both Mr. Bloom and Mr. Adelstein in their evidence that at different times they each asked the crowd in the entrance hall to vote upon proposals which included, as one alternative, that everyone should go to the Old Theatre and that when they did this they knew that entry by students into the Old Theatre would be contrary to the Director's order. Mr. Bloom made such a proposal at least once and Mr. Adelstein at least twice: Mr. Bloom knew when he put his proposal that the Director had refused to alter his decision and Mr. Adelstein certainly knew this when he put his proposal for the second time.

Both of them explained to us that the proposal was one of several alternative proposals which they were putting to the crowd: one alternative was to stay where they were, another was to go to the Three Tuns. They also told us, and we believe them, that at that stage they hoped the crowd would choose the Three Tuns. But at no stage did they suggest to the crowd that as the Director had banned the meeting the crowd should disperse.

In our view charges 1 and 9 are clearly proved: if any student publicly puts a proposal to other students which, if accepted, involves a clear breach of an order of the Director, he is in our view guilty of disobedience of that order. When the students concerned are the President of the Union and the President of the Graduate Students' Association, whose views carry considerable weight with other students, their disobedience is more serious. It is no answer to say that the proposal is only put as an alternative to a lawful proposal. Nor is it an answer to say that the meeting was disorderly and might well have broken into the Old Theatre had they not spoken at all: it was their clear duty, if they did speak, to tell the students present that the order of the Director should be obeyed and to refuse to put to a vote any proposal involving disobedience of that order.

Complaint No. 10 against Mr. Bloom requires us to be satisfied that (a) he convened and (b) he presided over 'that meeting', which in the context of the complaint means the meeting which was banned by the Director. The Director was himself present for a considerable part of the time whilst the gathering took place in the entrance hall and he told us that he did not regard that gathering as the meeting he had banned but that it was a group of students who wished to hold that meeting. The meeting which was banned was a meeting to discuss action against Dr. Adams: that subject was not discussed in the entrance hall, as the discussion there related to the Director's action in banning the meeting.

Mr. Bloom was the person who had originally called the 4 p.m. meeting: he was also the person who had received the Director's order that the meeting should not be held. In our view it was his clear duty to take all possible steps to call off the meeting and to discourage a crowd from collecting. He took no such steps but we do not consider that he convened and presided over the meeting which was banned by the Director, and we therefore do not consider that complaint No. 10 is proved.

There only remains complaint No. 11 against Mr. Adelstein which requires us to be satisfied that he 'encouraged' the gathering in the entrance hall to 'demand' admission to the Old Theatre.

In our view, his action in putting to the vote a proposal that the students should 'storm the Old Theatre' is sufficient evidence to justify this complaint but as he is separately charged for that action we consider that proof of the complaint involves us in examining his other actions at that gathering.

It should be mentioned that he arrived some time after the gathering had started and that his first intervention was to suggest that they all went to the Three Tuns.

A little later he made his first speech: by this time the gathering was beginning to get out of hand. The Director had only been heard with difficulty and Mr. Adelstein appears to have been the only speaker who was listened to without serious interruption. It is doubtful if anyone could have then persuaded the gathering to disperse peaceably but Mr. Adelstein had the last opportunity to do this: what he said must, in our view, have encouraged the crowd in their opposition to the Director's ban. He admitted saying that he regarded the ban as an arbitrary action which raised the principle of free speech and that in his opinion the meeting should be held in the Old Theatre.

One of the witnesses said that Mr. Adelstein told the crowd, 'If you hold to your principles you must go into the Old Theatre'. Another witness described Mr. Adelstein's words as, 'If you think it is a point of principle to hold the meeting you must hold it, and if you think it is a point of principle to hold it in the Old Theatre you must hold it there'. Having heard Mr. Adelstein's evidence we have no doubt that he said these words, or words to the same effect, and was clearly telling the crowd that he would not regard it as wrong for them to enter the Old Theatre if they thought fit to do so.

Before us Mr. Adelstein admitted that at no time did he suggest to the crowd that to go into the Old Theatre was contrary to the Director's order, or was wrong. He also told us that when he later used the phrase 'storm the Old Theatre' he did so to make it clear to the students what entering the Old Theatre would mean: and we accept that he was not personally in favour of going in himself. He appears to have regarded himself as a representative of the students rather than their leader and that it was his duty to ascertain 'the sense of the meeting' and to do what the meeting wanted even

N

though it involved disobedience of the Director's order. In our view a student who is President of the Union cannot shelter behind the wishes of his fellow students and if he speaks to them when they are clearly contemplating illegal action he must share responsibility for that action if he does not clearly dissociate himself from it and tell them not to do it.

Hence we find complaint No. 11 proved.

We now have to consider what penalties we ought to impose on Mr. Bloom and Mr. Adelstein for the offences which we have found to be proved against them.

At the outset we should make it clear that we do not regard them as the principal instigators of the disorders which occurred on 31 January: we accept that there are others, not identified before us, who by inflammatory leaflets and other means deliberately provoked conflict between the Director and the students. It would not be right for us to penalize Mr. Bloom or Mr. Adelstein for the acts of people other than themselves. They are not before us as representative of students generally but as persons who have themselves committed breaches of discipline.

But their own actions at the gathering at the entrance hall when they disobeyed the Director's order are serious offences. It was argued in mitigation that they were then in a difficult situation: the crowd was inflamed and out of hand and even if they had both then acted with perfect propriety it is doubtful whether the Director's order would have been obeyed. To some extent, however, their failure to call the meeting off at 3 p.m. contributed to their subsequent difficult position. We have found that their actions at 3 p.m. were not proved to be disobedience but in considering how far there are mitigating circumstances in relation to their later disobedience their earlier failure to take prompt action to foresee and avoid a situation likely to get out of hand is a relevant consideration.

After we had found the three complaints proved both Mr. Adelstein and Mr. Bloom made speeches to us in mitigation in which they emphasized that they regarded the Director's ban on the meeting as a denial of free speech. They alleged that the meeting was called only for purposes of discussion but we are satisfied that this was not the case. It is clear from the evidence that the meeting was called for the purpose of taking action to stop Dr. Adams from coming to the School and formed part of a campaign to prevent a person who had been duly appointed to an academic post from taking it up. Action of this kind is a denial of academic freedom and cannot be defended on the basis of a right to speak freely.

We have considered carefully whether we should distinguish between Mr. Bloom and Mr. Adelstein in the penalty to be imposed upon them. Mr. Adelstein has been found guilty of two complaints and Mr. Bloom of only one: Mr. Adelstein has also been before the Board on a previous occasion when another complaint of breach of regulations was proved against him but sufficient mitigating circumstances then justified the absence of any penalty: Mr. Bloom, however, is a graduate and should therefore exercise greater responsibility than an undergraduate and in examining the conduct of both of them prior to the disobedience which we find they each committed there appear to us to be greater mitigating circumstances for Mr. Adelstein than there are for Mr. Bloom. Hence we think the penalty should be the same on each of them and our unanimous decision is that both be suspended from the School forthwith until the end of the Summer Term 1967.

In conclusion we wish to add one general observation:

We expect, and indeed we hope, that the work and constitution of the School will continue to develop and change and that these changes will be debated widely, freely and sometimes passionately. Such debates and the changes they provoke have been a recurring theme in the life of the School since it began. It is not debate or change that disturbs us.

In fulfilment of the concept of a university the School embraces diverse schools of thought and many shades of opinion. This very diversity demands that debate and discussion should proceed in an orderly and rational manner with proper heed for the views and needs of everyone involved in the School. What is needed now is a conscious effort by everyone to think in terms of the well-being of the School as a whole: a School where the various purposes of an academic institution—learning, teaching and research—can all flourish.

BRIDGES
D. V. DONNISON
L. FARRER-BROWN
G. S. A. WHEATCROFT

13 March 1967

Appendix IV

Letter issued by the Students' Union on 20 March 1967

The following letter is being sent to the members of staff of the London School of Economics. Copies are also being distributed to the Board of Governors, the press, supporting universities in the U.K. and abroad, M.P.s and others who we believe have a genuine interest in the future of the L.S.E.

We have three main reasons for sending it:

1. The students of the college wish to state clearly that we are seeking a satisfactory settlement, not a victory, in the current turmoil.

2. The facts of the situation have been grossly mis-represented by the press and by others whose ignorance of our situation seems matched only by their willingness to offer easy disciplinarian solutions to a very difficult and trying situation. We have had to resort to a letter of this length so that our case can be accurately presented.

3. That we are anxious to prevent the further perpetration of blatant injustice.

We let the letter speak for itself.

To the staff at L.S.E.,

After much debate, Union decided on Saturday to continue the sit-in and boycott. We are very concerned that you as staff members understand why we have taken this decision, and appreciate the importance and seriousness to us of the issues on which our decision was based. We deeply resent being branded irresponsible (truants, Provos, American agitators, hard-core dissidents, etc.) and hope in this letter to demonstrate why we feel our course of action is justified and necessary under the circumstances.

We began these demonstrations in response to the Board of Discipline's decision to suspend David Adelstein and Marshall Bloom for three months. We opposed and rejected these decisions on three grounds.

1. We as a Union were responsible for the vote that was taken on 31 January. Of those students assembled outside the Old Theatre, some proposed challenging the Director's order. Therefore all present wished a vote to be taken so that a decision could be reached. All others present were no less responsible for the vote being taken than the chairmen who conducted it. It was consequently a clear case of victimization to single out two individuals for trial and punishment. It was indeed their *duty* as our representatives to act as they did.

2. Even if they had been solely responsible for administering the vote, the precise point on which the decision was based was a highly technical consideration. After the appeal, the one remaining charge—that of having disobeyed an order of the Director—was based only on the fact that they had tried to take a vote. *They had not been ordered not to take a vote.* But because

one of the possible outcomes of this vote would have been a decision to enter the Old Theatre, which would have been such disobedience, therefore, *for this reason alone*, they were suspended for three months. As the convictions were based on such a technicality, the sentences imposed seemed highly exorbitant and unjust.

3. The whole procedure, as well as the convictions, implied an attitude to students of singular disrespect. Both the Board of Discipline and the appeal board were clearly structurally biased against us. Also, we saw that, while we are expected to have responsibilities within the L.S.E., our rights to free speech and assembly, as embodied in this challenge to the Director's order, were completely denied.

These three considerations were fundamental in our minds as we began our demonstrations, and were indeed its causes.

Before these demonstrations began, we had pursued a conciliatory policy for fear that full expression of our objection to the original disciplinary proceedings might further prejudice the attitude of the Board towards the defendants. We had had a small silent vigil and had set up a conciliation committee which met informally with staff members in an attempt to communicate our objections in a gentle manner. After the harsh decisions of the Board of Discipline indicated to us that the administration had turned a deaf ear to the students' objections, we felt forced to begin the sit-in and the boycott. During the demonstration we have been making a great effort to communicate, both to the administration and to you the staff, our sense of urgency about these issues. This was indeed the central point of the sit-in and the boycott. It was also the point of numerous informal attempts at negotiation between staff and students. On Tuesday, thirteen students began a ninety-six-hour hunger strike. On Wednesday, an open invitation was sent to all members of the staff and administration to discuss these issues with students outside the Senior Common Room. (We are grateful for the response of about forty staff members at that time.) On Thursday, 330 of us even offered to suspend ourselves to indicate further how important we considered these matters to be, and to demonstrate our collective responsibility. On Friday, the fact that over 1,500 students from other universities supported us on the 'Daffodil March' showed that the principles we were upholding were shared by students throughout the country. Also on Friday,[1] Union officially sent a negotiating committee to discuss with representatives of the Standing Committee of the Board of Governors our concern with these matters, and particularly to discuss possibilities for an acceptable compromise on the relevant issues.

In addition to these efforts to communicate directly why these issues were so important to us as students, we tried to make evident our awareness of the responsibilities that went along with our demand for rights. We behaved in a most orderly fashion in the sit-in and the boycott. We forbade violence. We refused any consideration of destructive actions. We even organized our own policing to prevent any irresponsible behaviour by insiders or outsiders. *This* was our 'direct action'.

In the light of all these efforts to indicate to you how very seriously we considered our requests, we hoped to see some specific responses to them in

[1] Or Thursday? [H.K.]

the decisions of last Friday. On some of our long-range concerns, we had received a quite positive response from the Director in his statement of Thursday,[1] 17 March. Part 3 recognized our right to be represented on relevant School committees; and Part 4, our right to play a part in all future disciplinary structures and procedures. We appreciated these decisions, and felt that we had succeeded in some sense on the long-range concerns. And we became more hopeful that the decision, which was to be announced at 8 p.m. that evening, on the precipitating issue of the suspension of Adelstein and Bloom would contain acceptable modification of the sentences. About 800 people sat and stood in the Old Theatre for over three hours, and finally, at 11.20 p.m., Richard Kuper arrived with news of the decision.

The Standing Committee's report indicated 'that the charge against Mr. Adelstein of encouraging disobedience to an instruction given by the Director was not proved beyond reasonable doubt' (Point 2). It also assured that 'the Director will use his best endeavours to procure that the University of London will allow Mr. Bloom to sit for his proposed examinations notwithstanding his suspension' (Point 5). This report also 'unanimously confirmed the findings of the Board of Discipline that both Mr. Bloom and Mr. Adelstein were guilty of disobedience to an instruction given by the Director' (Point 1). But on the main substantive question—the question of the sentences imposed—this committee was singularly inflexible. The only modifications they offered were that instead of having to remain fully suspended until the end of the summer term 'as from 30 May 1967, Mr. Bloom and Mr. Adelstein may have access to school premises for the purpose only of visiting their respective tutors to receive instruction under arrangements approved by the Director, and making full use of the facilities of the Library' (Point 4). It was decreed that throughout the whole period of the suspension, they will remain unable to attend classes, seminars, or lectures; to visit the Union premises; or even to accept personal invitations from members of staff to visit them on school premises. In other words, even after the appeal, they are in a worse position than any ordinary member of the public.

The Union was in a state of tired and disappointed shock, and at about 2.30 a.m. voted to recess until the afternoon.

As the meeting began on Saturday, Mr. Kidd arrived with a statement from Lord Bridges, the Director, and himself. This statement reaffirmed somewhat ambiguously the principles in the Director's earlier message (Point A). It then (Point B) threatened us by saying that none of these principles would be implemented until the sit-in and boycott were halted. And finally, we were informed that the decision of the Standing Committee regarding the initial suspensions of Adelstein and Bloom will stand; that 'They have never been, and never will be, a matter for negotiation' (Point C). This announcement was greeted with cries of 'Shame!'. Mr. Adelstein said that 'This is perhaps the most incredibly disturbing thing that has happened.' Mr. Zander of the Law Department commented that 'Just at the very moment when the whole situation could conceivably be resolved, Mr. Kidd's wretched little statement has put the whole thing in jeopardy.' The previous evening, Dr. Patterson of the Sociology Department gave a brief but incisive analysis of the reciprocal nature of rules in any relationship. He

[1] In fact, Friday, 17 March.

suggested that the rules insisted upon by the administration were so unsatisfactory and unjust to the students in this situation as to make it impossible, if not degrading and dehumanizing, for us to pursue a policy of
'acquiescence' or 'withdrawal'. He could see no alternative but for us to
stand firm on our principles, and to continue our policy of 'rebellion'.

It was in the light of this verdict of the Standing Committee and the
announcement by Mr. Kidd, that the decision to continue the boycott and
sit-in was made.

We saw these pronouncements in relation to the three immediate issues
with which we began the demonstrations (page 184 above); and,

 1. we continued to see no justice in the victimization of Adelstein and
Bloom,

 2. the technical considerations remained quite as trivial,

 3. the attitude of singular disrespect for students and for their rights,
particularly in Mr. Kidd's statement, seemed to have changed not one
iota.

Independently of the Director's statement, we were told that negotiations
on long-range issues must be completed on their terms (i.e. the suspension
of the sit-in and boycott). Independently of our repeated demand throughout
these events that our central and immediate concern was with the severe
punishments on Adelstein and Bloom, we were told not only that they would
disagree with us, but also that they would not even negotiate with us about
these.

Furthermore, it was disclosed that in fact these suspensions had already
been a subject for negotiation with members of the Standing Committee
(Professor Roberts and Miss Seear—with the Director present). The
Students' Union had elected a delegation of nine to meet with these members.
This was in response to an invitation by the members to discuss ways of
finding a solution to the crisis at L.S.E. It was revealed that during the
course of these discussions these two members proposed a formula whereby
if the student representatives would agree to call off the sit-in and boycott
that night, they, Roberts and Seear (with the Director being present and
therefore complicit) would use all their power to persuade the Standing
Committee to modify the sentences significantly. We accept that some
semantic constructions could argue that these were not negotiations; but we
would see these constructions as niggling. We accept that some constructions
could say that Roberts and Seear were not official negotiators; but we would
then have to see their proposals as having been made in extreme bad faith.

We could see no way to accept the point that these suspensions had never
been a matter for negotiation. The Union resolution of 16 March under
which we elected our own representatives for these talks, read 'Union instructs Union Council and two other representatives (to be elected at this
meeting) *to enter into negotiation* with the Standing Committee of the Court
of Governors or its representatives, and any proposals obtained by the student
representatives must be ratified by the Students' Union.' After these negotiations had been completed we were told that in fact the subjects we had
negotiated about had never been subjects for negotiations. Richard Atkinson,
who had participated as a student representative in these talks, branded the

assertion by the Chairman of the Governors, the Director, and the Secretary 'a deliberate and outrageous lie'.

Union could not accept Mr. Kidd's statement as final; nor, in the light of the near total rejection of our three original points, could we accept as final the findings of the Standing Committee.

We trust that by now it will be clear to you why we decided that we must continue with the sit-in and the boycott. We felt not only a moral imperative to continue, but also a practical imperative, primarily in the interests of Adelstein and Bloom, but also to ensure that the more permanent reforms should be effected without threat. We would stress that we are very concerned about the long-range effects on the welfare of the School of our recent demonstration. But we feel most deeply that this welfare is indeed best served by not selling out on the principles and practices which have been at the basis of our recent actions. We continue the sit-in and boycott in a further attempt to communicate to you how very serious we consider these matters to be, and our determination to have some less inadequate response to our demands.

To facilitate our attempts to work constructively at this time, we have elected a committee of thirty-four to help organize and oversee our efforts. Twelve of these people are specifically appointed to further all attempts at negotiation with the staff and administration on the immediate and the long-term relevant issues. We trust and we hope that they will indeed be allowed to negotiate on these very issues.

We very much appreciate all efforts by staff members to help us on this, as we have appreciated all efforts that have been made to date. (We have enjoyed and profited from getting to know those of you who have participated with us outside the structured staff–student roles, and we hope this feeling has been reciprocated.)

A recent speech by Sir Maurice Bowra, Warden of Wadham College, Oxford, seems to us most appropriate (*The Times*, Wednesday, 15 March); 'I am sure that this is the thing that the young value most—that they know their own personalities, which are too serious to be badgered and pushed about by a lot of silly rules they do not agree with or understand or approve of; they want to be civilized members of a civilized society getting as much out of each other and everybody else as they can.'

We feel that these remarks apply to us. We would like L.S.E. to be a civilized society. For us this implies not 'being pushed about by a lot of silly rules'. In a civilized society, on our three initial issues,

1. elected representatives would not be victimized;
2. to take a vote would not be a crime;
3. staff and administration would quite naturally respect students' rights, including that of free speech.

In the spirit of Sir Maurice's remarks, we would invite those of you who are interested to participate with us in a series of informal discussions, meetings, and seminars which we are planning on the lines of an 'open university', and which we hope to begin this week.

Lastly, we would stress, as we have been trying to all along, the strength of our commitment to a healthy human and academic community at the

L.S.E. We sincerely hope that you will agree with our feeling that throughout the recent days our actions have been consonant with just this commitment. We would remind you of our three points, and we hope you will help
us now, in our effort with the administration, as there is nothing we want
more than an acceptable end to the present crisis.

The Committee of 34,
on behalf of the Students' Union.

19 March 1967.

Appendix V

Many students are dismissed or given heavy punishments for academic and non-academic offences. For many non-academic offences the punishments are merited. In some cases they are not. The head of a college is allowed to be prosecutor, judge and jury; often an enquiry leading to a dismissal or a heavy punishment is only nominal, quite arbitrary, and far removed from the code of natural justice.

A more enlightened code of discipline is required. With N.U.S. pressure, charters of the new universities of technology have made provisions that accused students will be given a fair hearing. For colleges of education the Weaver Report recommended that students 'should be granted, and know that they possess, a clearly defined right to be heard if their suspension or dismissal is in question'. After consultation with N.U.S., the D.E.S. is implementing this suggestion by the provision of a detailed regulation, the essence of which is that no student shall be expelled without being afforded an opportunity of appearing in person, accompanied if so desired by a friend, before a duly constituted meeting of the governors. Similar provision is made in the draft instruments of government for students in polytechnics sent out by the D.E.S.

We are leaving behind the arbitrary method of enquiry adopted in the past by college authorities. But the provisions so far made are of a general nature. Early this year N.U.S. published an 'Action' leaflet on disciplinary procedure (copies are available on request). Detailed procedures have now to be worked out, and this pamphlet sets out N.U.S. guidelines.

Differentiation should be made between academic and non-academic offences.

ACADEMIC OFFENCES

In purely academic offences—where the student does not reach the required academic standard—it is extremely difficult to challenge the assessment of an academic body. No court of law would question this unless there was *prima facie* evidence that there was prejudice and personal dislike, the burden of proof, according to law, being upon the student. Normally the only redress for such a student is the submission of an appeal or petition to the academic board to reconsider the case.

NON-ACADEMIC OFFENCES

The treatment of non-academic offences by college authorities has caused the National Union most concern. The following GENERAL PRINCIPLES should be observed:

1. Students should expect the same treatment before the law as any other citizens;

2. a college is not in general a competent body to sit in judgment on any non-academic offence committed by a student (with the exception of certain 'institutional' offences);

3. there must be no double punishment.

Distinguish between:

A. *Institutional non-criminal offences*

In every institution there are a number of rules and regulations which have no place in the criminal law of the country, but are nevertheless necessary for the smooth functioning of the institution. Most are of a minor nature, such as 'hours' rules in halls of residence, and detailed rules as to behaviour in libraries or union.

Offences committed on student union property, or within its jurisdiction, should be dealt with by the student union disciplinary committee. A model constitution for union disciplinary committees (embodying the principles stated below) is available from N.U.S. on request. Other 'institutional offences' of this kind should be dealt with by the college disciplinary committee.

No distinction should be made in procedure between these minor offences, and other offences.

B. *Institutional criminal offences*

i.e. those committed in connection with the accused's membership of the college (e.g. pilfering from a cloakroom, illegally supplying drugs to members of the college).

C. *Non-institutional criminal offences*

i.e. those committed outside the college (e.g. drunken driving, shop-breaking, disorderly conduct at a political meeting or demonstration).

If an offence falling within category B is brought to the attention of the college authorities they are obliged by law to refer it to the police if the offence is 'arrestable', in other cases they may either refer it to the police, or, if it is of a minor nature, deal with it through the college's disciplinary procedure.

Where a case is to be dealt with by a college's internal disciplinary machinery (this also applies to A) the status of the student charged—in particular his right to be on the campus and attend classes—should not be altered, pending the hearing.

If the offence is to be dealt with by the courts there are clearly no grounds for the college to intervene unless and until the accused is found guilty by a court of law.

If, under either B or C, the accused is found 'not guilty' or acquitted by a court of law, or if the police consider there is insufficient evidence on which to bring a charge, the college should take no further action. There must be no second trial by the college; it would clearly be a gross miscarriage of justice if the college were to accept a lesser burden of proof than a court of law, or make their own charges when the police had decided that there was insufficient evidence to bring a charge.

If the accused is found guilty (of an offence in either category B or C), the college authorities should take no further action unless it is absolutely clear that the continued presence of the accused within the institution would be detrimental to the well-being of the college community. Where the accused has been sentenced to a term of imprisonment (unlikely with a person under 21)—ideally he should not be expelled for good from the institution but suspended from it for a year or two. The effects of expulsion by his college will have in most cases a very grave effect on the accused. Rejection by his community may go a long way into making him a hardened criminal. Such action should only be contemplated in the severest of cases.

Within the above principle there is clearly no case for any further punishment except suspension or expulsion in the most exceptional circumstances. Additional punishment in the form of fine, gating, etc., would only be double punishment. In any event such punishment must only be imposed by a properly constituted 'disciplinary committee'.

DISCIPLINARY COMMITTEE
Constitution

(a) In all cases the charge should be heard by a properly constituted Disciplinary Committee.

(b) The Disciplinary Committee should be set up by the college authorities; it should consist of, say, five staff members and three student members, none of whom shall be an 'interested party' in the case. The college legal assessor should sit on the board in an advisory capacity. The vice-chancellor or principal should not sit on the committee, nor should any other interested parties.

(c) The penalties which may be imposed by the committee should be clearly specified in the constitution of the committee and may include reprimand, fine (to a specified maximum), suspension from academic or other privileges, rustication or expulsion from the university or college, as well as (in the case of damage to property or premises) requirement to make good the damage in whole or part.

Procedure

(a) The student should be informed in writing of the charge against him and allowed sufficient time (say 14 days) for his preparation for the hearing.

(b) The student should have the right to be assisted in his defence by an adviser (qualified or unqualified in the practice of the law) of his choice.

(c) The burden of proof should rest on the officials bringing the charge. The student should be given an opportunity to testify and to present evidence and witnesses; and to hear and question adverse witnesses. In no case should the committee consider statements against him unless he has been given copies of them and the names of those who made them, and has been given an opportunity to rebut unfavourable inferences which might otherwise be drawn.

(d) In all cases a verbatim record of the proceeding should be kept.

(e) The decision of the Disciplinary Committee should be final, subject to the right of appeal to an Appeals Committee external to the college. The Appeals Committee should be appointed after consultation between college governing body and student union, but should contain members of neither.

(f) After sentence by the Disciplinary Committee the student should be allowed a period of not less than 10 days in which to lodge, in writing, notification of appeal with the registrar or secretary of the college.

(g) Before the appeal hearing the student should be furnished with a copy of the minutes, and a verbatim record of the Disciplinary Committee hearing.

(h) Only witnesses and evidence heard at the hearing of the Disciplinary Committee may be heard at the Appeals Committee hearing. No new evidence should be allowed, except where the submission is for a re-hearing.

(i) The person bringing the charge and the charged student should be afforded the opportunity to make statements before the Appeals Committee.

(j) The Appeals Committee should have the power to confirm, set aside, or vary a finding of the Disciplinary Committee, or order a re-hearing by the Disciplinary Committee. Their decision should be final.

It may not be possible for all procedures outlined above to be fitted into the general regulations of a particular college, but it is hoped that every effort will be made by all colleges to ensure that the procedure advised above is conformed with substantially and the spirit of fair discipline maintained.

Index

Chronological Index